Exploring Children's Learning

3–11 years

Edited by
Christine Ritchie

Routledge
Taylor & Francis Group

LONDON AND NEW YORK

First published 2017
by Routledge
2 Park Square, Milton Park, Abingdon, Oxon OX14 4RN

and by Routledge
711 Third Avenue, New York, NY 10017

Routledge is an imprint of the Taylor & Francis Group, an informa business

British Library Cataloguing in Publication Data
A catalogue record for this book is available from the British Library

Library of Congress Cataloging in Publication Data
A catalog record for this book has been requested

ISBN: 978-1-138-19027-6 (hbk)
ISBN: 978-1-138-19030-6 (pbk)
ISBN: 978-1-315-64116-4 (ebk)

Typeset in Melior
by Saxon Graphics Ltd, Derby

Contents

Explor   rning

Exploring Children's Learning: 3–11 years is essential reading for those passionate about supporting children's learning environments from Early Years to Key Stage 2. By combining learning with important aspects of a broad curriculum content it will inspire and enhance an interest in supporting children's learning. Individual chapters focus on key areas of the curriculum such as literacy and history, numeracy and science, as well as more general topics such as creativity, assessment and the emotional and behavioural aspects of learning.

The book takes an objective view on control over curriculum and offers practical insights into how supportive learning opportunities can create enjoyable and satisfying lifelong learning habits, preparing children for the challenges they may face in their adult working life.

Whether you dip into chapters, or read through the book as a whole, you will develop your understanding of the complexity of learning and the lifelong effects implicit in this, not only from the individual basis that each child faces in terms of learning how to learn, but also concerning the differences in learning strategies required to successfully negotiate subject knowledge across a range of disciplines.

This book is a must-read for students of Childhood and Education Studies programmes, those undertaking Initial Teacher Training as well as general readers with an interest in supporting children's learning.

Christine Ritchie has enjoyed a long career in education, working in the UK and Europe, gaining experience in a variety of educational areas, starting as a primary school teacher and working in Early Years education. Now retired from full-time work, she continues to be involved in education and engages in related activities and research.

Acknowledgements

The contributors would like to thank families and friends for their support in the process, and, in some chapters, the content of writing this book. Thanks also to students, teachers and colleagues associated with Canterbury Christ Church University who found time to contribute their thoughts through discussion and case study evidence. Lastly, thanks to the PGCE/Primary Education History Group for their generous contributions to Chapter 11.

Contributors

Polly Bolshaw is a Lecturer in Early Years at Canterbury Christ Church University (CCCU), who teaches predominantly on the BA (Hons) Early Childhood Studies programme. She is also a committee member of OMEP (World Organisation of Early Childhood) UK. Prior to joining CCCU, she worked as an Early Years Professional in a Sure Start Children's Centre. Her academic interests include policy and practices impacting on the early years sector as well as services within the UK aimed at supporting young children and their families.

Jill Bussien has taught in a range of educational settings from early years to HE, with a background in Art, SEN and Deaf Education. She obtained qualifications from The Institute for Education, London University, The Open University and the University of Birmingham, where she obtained the mandatory qualification of a Teacher of the Deaf. Subsequently, she has been an Advisory Teacher and focused on Post-16 learning. Her professional interests include Applied Linguistics, the education of D/deaf learners, the training of Communication Support Workers and the impact of their work. Currently, she is Chair of ADEPT (Association of Deaf Education Professionals and Trainees), a member of the NEC of BATOD (British Association for Teachers of the Deaf) and a member of DESF (Deaf Education Support Forum).

Gary Callahan-Ferris is a Communication Support Worker, British Sign Language/ English interpreter, Teacher, Teacher of the Deaf and BSL assessor. He has worked in education supporting deaf students in a range of settings, ranging from pre-school to university and has a deaf family. He is a member of the Association of Deaf Education Professionals and Trainees (ADEPT), British Association of Teachers of the Deaf (BATOD), Society for Education and Training (SET) and the National Union of Teachers (NUT). He has a specialist interest in 'Inclusion' within education, including campaigning on lesbian, gay, bisexual and trans people issues as they affect education and those in education. He is an openly gay teacher and in a civil partnership with his lifelong partner Robert.

Chris Carpenter has been a senior lecturer at Canterbury Christ Church University since 2000. Before this he worked as a PE teacher at an Institute of Higher Education and then in four different schools across three authorities in the South of England. While in Oxfordshire he also worked part time as an advisory teacher of PE, working mainly with primary schools in the south of Oxfordshire. Since his appointment at Canterbury he has been the subject leader for the secondary Physical Education PGCE and has taught on a range of undergraduate and postgraduate courses, including the MA in education. He also teaches on two of the EdD modules and during the past five years he has worked on a school-based CPD project with the Department of Professional Development.

Anita Cooper, Senior Lecturer at Canterbury Christ Church University, has enjoyed 20 years' experience in the educational field but primarily has a background in early years/primary teaching and senior leadership. Before starting her academic career in 2010 she worked as an early years adviser with a primary focus on inclusion and early help for children with special educational needs and disabilities. Her academic areas of interest includes the voice of the child, equality and social justice, early years status in society, diversity and inclusion, community of practice, leadership, and the emancipatory potential of education.

Janice Gill is the Faculty Director of Childhood and Education Studies at Canterbury Christ Church University. She joined the University in 2004, working as a Senior Lecturer on postgraduate and undergraduate Initial Teacher Education Programmes. Prior to joining CCCU, she taught in Key Stage 2 in East and West Sussex primary schools for 18 years.

Peter Gregory has taught across all phases of education in the South East. In schools he has led subject development and curriculum design as well as undertaking local authority advisory work. He is currently Principal Lecturer in Education (Creative Arts) at Canterbury Christ Church University and regularly teaches and presents research across the UK, Europe and beyond. Peter is Vice President of the National Society for Education in Art and Design (NSEAD) and a World Councillor for the International Society for Education through Art (InSEA). He has many research interests – including creativity, visual arts and the leadership of art and design in schools, and has contributed to several publications. Peter also chairs the Expert Subject Advisory Group (ESAG) which was originally set up by DfE to advise schools on the implementation of the (then new) national curriculum.

Kristy Howells is the Faculty of Education Director of Physical Education at Canterbury Christ Church University and has taught across a range of undergraduate and postgraduate degree programmes and ITE provision that include Physical Education and Physical Activity. She is particularly passionate about Physical Education and Physical Activity, and these are the areas of her research. She has disseminated her findings to schools, through book chapters and national and international conferences.

Temi Ladenika, an educator since September 1985, is currently a part-time senior lecturer at CCCU and the Proprietor of Pulse and Water College, a small independent school providing for learners who thrive within small group learning. Her current scholarly activity centres on how tutor practices foster autonomous learning. Her paper on Globalization and International School Partnerships was accepted for presentation at the WCECC in Istanbul in 2010. Her views on learning and behaviour have developed within her scholarly activity, as well as experience of education spanning three decades across Secondary, Further and Higher Education.

Catherine Meehan is the Faculty Director of Early Childhood at Canterbury Christ Church University, Kent. She has worked in a range of early childhood educational settings and teacher education in Brisbane, Australia before moving to the UK. Catherine is on the OMEP UK committee and her research interests include children's voice in research, children's rights and participation in education and care. Catherine is a Principal Fellow for the Higher Education Academy.

Andrew Owen is a communication support worker, British Sign Language/English interpreter, consultant, trainer and author on deaf issues, based in London. He supports deaf students in sixth forms and universities around south east London. He has written seven books on deaf and interpreting issues, and contributes regularly to deaf-related magazines and conferences. He was co-founder of the Association of Communication Support Workers (ACSW) and is the current Vice Chair of the Association of Deaf Education Professionals and Trainees (ADEPT). He has a special interest in the language of examinations for deaf candidates and writes guidelines and consults over the national regulations.

Christine Ritchie has enjoyed a long career in education, working in the UK and Europe, gaining experience in a variety of educational areas, starting as a primary school/early years teacher. In 2000 she changed direction, moving to working as senior lecturer and Programme Director teaching mature students at university studying on a range of foundation degrees and BA (Hons) programmes related to childhood studies and the early years. Now formally retired, Christine continues to maintain links within higher education and has enjoyed the opportunity that retirement has given to further explore themes within education.

Lin Shaw has worked in England, Africa and Australia in various specialities as a clinical nurse manager and teacher. Specialism in Early Years educare has included Special Needs practitioner within a primary school, managing mother and toddler groups and international voluntary work. Lin has taught GCSE science equivalency and applied science in Further Education, and is currently Programme Director for the Education Foundation Year and a senior lecturer in Early Years Studies at Canterbury Christ Church University. In her spare time Lin assists ecology consultancy companies with the translocation of reptiles and protection of endangered UK wildlife, is an ambassador for a project on food, health and the planet, run by the Wellcome Trust, and an active member of a pre-school Parent Teacher Association.

Diana Strauss's first degree was in primary teaching, curriculum studies and special educational needs. She has maintained her specific interest in creativity as a dominant theme throughout her teaching career. Diana joined Canterbury Christ Church University in May 2010 and lectures across a range of modules, including child development, creativity, imagination and play and language acquisition. She is privileged to be an active participant, alongside colleagues, inspiring students and professionals alike in the field of early childhood education. Documenting children's creativity can be very challenging and Diana is encouraged by the emphasis on creative approaches to teaching. As the co-founder of Write Dance Training in the UK, she continues to promote music, dance and creative approaches to learning and teaching for inclusive practices.

Gemma van Vuuren-Cassar joined Canterbury Christ Church University in 2008 and is the Faculty Director of Learning, Teaching and Assessments. After a short stint teaching in primary and secondary schools, she pursued further studies and then joined the University of Malta in 1995. Assessment in Education is one of her key areas of research. She leads modules and work-based learning on assessments for undergraduates and postgraduates; and delivers continuous professional development courses to practitioners in the schooling settings in France, Germany, Italy, Malta and the United Kingdom. She is a Senior Fellow of the Higher Education Academy (UK).

Clare Wiseman is Programme Director for the Foundation Degree Childhood Studies in the School of Childhood and Education Sciences at Canterbury Christ Church University. Clare teaches predominantly on the Children Learning Literacy and Children Learning Mathematics modules. She previously taught on both the undergraduate and postgraduate Initial Teacher Education programmes. Prior to joining Canterbury Christ Church University, Clare was a Primary Education Consultant for Kent Local Authority. Previously, she had taught across Key Stage One and Key Stage Two in Kent primary schools for 12 years.

Introduction

Overview

The chapters in this book have been written by university tutors and professionals who share a range of experiences working with children from birth to adolescence in educational settings. All are passionate about the importance of supporting children within a learning environment in the best way that they can, for academic and lifelong learning development and for the positive feelings of self-fulfilment and excitement that can come with the acquisition of new knowledge, skill and understanding.

The fostering of the love of learning for its own sake requires to be balanced against the need to meet the government's testing demands on children. This has been one of the dilemmas and challenges discussed among the contributors, colleagues and students, as well as within the media as a concern for parents and future employers. Assessment is recognised by the authors as being an integral part of understanding and promoting learning, with formative assessment providing feedback to learners and offering planning opportunities to the educator to guide further learning. However, striking the balance between encouraging a love of all learning in curious children and providing evidence of meeting the criteria set by outside agencies through a rigorous testing regime is challenging. In a world where competency is questioned and a raft of paperwork can take precedence over time spent listening to children, educators cannot be blamed for looking for an easy-to-follow learning guide that requires minimum input. This book does not offer such a guide; rather, it is hoped that by reading these chapters your own interest is stimulated and enhanced so that you will find renewed vigour in supporting children as they explore learning throughout their formative years regardless of the challenges you, as the adult, may face in your working life.

No assumptions are drawn within the chapters as to whether political forces or professionals working in education should be given more control of the curriculum and assessment options, but it is assumed that all children are entitled to engage fully in learning across a wide field of subjects and interests. It is further assumed that learning will help create enjoyable and satisfying lifelong learning habits that will provide employment opportunities as well as answers to some of the environmental challenges which we, as a global nation, will face in the future.

Aims of the book, and readership

In writing each chapter, the authors all hoped to be able to persuade each reader of the importance of learning in all its forms and to share the enthusiasm for learning together with the excitement of watching children develop a sense of achievement as they unravel the rewards and feelings of satisfaction by being immersed in a love of learning. Some chapters, therefore, are dedicated to specific areas of the curriculum, such as literacy and history, and other chapters are devoted to addressing some of the important areas that impact upon learning, such as emotional development or assessment practices.

There is also, among the authors, the aim of wanting to share knowledge of theory and pedagogy with a range of readers who themselves search for ways to enhance learning for children. The book has therefore been designed to interest all who work, or plan to work, in education with children between the ages of 3 and 11; that is, from the Early Years through Key Stage 2. This group of educators includes students on Foundation degrees, BA (Hons) degrees, teacher training and other similar programmes of study. The wide age range targeted is deliberate, because the authors believe that learning needs to be understood as part of an ongoing process, and educators need to understand the age group that they are working with and the learning experiences before and after each particular stage. It is hoped, therefore, that readers will engage in the text at every level and reflect upon how one stage in a child's education leads on to the next and also understand how what happened may impact upon a child's future learning.

The organisation of the book

Each chapter begins with an overview, giving some of the key points that the text will cover and so set the scene. Within each chapter there are places that ask the reader to take a 'quick pause for reflection' and which then pose some questions or ideas to consider related to the text. These have all been kept fairly brief, but it is expected that there will be many other points where the reader will want to stop and consider the issues that have been raised and explored, and to form questions of their own. Tables and figures are also included, to clarify and illustrate some of the points made within chapters.

At the end of each chapter, there are some suggested texts and websites to check out for further study. Again, these have been kept to a minimum, as it is felt that the wide range of resources available online (or even in libraries!) will provide readers with the opportunities to follow their own interests for the age group of the children they are working with. The authors also considered that whatever future changes are made to curriculum or policy terms within education, readers will be prompted to search for the latest online documents. However, children do not really change; learning and growing still take place in similar ways to the past, so fundamental truths remain the same, and it is these fundamentals that each chapter explores and to which the recommended reading is directed to support.

Overview of each chapter

The chapters in this book fall into two categories; the first category looks at aspects of learning away from any curriculum concerns and the second focuses on particular challenges of learning in specific curriculum areas. What follows is a brief overview of each chapter.

Chapter 1 focuses on 'exploring learning' with its main themes being to explore how practice has been influenced by theory, including those of the 'traditional' development theories associated with Piaget, Vygotsky and also the behaviourists, such as Skinner. The chapter seeks to explain learning through consideration of how experiences and learning behaviours lead to the adoption of learning strategies, both by children themselves and by the adults guiding the learning. In this way, the chapter aims to provide an introduction to the rest of the book.

Chapter 2 takes a closer look at the importance of considering the voice of the young child in learning, and asks children 'What matters to you?'. It draws upon the Pedagogical Documentation originating in Reggio Emilia as a tool for assessing children and explores the tensions that exist for teachers/educators and practitioners working with young children when trying to include their voice in the planning and implementation of learning experiences.

Chapter 3 considers the important areas of behaviour and emotional intelligence within a learning framework based on critical learning theory. It indicates that, by centralising the learner, a view of the multifaceted experiences which revolve around the learner from a diversity of social interactions may be used to understand and interpret behaviour and so support the learner. The chapter not only looks at critical learning theory and emotional intelligence to show how these may have an impact on learning, but also explores guidance to identify perspectives of behaviour and emotion within formal learning situations.

Chapter 4 uses case studies to show how creativity can support important and significant learning experiences for both young children and adults. It takes as its premise the idea that creativity excites, motivates and challenges assumptions and so is able to push past the boundaries that can restrict and inhibit learning. The chapter provides an overview to understanding what is meant by 'creativity', and includes the difference between creative teaching and developing creativity for innovation.

Chapter 5 provides the reader with an overview of the aims and purposes of educational assessment related to practice along with how assessment activities serve both summative and formative purposes. The chapter puts forward the idea that educational assessment serves as a means of feedback on learning, both for the learner and the adult, although it also provides the means to make judgements about teacher accountability. Reading this chapter should provide a sound base from which to explore further the link between assessment practices and learner opportunities.

Chapter 6 considers the needs of the Deaf learner, and the discrete role of the Communication Support Worker (CSW) in providing the support needed to facilitate learning for children in a hearing world. It tackles the complexity of delivery of the curriculum through the medium of spoken and written English to Deaf children and highlights the importance of being 'Deaf-friendly' in modifying teaching resources to make the curriculum accessible to all. The chapter offers advice for those wishing to train as a CSW and outlines the duties the role entails in a changing educational world.

Chapter 7 is the first of the chapters to consider a specific curriculum subject, namely the importance of learning to be literate. The chapter not only considers the traditional understanding of literacy – that is, reading, writing and communication – but also looks at other ways in which children learn to be literate. The chapter therefore also considers emotional literacy, digital literacy and ecoliteracy, illustrating how these interpretations of literacy contribute to the 'wholeness' of a child's learning.

Chapter 8 examines the way in which children learn mathematics and how a child's early experiences provide opportunities to begin to explore mathematical ideas and concepts inherent in their world. The chapter endeavours to show how the early everyday encounters with mathematics lead to an increase in knowledge and skills that pave the way to more formal mathematical thinking and problem solving. It also provides suggestions for using a variety of resources to stimulate mathematical exploration and experiences to positively enrich the learning for children and to move them forward in their thinking.

Chapter 9 investigates how children gain scientific knowledge, skills and understanding, offering an historical overview of science in early years and primary education. The chapter stresses the importance of science in the modern world and in ensuring that children develop prerequisites for lifelong learning and employability in a rapidly evolving environment, where understanding scientific concepts is essential. The chapter also explores the visionary pedagogy for Early Years science that supports enquiry skills and a child's way of knowing, rather than pushing the theories of science for their own sake. It shows how promoting enquiry into the environment can combat any poor cultural attitudes attached to scientific study brought about by the use of scientific language or a cultural concept of the type of person who becomes a 'scientist'.

Chapter 10 takes as its theme the ways in which adults can support the physical development, health and well-being in Early Years and primary-aged children, especially through the use of the outdoor environment. The chapter explains the requirements for physical activity set out in the NHS guidelines as well as defining the term 'physical activity'. It suggests a wide range of activities for children, with the aim to demonstrate the importance of physical activity for health, and also how this is related to learning in other curriculum areas. It provides the reader with ways to support children's learning through the use of key vocabulary through providing positive role models, and suggests starting places for observations that might lead to formative assessment opportunities.

Chapter 11 explores teaching and learning in the curriculum for history and geography that leads to an understanding of people and places in the world today. It explores some of the key issues and challenges linked to these subject areas, and the challenges that teachers/educators and practitioners face when supporting children's learning. There is consideration of the methods of supporting learning, including those of the more traditional 'teaching methods' and more 'creative' pedagogical approaches, with many strategies and ideas gathered from case studies and examples from practice to highlight the different ways in which children may be encouraged to explore learning for themselves.

Last word

The topic range of the chapters and the focus on children aged 3 to 11 will provide the reader with a wealth of information relating to learning for children today. Whether readers dip into chapters or read through the entire book, they should derive an understanding of the complexity of learning not only from the individual basis that each child faces in terms of learning how to learn, but also from the differences in learning strategies required to successfully negotiate subject knowledge across a range of disciplines. All, of course, enhance the core of the individual learner, making the world a more interesting and rewarding place to be, with challenges and opportunities at every stage of life and learning.

It would, however, be simplistic to assume that one book could answer all the questions about learning or about the strategies for learning used within different curriculum areas. Each chapter provides a sound background to an aspect of learning that the reader can use as a springboard for further study. Having such a wide overview in one book will provide material for both the specialist and the generalist within an educational framework. The authors hope that, as the reader, you will gain insight into the world of learning for children at the crucial early stages of their educational experiences.

Exploring learning theory and its significance in education

Christine Ritchie and Anita Cooper

Chapter overview

This chapter focuses on 'exploring learning' and considers three main themes: first, how theory has provided a basis for understanding the processes of constructing learning; second, how during this process children develop learning strategies and build a learning identity, and third, to examine ways in which adults support learning through the use of learning and teaching strategies. Examining theories about how children learn will indicate how belief in the ways children learn has determined past and current educational practice. The aim is to encourage readers to consider their own beliefs and practices related to children's learning and to recognise aspects of theory when observing children in learning situations, and so be able to make conscious decisions when selecting strategies that promote learning in general and for individual children, regardless of the curriculum content.

Why understanding children's learning matters

The quest to determine how a child learns has occupied the minds of great thinkers, and theories about how children learn have influenced educational practice in ways that can be easily traced through history. The idea that children were 'empty slates' or 'empty vessels' as suggested by John Locke in the seventeenth and eighteenth centuries, where children were born waiting to be written on or filled up with knowledge, contributed to the teaching methods of the past where children were mostly silent and expected to listen to the adult and then regurgitate knowledge in a rote-learning scenario. This method of teaching children was slow to change, and in many ways was influenced by the behaviourist theories of Pavlov and Skinner, with the idea that behaviour (including learning) could be conditioned through a process of reinforcement. From the 1960s onward the influence of Piaget changed educational ideas, and *The Plowden Report* (HMSO, 1967) moved towards a more exploratory form of learning, with a more child-centred approach that encouraged children to discover knowledge for themselves through experimentation within their environment, with the adult being the facilitator of the learning experience rather than just the expert. Similarly, when the writings of Vygotsky became more widely discussed, the importance of learning together, socially and in groups with the learning scaffolded by a 'more knowledgeable other', brought further changes to teaching methods. Theories, including Jerome Bruner's 'spiral curriculum', are so embedded in educational practice that the ideas are taken for granted and not always consciously explored (Gibbs, 2014, p. 42).

The traditional theories adopted by schools brought significant changes not only to the thinking about how children were learning, but also to the physical layout of classrooms, with rows of desks facing the teacher being replaced by tables arranged to accommodate group learning; walls with a few charts on display were replaced with brighter, changeable wall displays and resources that children could use independently from adults to aid their learning. Changes in the beliefs about children's learning behaviours also saw the introduction into the classroom of more adults; no longer seen as sufficient, the one adult to 35+ children ratio has given way to smaller classes with several adults supporting learning, particularly for younger children.

Although, arguably, Piaget and Vygotsky may be considered as the 'fathers' of modern understanding of both development and learning, together with researchers such as Pavlov and Skinner (Skinner, 1953, 1971), who argue that learning is a change in behaviour brought about by reinforcement and conditioning, other key writers and researchers have continued to influence the way in which children's learning is approached in educational situations. Words and terms abound that have resonance for the teacher and parent from such developments, including emotional literacy, behaviour for learning, thinking skills, modelling behaviours, teaching and learning strategies to name just a few. All reflect the notion that the child is unique, an active member of the community and that learning is more complex and holistic than perhaps previously considered. Understanding some of the complexity surrounding learning allows us to understand the child and so meet their needs in an increasingly complex world.

Teaching versus learning

Before continuing the exploration of learning in this chapter, the distinction between 'learning' and what constitutes 'teaching' deserves consideration. Within education, it is perhaps impossible to separate one from another as teachers and practitioners are as involved in what should be taught as in what should be learned. Issues of adult and school accountability examine planning and intent as well as how much children know, especially in the core curriculum subjects of literacy and numeracy. Emphasis on knowledge-based assessment adds pressure to adults to 'teach' children facts to a set timetable, although teachers and practitioners who understand children's ways of learning will plan creative activities to engage children in learning. Research seems to indicate that national curriculum testing does inhibit some forms of teaching that may support children in their learning; for example, Jones (2010) found that the teaching of thinking skills in primary schools has suffered as a result of an education system that is dominated by tests and league tables. Encouraging children to think and question is often seen as a fundamental part of learning, so any teaching that prevents children from learning to think for themselves indicates some of the challenges facing educationalists as they ponder the balance between teaching and learning.

Teaching methods are founded on the drive to acquire knowledge and conform to patterns of behaviour that are generally based on behaviourist theories. Such theories are based on assumptions of conditioning and a cycle of reinforcement for certain accepted behaviours that followed the work of Burrhus Frederic Skinner, and others, known as 'operant conditioning'. This theory is based on the study of actions and their consequences, and is often used in schools as part of a system of rewards and punishments. Through reinforcement of certain behaviours, children can be manipulated or programmed into working in ways that support learning in predetermined directions. This is an effective way to manage a class and feedback on learner performance (e.g. encouragement, approval, praise, affirmation) providing reward and also reinforcement to ensure repeat performances.

Learning could perhaps be considered as something that brings its own rewards and reinforcement, but it comes from within the individual rather than being imposed from outside. Perhaps this is the distinction between learning and teaching; one comes from within and the other is controlled and determined by others.

Some traditional views of learning

What is learning? A pause for reflection

Before you read this chapter, pause and consider what you think learning is. How do children learn? What do they learn? How do we know that children are learning?

And then, consider how 'teaching' fits into the picture of learning …

The processes involved in understanding how children learn are complex, and there are differing views that try to satisfactorily answer the fundamental question, 'What is learning?'. Many academic papers and books on learning seem to hesitate to explicitly define the meaning or agree on a definition (De Houwer *et al.*, 2013; Wirth and Perkins, 2008). However, any attempt at a definition usually encompasses the idea that learning involves the acquisition of new knowledge and a change in behaviour, often as a result of experience being internally assimilated in the mind by the individual, either by solitary activity or through interaction with another person or the environment. Dewey (1998) famously links learning to experience, but not to all experiences; he equated learning from experience as the ability to reflect upon the experience in a personal way, thus enabling learning to take place. This idea that experience precedes learning is extended in the notion that 'learning is a consequence of thinking' (Perkins, 1992, p 31; Ritchhart and Perkins, 2008), which stresses the importance of not only educators presenting children with opportunities to experience but to then talk/think/reflect in order to bring about learning.

Our understanding of the role of learning within child development made significant strides with the influential work of Jean Piaget and his interest in cognitive development. His work outlining stages of development related to a child's age showed how children were able to build upon existing knowledge to assimilate and accommodate new learning. In this way, his contribution demonstrates the cumulative and constructive nature of learning; that is, that as new experiences and ideas are explored and assimilated into new mental pictures, the child's view of the world changes and a new layer of knowledge and understanding is established.

Piaget essentially saw learning as a solitary, cognitive activity, with the role of the adult being a facilitator of learning, giving the child experiences and opportunities to explore the world and build knowledge and understanding for themselves. Vygotsky brought a new dimension to such constructivist theories, by stressing the importance of the adult or 'more knowledgeable other' in the learning process. Vygotsky's ideas were based around the way in which a more learned partner can encourage and anticipate the next step in learning and so enhance the learning experience. This led to an appreciation that a difference can be made to the learning process through social interaction. Vygotsky succinctly voiced the idea that 'what the child is able to do in collaboration today he will be able to do independently tomorrow' (Vygotsky, 1987, p. 211; 1998, p. 202) giving value to social learning and talking about learning. This change, from a child working independently to a child learning cooperatively with others, is significant, not only within research, but also in the way children are educated.

Jerome Bruner famously wrote, 'We begin with the hypothesis that any subject can be taught in some intellectually honest form to any child at any stage of development' (Bruner, 1960, p. 33). The intellectual stages on which Bruner based this statement are those established by Piaget, and Bruner valued the observations of a teacher, who told him, 'as far as I am concerned young children learn almost anything faster than adults do if it can be given to them in terms they understand' (David Page in Bruner, 1960, p. 40). This suggests that with relevant and appropriate questioning, the use of an appropriate vocabulary paired with resources that a child can handle themselves will not only speed up learning but will, as Vygotsky also indicated, allow children access to knowledge and skills that may previously have been thought to be beyond their capabilities (Bruner, 1960, pp. 41–4). However, Bruner suggests that it takes many similar experiences to layer knowledge to make 'an educated man' (Bruner, 1960, p. 52); he termed this revisit to similar experiences and knowledge the 'spiral curriculum'.

Bruner (see Wood *et al.*, 1976) also contributed the term 'scaffolding' to the process of learning, following Vygotsky's earlier theories of how a child is supported by the adult in what Lev Vygotsky, writing in the 1930s, called 'the zone of proximal development (ZPD)' (Vygotsky, 1978, pp. 84–8). Vygotsky suggested that using tests could only determine the starting place, or actual development level, of a child's mental ability. This actual development, Vygotsky surmised, only considers the learning that has been fixed in the child's mind and does not take into account the learning that is in an embryonic stage, the potential that may soon be fulfilled. Regardless of the child's age, Vygotsky considered that potential learning was greater than actual learning and that the distance between the two, or zone of proximal development, could be breached 'through problem solving under adult guidance or in collaboration with more capable peers' (Vygotsky, 1978, p. 86). Understanding the gap between the actual learning and the potential, embryonic learning of the child is still a key aspect of the educator's role, and knowing the child well enough to bridge the gap by scaffolding the learning experience that remains a fixture in any learning environment today.

Scaffolding learning: a pause for reflection

Below are some basic steps when scaffolding learning. Consider a situation where these steps have been followed and what the outcome of the learning might have been/not been as a result of the scaffolding process:

- Arouse interest
- Set goals
- Give feedback to keep on task
- Provide assistance when required
- Maintain interest and on-task behaviours
- Control frustration and risk of failure
- Assist internalisation of learning through discussion and questioning.

What happens if you take one or more steps away from the scaffold?

And what is the purpose of the scaffold?

More recent trends in learning theory

The assumptions from Piaget and Vygotsky, namely that learning is constructed internally in the mind as a result of experience and problem solving in the real world, has become the cornerstone of much research. Piaget and Vygotsky were both interested in learning as a part of cognitive development, and Piaget in particular was interested in defining 'stages of development' and linked this to the chronological age of the child and to how children 'perform'. The importance Vygotsky placed upon the social aspects of learning, rather than Piaget's suggestion that the learning is more of a solitary process, has found resonance within education and is supported by other influential writers in the field. The idea of learning with and from others has also been the focus of Bandura's work on social learning, where he comments, 'new patterns of behaviour can be acquired through direct experience or by observing the behaviour of others' (Bandura, 1971, p. 3). Such 'behaviours' encompass not only social cultural norms, but also the actions and attitudes of learners as the child observes and copies significant figures in their lives. Reinforcement of how a learner behaves through both modelling and the consequences of reward or punishment serve to point children towards learning in a direct and efficient way, providing that the child is a willing partner in the process. It is much easier to copy what someone has done previously than to work it out for yourself. Etienne Wenger also added much to our understanding of social learning in his 'community of practice' (Wenger, 1998) theory. This idea is important within education, as it shows that 'learning takes place through ... participation in multiple social practices, practices which are formed through pursuing any kind of enterprise of times' (Farnsworth et al., 2016, p. 2). Encouraging children to bond with each other as they learn will help to establish a 'community of learning', which if children feel they belong will support children's learning disposition and help to create their identity within the community of practice (Wenger in Farnsworth *et al.*, 2016, p. 7).

Social learning theory considers learning in a more holistic manner rather than getting to grips with the details of cognitive development and the acquisition of knowledge. Wenger's 'community of learning' also covers adult behaviours and learning as well as that of a child. Children's learning as a research subject seemed to change from the mid-1970s with the emphasis shifting to ways of thinking (Stevenson, 1983; Siegler, 2000; Jones, 2010) rather than pure 'learning'. This apparent neglect of learning as a research focus is suggested by Siegler (2000) as a result of Piaget's writings where he 'frequently distinguished between development, by which he meant the *active* construction of knowledge, and learning, by which he meant the *passive* formation of associations' (Siegler, 2000, p. 26). Siegler argues that the term *active* was more tempting to researchers to follow up than the term *passive* and so cognitive development of 'thinking skills' became of greater interest. The research into children's cognitive skills led to the inclusion of 'thinking skills' into the National Curriculum (Jones, 2010, p. 70) and a large amount of support material is available to teach such skills, including that produced by Robert Fisher (see Fisher, 2011). Bloom's *Taxonomy*, in which he sets out a hierarchy of six categories in the cognitive domain, was originally intended to test the depth of understanding of students' knowledge (Krathwohl, 2002). The categories were quickly adapted to structure questions for children not only to assess their knowledge but also to promote deeper thinking and reflection. Questioning, and requiring children to think critically about stories, information and experiences, continues to be used across the curriculum. Thinking, and promoting thinking, is not just for older children and adults; Salmon (2016) argues for expanding children's learning during play by probing their experiences and inviting them 'to question, find problems and explore solutions [so] they can get into a deeper level of learning' (Salmon, 2016, p. 481).

During the 1990s, new research into the *process* of learning also became more of a focus in research that has affected our thinking about learning and how to support learning within education. This new approach to investigating children's learning resulted in looking at strategies of learning, and, according to Siegler (2005), had three main assumptions:

1. Children were recognised as using both active and passive learning mechanisms.

2. Children were active in selecting strategies to solve problems and reflected upon their successes and failures.

3. Children also benefited from statistical learning, associative learning and pattern recognition.

(Siegler, 2005, p. 769)

One of the key concepts here that has had the most influence on our understanding of the process of learning today and one that is commonly used within education is the idea of employing 'strategies for learning'. Strategies, however, within the research apply not only to the way in which adults might support learning, but more importantly to how children actually learn. Microgenetic studies (i.e. closely analysed observations) have formed the basis of research projects and it has found that children use a range of strategies in their own learning as they solve a problem or engage in personal, meaningful activity (Siegler, 2005). Research indicates that not only do children use a range of strategies as they learn but they also continually develop new strategies to fit new situations (Siegler and Svetina, 2006; Siegler, 2005). Children who develop strategies for learning at an early age also appear to become more able learners later on in life. Research shows that although typically the number of strategies used to learn may increase with age and experience, children aged 1 to 10 years are commonly found to use the same pathway of strategies (Siegler, 2005, p. 773). The idea that differently aged children use a similar range of strategies could be taken further. Consider the notion that the only difference between a child and an adult is that the child has more learning to do and so is at the early stages of developing a range of strategies, whereas an adult has already developed the (same) range of strategies and may use them unconsciously.

In a similar comparison, adults are more interested in the *products* of learning, whereas young children, in particular, are more interested in the doing, the *processes* of learning as they acquire new learning strategies and understanding. If this assumption is correct, then learning strategies are common to all, regardless of age or stage of development. The strategies may be refined and expanded but the development of strategies can be mapped into future learning or 'lifelong learning'.

Strategies: a pause for reflection

Think of one learning situation you have experienced; which strategies did you use to learn?

Can you list these strategies in the order that they were used? How do you know if they were effective in promoting your learning? Was there any barrier to stop you learning?

Building a learning identity

If children are developing strategies in their own learning, they are also conceivably developing their personal learning identity. This is important, as understanding yourself as a 'learner' and being aware of how you learn is likely to influence beliefs and attitudes. The person who engages in self-talk that says 'I am a poor learner' or 'I am quick to learn new things' is likely to be right. This idea is encapsulated in the 'I can' initiative (www.ican.org.uk) and other schemes designed to promote positive and affirmative thinking.

Figure 1.1   'I can do it!' positive thinking enhances learning

Children seem to have their own ideas as to what learning is, and also know who is 'good' at learning. Consider the responses to the questions that were given by children and pick out some of the comments to reflect upon that are meaningful to you (Table 1.1).

Table 1.1 First thinking: What is learning?

What is learning? (Responses from a group of Year 5 and Year 6 children)

- Learning is where you're finding things out for yourself but having fun at the same time.
- Learning is writing, doing practical things and having fun.
- Stuff that helps your life.
- I think learning is for the students who never know the thing before, and they know it after the lesson.
- Learning is when you get told something and you remember it.
- Learning is when you learn something new for the very first time.
- Learning is education: education is learning.
- When you do something you have never done before, or when you spell a word wrong, or when you MAKE A MISTAKE.
- Learning is when the teacher teaches you something and you do it yourself.
- Learning is something that gets you a good job.
- It is something that helps you through daily life and when you get something wrong you know how to do it next time.
- Learning well is hard work.
- I learn best by finding things out by myself and by asking questions.
- I feel that a lot of people outside of school help me learn. You don't stop learning as soon as school ends. I feel I learn most when I am enjoying the subject and also when it has a physical aspect to it.

What helps you to learn? (Responses from a group of Year 5 and Year 6 children)

- Doing practical things.
- Concentration.
- Groups and team work.
- Learning in a fun way.
- My teacher.
- Helping me learn is when I am happy but also when I work with someone (a girl though).
- A quiet environment.
- Using laptops, watching TV and looking at clips help me to learn and when I can discuss things with my friends.
- Resources around the class help me with my work.
- Using the Internet and books helps me.
- Displays help me to learn because sometimes they give you the answers.
- The classroom helps me because I'm next to a girl and I won't talk to a girl.
- My friend; she tells me the answer and then shows me how to work it out.

How do you learn? (Responses from younger children)

- ▪ I learn when my teacher asks me questions (boy, aged 5).
- ▪ I learn when Mrs R. writes on the big white board (girl, aged 5).
- ▪ I learn with a partner (boy, aged 7).
- ▪ On my own when it's quiet. When I've finished and I've got it all right and the teacher tells me it is good (boy, aged 7).
- ▪ I learn best when I'm working with a partner or a grown up (girl, aged 6).
- ▪ I like to work in peace and quiet because I can concentrate better (girl, aged 8).
- ▪ I like to know what to do before we do it (boy, aged 8).

All the responses shown in Table 1.1 indicate that children know that they are learning.

Children are also aware of times when they do not learn; consider these responses from children:

- ▪ I'm not fond of maths because I don't think the teacher likes me (boy, aged 8).

- ▪ When I am sad (aged 10).

That children are aware of their own learning is perhaps not surprising, although Colliver and Fleer (2016) express the opinion that children are not often asked about learning in the belief that the subject is too complex for children to understand. However, Colliver and Fleer (2016) maintain that children from the age of 2 to 5 years were clearly able to perceive their learning through play activities. Understanding how they learn suggests that children also develop a sense of a learning identity and may also consciously develop learning strategies as opposed to using trial-and-error methods of learning.

An earlier study (Sobel *et al.*, 2007) also started with the body of research which suggests that children lack the metacognitive abilities that prevent them from reflecting upon the process of learning (Sobel *et al.*, 2007, p. 346). Sobel and colleagues were interested in finding out what young children know about the process of learning, and more specifically 'about how, when and why learning takes place' (Sobel *et al.*, 2007, p. 346). They concluded that young children (aged from 3 years) are able to explain how learning takes place, and moreover conclude that as children develop they increasingly recognise that the 'desire to learn' promotes more learning. This is important, as children who want to learn and have a positive view of themselves as learners are more likely to achieve success in future learning.

Strategies for learning: adults supporting learning

Adults promoting learning may have many agendas, not least the need to prove their effectiveness as teachers driven by the testing of the results of learning within educational establishments. If, as suggested earlier, learning is a change in behaviour as a result of experience or the acquisition of knowledge, then adults supporting learning strive to have control of behaviour, experience and the new knowledge designed to make children 'better' learners. Behaviourist theories (e.g. Skinner) and those of cognitive, constructive learning researchers (e.g. Piaget) help to shape the way in which adults mould children into thinking, questioning and learning-directed beings. Towards this end, the identification of 'types of learners' and learning styles has been promoted within education. Pritchard (2009) offers a comprehensive guide to 'ways of learning' based on the work of key researchers, defining learning style as being:

- a particular way in which an individual learns;

- a mode of learning – an individual's preferred or best manner(s) in which to think, process information and demonstrate learning;

- an individual's preferred means of acquiring knowledge and skills;

- habits, strategies, or regular mental behaviours concerning learning, particularly deliberate educational learning, that an individual displays.

(Pritchard, 2009, p. 41)

From these various parts of the definition of learning style, it is clear that the teacher/practitioner's first task is to get to know the child. The second task, of course, is to recognise when 'significant learning' takes place (Wirth and Perkins, 2008, p. 10). Only by understanding the individual, unique aspects of each child can the adult begin to consider strategies and support for learning.

Commonly, 'strategies' are listed as ways for adults to prompt learning in children but it is also important to remember that children do develop learning strategies themselves (Kirsch, 2012, p. 383) naturally, as a result of experience when satisfying the natural curiosity about the world in which they live. Initial self-regulated learning (SRL) strategies could be considered as being prompted by a sense of curiosity and a desire to know; children become active and purposeful in their intent to achieve their goals and apply 'domain-appropriate learning strategies' to their acquisition of knowledge and learning (Donker et al., 2014, p. 2). Donker and colleagues (2014), in their study of the effectiveness of learning strategy instruction, offer three broad categories of strategies, each having several components:

- Cognitive strategies: including rehearsal, elaboration and organisation of tasks.

- Metacognitive strategies: including planning, monitoring and evaluation.

- Management strategies: including effort, working with peers and using the environment.

(Donker et al., 2014, p. 3)

It is suggested that children use different strategies, or adapt strategies, in different subject areas or situations; as you read through the chapters in this book, you will find different strategies suggested for different subject disciplines as these three groups of strategies are also employed within education to promote children's learning.

Zhou and Urhahne (2016, p. 1) recognise the rise in the study of self-regulated learning (SRL) strategies as being the focus of many recent studies across a range of research disciplines (Nota *et al.*, 2004; Cleary, 2006; Leidinger and Perels, 2012; Karlen, 2016). SRL strategies are those which encourage learners to be more autonomous and to direct their own strategies for learning. Although seen as being complex (Boekaerts, 2005), the various definitions of SRL may be summarised as active goal-directed learning in which learners make plans, monitor and adjust their learning and behaviour, and then reflect and evaluate learning (Schunk, 2005). Such definitions more than hint that learning is a cycle, as suggested by Kolb (1984) and later by Honey and Mumford (1986) in their learning questionnaire. Considering the individual in the learning process shows the importance of observation and relationships in learning; that need to belong to the social group or community of learners.

The three categories of learning strategies do not initially appear to take into account motivational aspects of learning, such as self-efficacy, persistence, resilience and a general disposition towards learning. Such motivational characteristics may be assumed to lie within a child's natural curiosity and exploration of the world; learning may be self-directed as well as employing self-regulated strategies. Donker and colleagues (2014) consider the importance of the motivational aspects of learning, such as self-efficacy, the value of the task and the goal orientation in learning. In determining *what* (rather than *how*) things are learned, many writers argue that motivation, interest and a disposition towards learning are important prerequisites for learning, and the use of strategy comes second. The more holistic wrap-around approaches to learning that consider the social, emotional aspects of learning (SEAL) have also become a part of learning strategy in many educational environments (DfES, 2005). Oberle and colleagues credit social and emotional learning (SEL) as a 'fundamental part of education' (Oberle *et al.*, 2016, p. 1), and go on to argue that SEL is an essential process in providing all children with the opportunities to learn (Oberle *et al.*, 2016, p. 3).

Strategies, then, to promote learning should combine a more holistic, 'soft' approach than merely a mechanical approach. Becoming a member of the learning community is as much of a social, emotional experience as it is a cognitive or ability-based set of skills.

Conclusions and implications for promoting learning

The chapters in this book consider the different aspects of learning from a range of perspectives, all directed towards promoting learning. Figure 1.2 provides a summary.

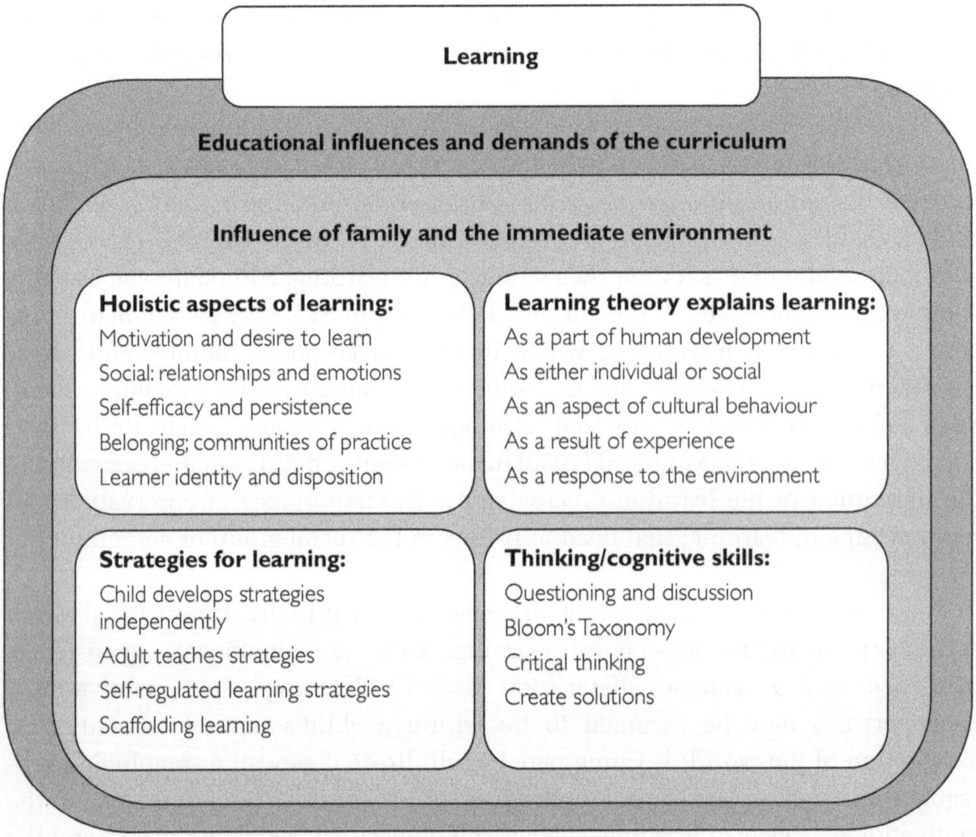

Learning

Educational influences and demands of the curriculum

Influence of family and the immediate environment

Holistic aspects of learning:
Motivation and desire to learn
Social: relationships and emotions
Self-efficacy and persistence
Belonging; communities of practice
Learner identity and disposition

Learning theory explains learning:
As a part of human development
As either individual or social
As an aspect of cultural behaviour
As a result of experience
As a response to the environment

Strategies for learning:
Child develops strategies independently
Adult teaches strategies
Self-regulated learning strategies
Scaffolding learning

Thinking/cognitive skills:
Questioning and discussion
Bloom's Taxonomy
Critical thinking
Create solutions

Figure 1.2 Some of the different aspects and influences on learning

The different aspects of learning all offer key suggestions for those wishing to support learning within education. The chief points from these suggestions indicate four main strands in learning.

First, learning is about experience in all its forms, from play (Salmon, 2016, p. 481) through to carrying out experiments in a science laboratory. Roberts (2005) lists six ways in which experience is frequently introduced into the curriculum:

- 'Hands-on' activities to liven up the curriculum.

- Field trips to take learning out of the classroom.

- Experiential activities (for example, to reach different learning styles).

- 'Learn-by-doing' to cement certain concepts or principles (for example, in science).

- Bringing personal experiences into the classroom – visiting speakers, drama, exhibitions.

- Use of narratives as part of the social process of schooling.

(adapted from Roberts, 2005, p. 15)

Second, the idea that 'learning is a consequence of thinking' (Perkins, 1992, p. 31) demands that an educator creates situations where children's thinking is pushed past the obvious into deeper, more critical thinking. Thinking is not seen here as a solitary activity but as a part of an interactive activity, where there is an exchange of ideas with specialised vocabulary and sharing of knowledge among children and adults (Ritchhart and Perkins, 2008, P. 57). The notion that thinking is linked to experience is also highlighted by Kuhn when she writes 'that students' learning is enhanced when they have identified a question or a problem' (Kuhn and Deary, 2005 in Kuhn, 2007, p. 109), showing the need for the educator to set meaningful tasks for children that are relevant and appropriate for their age and stage, but that are also tasks that stretch their thinking and capabilities.

Third, educators need to build on the strategies that children have already developed and to create interventions where children can be taught and then explore new strategies for learning. There are many strategies for learning, some subject specific, but Donker *et al.* (2014) list some used within primary and secondary settings that may lead to, or build on, self-regulated learning patterns. These strategies include the following:

- Planning of learning tasks.

- Goal setting, including monitoring progress and making adjustments.

- Evaluating learning and outcomes.

(Donker *et al.*, 2014, pp. 2–3)

Although these strategies may be thought of in terms of older children, the 'Plan, Do, Review' cycle established by HighScope Educational Research Foundation for the early years indicates that very young children can also adopt and use such strategies. Other key strategies that children use involve memory and recall which teachers can model and teach; for example, mnemonic actions (Paris *et al.*, 1982; Ghatala, 1986), including clustering, association, humour and rehearsal to aid memory and the learning of tricks and rhymes (such as ROYGBIN for rainbow colours).

Finally, it is important to consider the learner in the learning process; this seems obvious, but it is sometimes easy to become immersed in the curriculum and the accountability of assessment procedures and to overlook the importance of really getting to know children and their learning disposition. Understanding learning, as a process and an outcome, must make for greater awareness of how best to provide children with opportunities for learning how to learn. As Claxton (2007) reminds us, effective learners are capable of being:

- curious, adventurous and questioning

- resilient, determined and focused

- open-minded, flexible, imaginative and creative

- critical, sceptical and analytical

- both methodical and opportunistic

- reflective, thoughtful and self-evaluative

- keen to build on their products and performances

- collaborative but also independent.

(Claxton, 2007, p. 117)

This chapter has considered learning theories but cannot present all the different ideas and theories associated with learning and those that are continuing to be explored, including new evidence from neuroscience and research. However, it has attempted to cover important developments that have influenced educational practice. As you read through the following chapters, some of the ideas presented here will be augmented, together with some additional material related to how children learn in different areas of the curriculum and at different stages in their development.

Suggested further reading

Bates, B. (2016) *Learning Theories Simplified …and how to apply them to teaching.* London: Sage.
   This text offers an overview of all the traditional theories, plus those relating to teaching (rather than learning!). Altogether, it includes '100 theories and models from great thinkers'.
Wirth, K.R. and Perkins, D. (2008) *Learning to Learn.* Online document available from: www.macalester.edu/academics/geology/wirth/learning.pdf (accessed 29 April 2016).
   This gives an overview of key aspects of learning, ranging from thinking skills to research findings from neuroscience.

Websites

The Open University has a free learning website, OpenLearn, where one course, 'Exploring children's learning', provides information on four traditional key learning theories. Visit www.open.edu/openlearn/education/educational-technology-and-practice/educational-practice/exploring-childrens-learning/content-section-0
Try a search for Robert Fisher's stories for thinking and other resources; these will provide ideas for how to promote thinking and discussion using stories that can be adapted for different ages and subjects.
The National Association of the Education of Young Children (NAEYC) offers ten strategies to use with Early Years. Visit www.naeyc.org/dap/10-effective-dap-teaching-strategies to read more.

References

Bandura, A. (1971) *Social Learning Theory*. New York: General Learning Press.

Boekaerts, M. (2005) Self-regulation in the classroom: A perspective on assessment and intervention. *Applied Psychology: An International Review*, 54(2), pp. 199–231.

Bruner, J. (1960) *The Process of Education*. Cambridge, MA: The President and Fellows of Harvard College.

Claxton, G. (2007) Expanding young people's capacity to learn. *British Journal of Educational Studies,* 55(2), pp. 115–34.

Cleary, T.J. (2006) The development and validation of the Self-Regulation Strategy Inventory – Self-report. *Journal of School Psychology*, 44, pp. 307–22.

Colliver, Y. and Fleer, M. (2016) 'I already know what I learned': Young children's perspectives on learning through play. *Early Child Development and Care*, pp. 1–12. Available from www.tandfonline.com/eprint/mRhIrkr4eFv88ecbmzzg/full (accessed 21 April 2016).

De Houwer, J., Barnes-Holmes, D. and Moors, A. (2013) What is learning? On the nature and merits of a functional definition of learning. *Psychonomic Bulletin & Review*, 20(4), pp. 631–42.

Dewey, J. (1998) *Experience and Education: The 60th Anniversary Edition*. Indiana: Kappa Delta.

DfES (Department for Education and Science) (2005) *Primary National Strategy: Excellence and Enjoyment: Social and Emotional Aspects of Learning Guidance*. London: HMSO: DfES Publications.

Donker, A.S., de Boer, H., Kostons, D., Dignath van Ewijk, C.C. and van der Werf, M.P.C. (2014) Effectiveness of learning strategy instruction on academic performance: A meta-analysis. *Educational Research Review*, 11, pp. 1–26.

Farnsworth, V., Kleanthous, I. and Wenger-Trayner, E. (2016) Communities of practice as a social theory of learning: A conversation with Etienne Wenger. *British Journal of Educational Studies*, pp.1–22.

Fisher, A. (2011) *Critical Thinking: An Introduction* (2nd edn). Cambridge: Cambridge University Press.

Ghatala, E.S. (1986) Strategy-monitoring training enables young learners to select effective atrategies. *Educational Psychologist*, 21, pp. 1–2, 43–54.

Gibbs, B.C. (2014) *Reconfiguring Bruner: Compressing the Spiral Curriculum*. The Phi Delta Kappan, Vol. 95, No. 7 (April 2014), pp. 41–44. Published by Phi Delta Kappan International Stable. Available from www.jstor.org/stable/24374719 (accessed 3 April 2016).

HMSO (1967) *The Plowden Report: Children and their Primary Schools: A Report of the Central Advisory Council for Education (England)*. London: Her Majesty's Stationery Office. Available from www.educationengland.org.uk/documents/plowden/index.html (accessed 30 March 2016).

Honey, P. and Mumford, A. (1986) *Manual of Learning Styles (2nd edn)*. Maidenhead, Berkshire: P. Honey.

Jones, H. (2010) National Curriculum tests and the teaching of thinking skills at primary schools – parallel or paradox? *Education 3–13*, 38(1), pp. 69–86.

Karlen, Y. (2016) Differences in students' metacognitive strategy knowledge, motivation, and strategy use: A typology of self-regulated learners. *The Journal of Educational Research?*

Kirsch, C. (2012) Developing children's language learner strategies at primary school. *Education 3–13*, 40(4), pp. 379–99.

Kolb, D. (1984) *Experiential Learning: Experience as the source of learning and development.* Englewood Cliffs, NJ: Prentice-Hall.

Krathwohl, D.R. (2002) A revision of Bloom's Taxonomy: An Overview. *Theory Into Practice*, 41(4), pp. 212–18.

Kuhn, D. (2007) Is direct instruction an answer to the right question? *Educational Psychologist*, 42(2), pp. 109-13.

Leidinger, M. and Perels, F. (2012) Training self-regulated learning in the classroom: Development and evaluation of learning materials to train self-regulated learning during regular mathematics lessons at primary school. *Education Research International. Vol. 2012, Article ED735790.*

Nota, L., Soresi, S. and Zimmerman, B.J. (2004) Self-regulation and academic achievement and resilience: A longitudinal study. *International Journal of Educational Research*, 41, pp. 198–215.

Oberle, E., Domitrovich, C.E., Meyers, D.C. and Weissberg, R.P. (2016) Establishing systemic social and emotional learning approaches in schools: A framework for schoolwide implementation. *Cambridge Journal of Education*, 45(3), pp. 277–97.

Paris, S.G., Newman, R.S. and McVey, K.A. (1982) Learning the functional significance of mnemonic actions: A microgenetic study of strategy acquisition. *Journal of Experimental Child Psychology*, 34, pp. 490–509.

Perkins, D.N. (1992) *Smart Schools: Better thinking and learning for every child.* New York: Free Press.

Pritchard, A. (2009) *Ways of Learning: Learning theories and learning styles in the classroom (2nd edn).* London: Routledge.

Ritchhart, R. and Perkins, D. (2008) Making thinking visible. *Educational Leadership*, 65(5), pp. 57–61. Available from www.visiblethinkingpz.org/VisibleThinking_html_files/06_AdditionalResources/makingthinkingvisibleEL.pdf (accessed 21 April 2016).

Roberts, J.W. (2005) Disney, Dewey and the death of experience. *Education and Culture*, 21(2), pp. 12–30. Available from www.jstor.org/stable/42922572 (accessed 16 April 2016).

Salmon, A.K. (2016) Learning by thinking during play: The power of reflection to aid performance. *Early Child Development and Care*, 186(3), pp. 480–96.

Schunk, D.H. (2005) Self-regulated learning: The educational legacy of Paul R. Pintrich. *Educational Psychologist*, 40(2), pp. 85–94.

Siegler, R.S. (2000) The rebirth of children's learning. *Child Development*, 71(1), pp. 26–35.

Siegler, R.S. (2005) Children's learning. *American Psychologist*, 60(6), pp. 769–78.

Siegler, R.S. and Svetina, M. (2006) What leads children to adopt new strategies? A microgenetic/cross-sectional study of class inclusion. *Child Development*, 77(4), pp 997–1015.

Skinner, B.F. (1953) *Science and Human Behaviour.* New York: The Free Press, Simon & Schuster Inc.

Skinner, B.F. (1971) *Beyond Freedom and Dignity.* Middlesex: Penguin Books.

Sobel, D.M., Li, J. and Corriveau, K.H. (2007) They danced around in my head and I learned them: Children's developing conceptions of learning. *Journal of Cognition and Development*, 8(3), pp. 345–69.

Stevenson, H. (1983) How children learn: The quest for a theory. In W. Kessen (ed.) and P.H. Mussen (series ed.) *Handbook of Child Psychology, Vol. 1. History, Theory and Methods* (pp. 213–36). New York: Wiley.

Vygotsky, L.S. (1978) Interaction between learning and development. In M. Gauvain and M. Cole (eds) (1997) *Readings on the Development of Children* (pp. 29–36) (2nd edn). New York: Freeman & Company. This chapter was originally published as ch. 6, pp. 79–91, in Vygotsky, L.S. (1978) *Mind in Society: The development of higher psychological processes* (edited by M. Cole, V. John-Steiner, S. Scribner and E. Souberman). Cambridge, MA: Harvard University Press. (Original manuscripts [*c.* 1930–4]).

Vygotsky, L.S. (1987) *Thinking and Speech* (trans. N. Minick). In R.W. Rieber and A.S. Carton (eds), *The Collected Works of L.S. Vygotsky: Vol. 1. Problems of General Psychology* (pp. 39–285). New York: Plenum Press. (Original work published 1934).

Vygotsky, L.S. (1998) *The Problem of Age* (trans. M. Hall). In R.W. Rieber (ed.) *The Collected Works of L.S. Vygotsky: Vol. 5. Child Psychology* (pp. 187–205). New York: Plenum Press. (Original work written 1933–4).

Wenger, E. (1998) *Communities of Practice: Learning, Meaning, and Identity*. New York: Cambridge University Press.

Wirth, K.R. and Perkins, D. (2008) *Learning to Learn*. Available from www.macalester.edu/academics/geology/wirth/learning.pdf (accessed 29 April 2016).

Wood, D., Bruner, J.S. and Ross, G. (1976) The role of tutoring in problem solving. *British Journal of Psychology*, 66, 181–91.

Zhou, J. and Urhahne, D. (2016) Self-regulated learning in the museum: Understanding the relationship of visitor's goals, learning strategies, and appraisals. *Scandinavian Journal of Educational Research*, pp. 1–17. Available from www.tandfonline.com/doi/full/10.1080/00313831.2016.1147071 (accessed 25 April 2016).

Children's views on what matters in learning and life

2

Catherine Meehan

Chapter overview

Using Pedagogical Documentation as a tool for assessing children, this chapter reports on research conducted with children, asking the question 'What matters to you?'. The chapter describes the origins of Pedagogical Documentation from Reggio Emilia, and presents a justification for its use by early childhood educators. Drawing upon current research, theory and policy, this chapter explores the tensions that exist for teachers/educators and practitioners working with young children and including their voice. Children's words, drawings, photographs and artefacts will be used to narrate five themes from the data about what is important to children in their lives.

Introduction

> Documentation is key to a practice which genuinely unites thought with action, belief with rituals, philosophy with pedagogy, and perhaps aesthetics with the mundane.
>
> (Lawson, 2000)

Other chapters in this book explore learning and pedagogy for young children from a range of perspectives within early childhood education and care settings, with links to curriculum and the Early Years Foundation Stage and the National Curriculum. Pedagogical Documentation has its origins with educators from Reggio Emilia. In this chapter, Pedagogical Documentation is used as a mode for assessing children's learning. It is underpinned by a set of values and beliefs about children.

The chapter discusses this specific approach to early childhood pedagogy which relates to documenting children's learning through observation and an alternative method for assessment. This approach is firmly founded within a pedagogical framework underpinned by values about children, their learning, the learning environment and those adults who work with children. The educational philosophies unique to Reggio Emilia were first reported in the literature in the early 1990s and have since been influential around the world in terms of curriculum, policy and practice.

Underpinning this pedagogical practice are the historical, theoretical, economic, political, social and educational factors which saw the emergence of this practice and how this has informed the development of curriculum internationally and the features of Pedagogical Documentation which are embedded in the Early Years Foundation Stage.

The background to Pedagogical Documentation in practice will also be considered in the context of the United Nations Conventions on the Rights of the Child (UNCRC); and as a means for communication and advocacy about young children's abilities rather than deficits.

Three case studies will be presented in this chapter to illustrate how Pedagogical Documentation may be used in practice to make children's learning visible. The case studies come from a project undertaken with university students in which Pedagogical Documentation was used as a form of assessment in Early Childhood Studies (Meehan, 2015b).

The chapter aims to help you to:

- Understand the origins and theoretical perspectives of Pedagogical Documentation.

- Consider how Pedagogical Documentation may be used with children, families and communities as a form of communication.

- Explore how this method of assessment can engage children in reflecting on their own learning.

Reflection: photographs and stories are shared memories of people, places and learning together

In January 2006, my family travelled with me to Reggio Emilia to attend a study tour in the schools. It was an opportunity to explore part of Italy, experience culture, music, art and traditions, and to be immersed in a place that was familiar but also unfamiliar. Reflecting on Figures 2.1 and 2.2, there is a narrative around these: buying a winter coat in the market, my daughter climbing on the lion statues, writing on the footpath 'Let it Snow' in the dusting of snow and waking up to the snowstorm which dumped a metre of snow in Reggio Emilia. The photos and stories capture a time and place and, in sharing them, I am making visible to a wider audience the environment and relationships that shaped my learning.

My experiences of this place, the photographs, the stories, the people I met, discussions and debates I was involved in have all shaped me as an educator, researcher and person. As I listened to Italian colleagues talking about their

Figure 2.1 The Lion statue in Reggio Emilia provides artistic inspiration and a tactile climbing experience for children

Figure 2.2 Market day in Reggio Emilia: a family shopping experience

approaches to teaching and learning, views on children, the environment and relationships with families, I felt at home but at the same time I felt challenged. This event was pivotal in terms of reinforcing my values and principles about young children, their learning, the role of the teacher and the value of Pedagogical Documentation in making children's learning visible. It shaped me and the experiences of Reggio Emilia continue to challenge me as an educator.

Framing Pedagogical Documentation

In many assignments I have read from students in the past, there have been some myths about Reggio Emilia. For the record, Reggio Emilia is not:

- a person, an Italian philosopher, someone like Montessori, Dewey, Vygotsky;

- a curriculum, syllabus, recipe for effective, successful early childhood curriculum;

- a centre for specialised training;

- the Reggio Emilia approach;

- a quaint village with one fantastic school.

Reggio Emilia is a vibrant city in the north of Italy. It came to the world's attention in 1991, when the American magazine *Newsweek* featured the schools of Reggio Emilia on the cover as 'an exemplary model of early childhood education'. The article applauded the schools for their commitment to creating learning environments that facilitated children's learning and thinking. The schools in Reggio Emilia are run by the city (municipality) and they cater for children from birth through to 6 years of age.

Historical, political, economic and social context as the backdrop for understanding the education and schools in Reggio Emilia

This chapter focuses specifically on the pedagogical approach derived from Reggio Emilia. This approach is situated within the socio-cultural theoretical perspectives. The time and place is of great importance in appreciating the context in which an educational approach is developed. Like other great educational pioneers, such as Maria Montessori, Friedrich Froebel and Robert Owen; Loris Malaguzzi, the founder of the schools in Reggio Emilia, had a profound influence in establishing an educational philosophy which continues to develop long after his death. The schools in Reggio Emilia are dynamic learning communities that continue to evolve but share a common set of values which underpin teaching and learning. In order to understand those values, it is important to reflect on the foundations and origins of the schools.

The story of Reggio Emilia is well documented in the literature (see e.g. Edwards *et al.*, 2012; Thornton and Brunton, 2014). Following liberation in 1945, this northern Italian town like many others in Europe had been decimated, and many of the locals had emigrated. Those who remained had to rebuild their lives, literally from the ruins. The people of Reggio Emilia decided in the rebuilding process that never again did they want their community to face war, and set about building a city that valued social democracy. Between 1947 and 1963, the National Women's Union oversaw the process and the first municipal school of the city was opened in 1963. The Diana school was established for 3- to 6-year-old children and remains one of the well-known schools in the heart of the city in a park adjacent to the Opera House. In 1971, the first school for children from birth to 3 years was opened (Reggio Children, 2008).

The northern part of Italy historically has been more socialist than further south. The collective approaches to decision making and distribution of city finances have focused on those who needed the resource. For example, the city funds early childhood education for children from birth to 6 years (approximately 14%) and the care of the elderly more highly than other municipalities around the world. The city recognised the necessity for both men and women to work in rebuilding the city and therefore child and elder care was supportive of these aims (Edwards *et al.*, 2012; Reggio Children, 2008).

Considering priorities: a pause for reflection

Find out from your local council how much of the budget is spent on the education and care of young children. Look at what the priorities are in your local area and consider the reasons why the funding may be more or less than the 14 per cent that the city of Reggio Emilia spends on child care and education.

Pedagogy and the principles of education in Reggio Emilia

Underpinning theoretical perspectives

Loris Malaguzzi was born in 1920. He is the founder of Reggio Emilia schools and was a contemporary of Piaget, but they had very different outlooks on children, learning and education. Malaguzzi trained in pedagogy and specialised in psychology. He worked as a primary school teacher in Italy and in the late 1940s started to work in the Villa Cella community to rebuild the first school from the rubble of bombed houses. He was a writer, consultant and advisor for schools in the Emilia-Romagna region, and was inspired by the local community building the new schools together and without the formalities of building authorities (Reggio Children, 2008).

Mantovani (2007) describes the core themes that characterise the pedagogy of Reggio Emilia. These themes include the pedagogy of well-being, 'good taste' (aesthetics), relationships, continuity, participation, documentation and culture. These themes emanate throughout the schools in Reggio Emilia and are evident in research about Reggio Emilia and observed in practice. The themes are based on social-constructivist views of children and also appreciate the 'multiple intelligences' or 'hundred languages' of children in the way they communicate and express their ideas and themselves. Politically and ideologically, the ideas associated with democracy, rights, access, inclusion and participation are all fundamental to the approach to education in schools in Reggio Emilia.

Malaguzzi made some profound statements about teaching and learning, and with other educators established a set of principles which underpin the education of children from birth to 6 years. For example, this quote highlights his beliefs about teaching, the role of teachers and the learning environment:

> Learning and teaching should not stand on opposite banks and just watch the river flow by; instead, they should make together a journey down the water. Through an active, reciprocal exchange, teaching can strengthen learning and how to learn.
>
> (Malaguzzi, 1993, cited in Edwards *et al.*, 2012, p. 83)

There are seven interrelated principles which underpin education in Reggio Emilia schools:

1. Pedagogy of relationships which includes relationships between children, educators, parents and families, the local community and the social/emotional and physical environment.

2. Pedagogy of listening has been described by Rinaldi (1998) who suggests that listening facilitates relationships within the social and physical environments and enables a range of 'voices' or perspectives to be considered.

3. Communication and collaboration is linked to both the pedagogy of relationship and listening. This principle values the contribution of every person and asserts the right for all to be heard. Collaboration provides opportunities for people to gain new understandings, perspectives, interests, abilities, and attitudes for both children and adults.

4. Pedagogical Documentation is a tool used by teachers to provide opportunities for reflection. It can be a communication tool for parents and promotes the potential of children.

5. Projects are a vehicle for collaboration and exploration of children's theories and provide opportunities for theories to be tested.

6. The hundred languages are the many ways in which children communicate and the pedagogy of listening should support children in having responsive adults who recognise the many ways in which children communicate.

7. The environment, both social/emotional and physical, is known as the 'third educator', the child and the adult being the other two educators. Learning occurs through social interaction and exploration (Caldwell, 1997; Gandini, 1997; Hill *et al.*, 2005).

Edwards and colleagues (2012) attribute a lot of vocabulary that is used in contemporary early childhood education and care policy and curriculum to ideas grounded in the values and philosophy of the schools in RE. For example, terms such as 'visibility, context, Pedagogical Documentation, projected curriculum, image of the child, education as a relationship and participation' are used interchangeably. For example, Hill and colleagues (2005, p. 17) described education in Reggio Emilia schools as a:

> System of relationships that foster the implementation of a social-constructivist, inquiry based approach to teaching that takes into account the cultural transmission of learning and the transformation of self as teachers and learners.

Similarly, children have been constructed as 'protagonists, collaborators and communicators' in the learning process whereas adults are constructed as partners and guides in children's learning (Caldwell, 1997; Gandini, 1997; Hill *et al.*, 2005).

Defining Pedagogical Documentation

Is Pedagogical Documentation a noun or a verb? Is it an object or an action? As a noun and an object it is a visual narrative, an artefact which captures a moment of children's learning. When thinking about Pedagogical Documentation as a verb or a 'doing' word, it becomes an action of the educator or teacher which includes close observation, consideration of the next steps in learning and then narrating the story of the learning and teaching interactions (Pelo, 2006 in Fleet *et al.*, 2006).

Educators at the schools in Reggio Emilia view education as a construction of relationships and documentation as narrative, telling the story of the children, the place and the new relationships, and interacting with objects and the learning and meaning making that occurs in that time and space (Rinaldi, 1998). Dahlberg and colleagues (1999) define Pedagogical Documentation as a process and content produced as part of that process. It is the relationships between children and their teachers, and the environment and objects create a climate for co-construction and reflection on learning.

To 'document' is to provide support with evidence of an assertion (Helm *et al.*, 1998). As evidence that children are actively engaged in learning, in meaningful experiences and construction of knowledge through interactions with their environments and each other, a teacher uses documentation to make this visible. At a time when teachers need to be accountable for their work with children, documentation meets this demand (Helm *et al.*, 1998). Documentation is a way of making visible the often invisible learning and teaching that occurs every day.

The educators of Reggio Emilia, drawing upon their principles of education, view Pedagogical Documentation as a means of making their practice public, by leaving it open to interpretation, challenges and as a provocation. Robertson (2006) asserted that Pedagogical Documentation was more than a classroom display. She suggested that it would be easier for teachers to keep things private and away from scrutiny; however, teachers cannot escape the fact that their 'knowledge, subjectivities and theoretical paradigms drive every decision they make about how a child will learn' (Robertson et al., 2006, p. 52).

Pedagogical Documentation and the UNCRC

> Each new generation offers humanity another chance. If we provide for the survival and development of children everywhere, protect them from harm and exploitation and enable them to participate in decisions directly affecting their lives, we will surely build the foundation of the just society we all want and children deserve.
>
> (Rights of the Child Factsheet 10, UNICEF)

The foundational values and philosophy of the schools in Reggio Emilia are an embodiment of the principles of the UNCRC. The quote above from UNICEF is apt, as it captures the intentions of the pioneers of education in the schools of Reggio Emilia. They built the schools from ruins following the Second World War, and the pioneers of education in Reggio Emilia vowed never to experience war again; they wanted peace for their children. This was to be the foundation of their philosophy and approach to schooling. They set up schools based on human rights and situated their practice to uphold the rights of children and to promote tolerance and democracy. Rinaldi (1998, p. 114) describes children as:

> Rich in resources, strong and competent ... unique individuals with rights rather than simply needs. They have potential, plasticity, openness, the desire to grow, curiosity, a sense of wonder, and the desire to relate to other people and to communicate ... children are also very open to exchanges and reciprocity as deeds and acts of love that they not only want to receive but also want to offer.

The educators from the schools in RE value children's rights and voice. This is evident in their practice and in the way in which children's learning is made visible through Pedagogical Documentation.

Case study 1: Children's views about learning and education

Children between the ages of 5 and 8 were asked what they thought learning and education was all about and how they thought education could be improved. A student, Natalie, asked children to draw their ideas and as they drew they told her their thoughts.

Learning is:

> 'It's when you find new things out!'
> 'Learning isn't always done at school. We never stop learning.'
> 'I think it's taking in information and understanding new things.'

Education is:

> 'Education is the reason we go to school so we can get jobs when we grow up.'
> 'It's like learning. It's what school is for.'
> 'It's what school gives us.'

We can improve education by:

> 'Letting children work stuff out for themselves.'
> 'I wish I could ask for help more because I am too shy.'
> 'Have more teachers like mine.'

Listening to children's voices: a pause for reflection

Thinking about Case study 1, what has the process of 'listening' to children taught us about what they know? When we consider the children's ideas about learning and education and how to make school better, it provides some challenges for those teaching in schools and early years settings. Think about what you can do in your practice to improve education for young children by listening to their voices.

Pedagogical Documentation in practice

There are many benefits of using Pedagogical Documentation in practice for children, their teachers and their families. When used as an artefact or commemoration of a project, it makes the learning visible for all to see and recall. Children are able to reflect on their learning and acquisition of knowledge, and documentation can provoke new learning and possibilities (Hill *et al.*, 2005, p. 186).

For teachers, documentation may be used as part of an assessment process to identify children's strengths and areas for development, or highlight aspects of their practice or policy which may need to be reconsidered. Documentation creates an archive or visual/narrated history of the class or group. It is a powerful advocacy tool for early childhood educators and practitioners, as it makes highly visible the learning and teaching, the co-construction of knowledge for families, the local community, other colleagues, policy makers and those who are sceptical about learning and teaching approaches which are advocated for young children (Hill *et al.*, 2005). Malaguzzi (1996, cited in Edwards *et al.*, 2012) suggested that Pedagogical Documentation should be an expected function of early years' practitioners' lives working with young children to learn and relearn with children through observation, reflection, speculation, questioning and theorising.

Three critical elements for adopting Pedagogical Documentation in practice are as follows:

- An understanding that adults and children are active learners, collaborators and co-conspirators in the negotiation of a curriculum.

- An understanding of the importance of observation, reflection, self-awareness and interpretation as the foundation of learning in the classroom.

- An understanding of the documentation process as a cycle of inquiry involving questioning, observation, organisation of data, analysis, interpretation and theory building, reframing of questions and assumptions, planning and evaluation (Gandini and Goldhaber, 2001).

An inquiry-based approach to implementing Pedagogical Documentation as a process adapts a model developed by Gandini and Goldhaber (2001). The model shown in Figure 2.3 is cyclical, and reflects the continuous process of reflecting, looking and listening, questioning, theorising, learning, teaching and documenting. The educator or teacher as researcher engages in an ongoing dialogue with children about their learning and pedagogy.

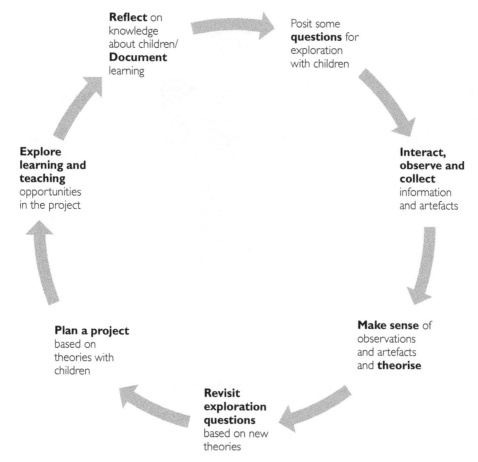

Reflect on knowledge about children/ **Document** learning

Posit some **questions** for exploration with children

Interact, observe and collect information and artefacts

Make sense of observations and artefacts and **theorise**

Revisit exploration questions based on new theories

Plan a project based on theories with children

Explore learning and teaching opportunities in the project

Figure 2.3 A cyclical model representing the continuous process of a learning dialogue

Case study 2: Project on children's views about safety

When we think about children and keeping them safe, most adults would think about protecting children from crime, those people who harm children and ensuring that children are in safe environments. When children are asked about how they can stay safe, where they feel safe and who they feel safe with, they have some interesting responses.

One child responded by drawing a picture of a fly swatter and said, 'Kill nasty bugs using a fly swatter not your hands as you might get stung.'

Sophie responded by drawing a picture of herself and saying, 'No nuts!'. For her, safety is about avoiding nuts because she will have a potentially life-threatening allergic reaction.

Another child responded by drawing two pictures and saying: 'Don't talk to strangers and don't play with matches.' This child's views show the influence of adults in what it means for him to be safe.

Figure 2.4 'No nuts!' Being aware of personal threats and keeping safe

Children's views: a pause for reflection

Consider the children's views above on safety and how their perspective differs from adults. Yet it is the adults who frequently make decisions on behalf of children, often without considering the child's voice.

Case study 3: Reflection on learning through the use of Pedagogical Documentation

As a result of working with children and creating an artefact to represent Pedagogical Documentation, the word cloud (Figure 2.5) was developed with the 50 most common words from quotes from Early Childhood Studies students. The word cloud highlights some of their learning as a result of the project.

The students involved in the Pedagogical Documentation project found the experience to be extremely beneficial. It taught them to take time to listen to children's views and perspectives on matters of importance to young children. They anticipated that Pedagogical Documentation will be a useful tool for their future work with young children and families and will help them embed theory into making sense of their practice. They learned how Pedagogical Documentation could become a legacy for children, and that 'traces of the children' can remain in the settings to share with other children. As a tool, Pedagogical Documentation can make learning visible to parents, to the children and to other professionals involved in children's lives, and this supported a collaborative approach to working with young children.

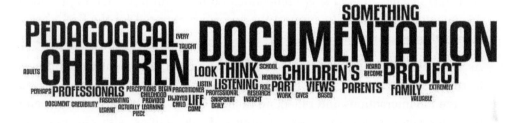

Figure 2.5   A pedagogical word cloud: 50 common words used by students

Considering words: a pause for reflection

Reflect on the words in the word cloud and the summary above it. Think about a small project you could do with children and then 'document' the learning that occurred. Perhaps you could start with some reflective questions, such as:

- What was the activity you observed like for children? What did they say? How did they act?

- What was the activity like for you? What did you do? What did you say? How did you feel?

- What decisions did you make during the activity? Why?

- What did you learn? What did the children learn? What did you learn together?

Concluding comments

At a time of rapidly changing landscapes in the field of early childhood (Meehan, 2015a), those adults working with children need to engage in advocacy, to articulate and promote practices and share knowledge that value children, their learning and development while upholding the UNCRC. This chapter has presented an overview of Pedagogical Documentation and provides three case studies for reflection. Pedagogical Documentation is one way in which children's learning can be made visible to families, communities and those who evaluate the quality of early childhood education and care settings.

Key points to remember

■ The approach adopted for educating children in the schools in Reggio Emilia needs to be understood in the context of its time and place. This chapter has demonstrated how this approach to education views children and the way in which children's learning and development is documented and shared.

■ This chapter has offered some reflections on how children's learning can be documented and shared to support the outcomes required for the Early Years Foundation Stage.

■ As a teacher or practitioner, you are a central part of documenting children's learning, since you will learn from the children and the environment as you observe the interactions and reflect on them. You are an action researcher, and this approach can support your teaching and interactions with children and their families.

Points for discussion

■ How could Pedagogical Documentation enhance the assessment processes?

■ As an educator, how could Pedagogical Documentation support your role as a reflective practitioner researcher?

■ How could Pedagogical Documentation be used to support the development of partnerships with parents, other agencies and the local community?

Suggested further reading

Books

Edwards, C., Gandini, L. and Forman, G. (2012) *The Hundred Languages of Children* (3rd edn). Santa Barbara, CA: Praeger.

Hall, K., Horgan, M., Ridgway, A., Murphy, R., Cunneen, M. and Cunningham, D. (2010) *Loris Malaguzzi and the Reggio Emilia Experience*. London: Bloomsbury.

Miller, L. and Pound, L. (2011) *Theories and Approaches to Learning in the Early Years*. London: Sage.

Thornton, L. and Brunton, P. (2014) *Bringing the Reggio Approach to Your Early Years Practice* (3rd edn). London: David Fulton.

Journal articles

Alasuutari, M. (2014) Voicing the child? A case study in Finnish early childhood education. *Childhood*, 21, 242–59.

Cox Suárez, S. and Daniels, K.J. (2008) Listening for competence through documentation: Assessing children with language delays using digital video. *Remedial and Special Education*, 30, 177–90.

Elfström Pettersson, K. (2013) Children's participation in preschool documentation practices. *Childhood*, 1–17. DOI: 10.1177/0907568213513480.

Parnell, W. (2012) Experiences of teacher reflection: Reggio inspired practices in the studio. *Journal of Early Childhood Research*, 10, 117–33.

Vallberg Roth, A.C. and Månsson, A. (2011) Montessori- and Reggio Emilia-profiled preschools in Sweden: Individual development plans. *Journal of Early Childhood Research*, 9, 247–61.

Useful websites

Reggio Children. Available at: www.reggiochildren.it/?lang=en (accessed 1 November 2014).

Reggio International Network. Available at: www.sightlines-initiative.com/index.php?option=com_content&view=article&id=19&Itemid=82 (accessed 1 November 2014).

UK RE Sightlines Initiative. Available at: www.sightlines-initiative.com/index.php?option=com_content&view=article&id=2&Itemid=4 (accessed 1 November 2014).

Education Scotland. Available at: www.educationscotland.gov.uk/learningteachingand assessment/approaches/reggioemilia/index.asp (accessed 1 November 2014).

References

Caldwell, L. (1997) *Bringing Reggio Emilia Home*. New York: Teachers' College Press.

Dahlberg, G., Moss, P. and Pence, A. (1999) *Beyond Quality in Early Childhood Education and Care*. London: Routledge.

Edwards, C., Gandini, L. and Forman, G. (2012) *The Hundred Languages of Children* (3rd edn). Santa Barbara, CA: Praeger.

Fleet, A., Patterson, C. and Robertson, J. (2006) *Insights: Behind Early Childhood Pedagogical Documentation*. Castle Hill: Pademelon.

Gandini, L. (1997) Foundation of the Reggio Emilia Approach to early childhood education. In J. Hendrick, *First Steps Toward Teaching the Reggio Way*. Upper Saddle River, NJ: Prentice-Hall, pp. 14–25.

Gandini, L. and Edwards, C. (2001) *Bambini: The Italian Approach to Infant/Toddler Care.* New York: Teachers' College Press.

Gandini, L. and Goldhaber, J. (2001) Two reflections about Documentation. In L. Gandini and C. Edwards, *Bambini: The Italian Approach to Infant/ToddlerCcare.* New York: Teachers' College Press, pp. 124–45.

Helm, J., Beneke, S. and Steinheimer, K. (1998) *Windows on Learning: Documenting Young Children's Work.* New York: Teachers' College Press.

Hendrick, J. (ed.) (2003) *Next Steps Toward Teaching the Reggio Way: Accepting the Challenge to Change.* Columbus, OH: Prentice Hall.

Hill, L., Stremmel, A. and Fu, V. (2005) *Teaching as Inquiry: Rethinking Curriculum in Early Childhood Education.* Boston, MA: Pearson.

Lawson, L. (2000) Personal communication. Burlington, VT: University of Vermont.

Malaguzzi, L. (1996) Catalogue of the exhibition *The Hundred Languages of Children* cited in *Reggio Children* (2008). Available at: https://zerosei.comune.re.it/pdfs/foldrerch/RCH_ENGLISH.pdf (accessed 12 October 2016).

Mantovani, S. (2007) Italy: Pedagogy and curriculum. Infant/toddler care. In R. New and M. Cochran (eds), *Early Childhood Education: An International Encyclopaedia, Vol. 4: The Countries.* Westport, CT: Praeger, pp. 1113–18.

Meehan, C. (2015a) Challenging the workforce: Themes for working with children from birth to 8 years. Early Years Workforce: Introductory Chapter. In C. Ritchie, *Challenges and Change in the Early Years Workforce.* London: David Fulton, Taylor & Francis.

Meehan, C. (2015b) Every child mattered in England: But what matters to children? Early Development and Care. Available from: http://dx.doi.org/10.1080/03004430.2015.1032957.

Reggio Children (2008). Available at https://zerosei.comune.re.it/pdfs/foldrerch/RCH_ENGLISH.pdf (accesed 12 October 2016).

Rinaldi, C. (1998) The projected curriculum and Documentation. In C. Edwards, L. Gandini and G. Forman (eds), *The Hundred Languages of Children.* Greenwich, CT: Ablex, pp. 113–26.

Robertson, J., Fleet, A. and Patterson, C. (2006) *Insights: Behind Early Childhood Pedagogical Documentation.* Sydney: Pademelon Press.

Thornton, L. and Brunton, P. (2014) *Bringing the Reggio Approach to Your Early Years Practice* (3rd edn). London: David Fulton.

3 Behaviour, learning and emotional intelligence
A critical learner perspective

Temi Ladenika

Chapter overview

Critical learning is underpinned by critical theory; in line with its critical social theory underpinning, critical learning theory places the learner at the centre of learning. By centralising the learner, a critical learning perspective provides a view of the multifaceted experiences which 'revolve' around the learner which makes visible a diversity of social interactions informing how behaviour may be understood and interpreted within these interactions.

This chapter provides a brief clarification of critical learning and how it is contextualised within critical theory; it engages a number of relevant theories, including behaviourist, interpretivist, emotional intelligence theories as well as critical learning theory to provide an explanation of how the behaviour of a learner is a product of their physical – mental, social – emotional and psychological states. It explores current systemic documentation, including statutory and non-statutory guidance, to identify perspectives about behaviour and emotion within formal learning systems. It ends in a summary of key ideas to enable a broad and balanced understanding of the relationship between behaviour, emotion and learning.

Introduction

Critical learning (CL) provides a perspective for exploring the management of learner behaviour and emotion in educational organisations. This exploration includes brief theoretical explanations of learner behaviour and emotion from behaviourist and constructivist perspectives as well as issues relating to emotional intelligence. It culminates with a brief review of systemic documentation which influences approaches to managing behaviour and emotion within formal learning environments.

Critical learning is an abduction founded in Habermas' critical social theory (CST) (Habermas, 1990, 1991; McCarthy, 1978); it is an application of critical social theory to educational environments. Critical learning places the learner at the centre of learning. By centralising the learner, a critical learning perspective provides a view of the learner's experiences through four key social interactions. In this chapter, emotion and behaviour are understood and interpreted within these interactions which include engagement, representation, emancipation and transformation.

Critical learning is a perspective on the experience of a learner within an educational environment. The difference between the terms 'critical learning' and 'critical learner' are syntactic i.e. synonymous and are used interchangeably within this chapter. A critical learning perspective is necessary as it provides an alternative view to understanding behaviour and emotion in schools. Prevalent approaches are predominantly positivist (i.e. behaviourist) in terms of management and accountability structures seen in statutory guidance and non-statutory advice. Other approaches which obtain largely at teacher-student level are interpretive (for example, strategies developed from the work of Rogers, 2012). A critical learner approach challenges assumptions that are implicit or explicit in these approaches by centralising the learner rather than the system or social relationships.

Historically, learning environments have been explained, in some cases designed, and to a significant extent shaped, by theoretical influences largely from psychology and sociology and to a lesser extent disciplines such as anthropology. These influences account for perspectives on the learner–teacher relationship, assumptions about how learning takes place, what constitutes teaching and learning as well as systems put in place to facilitate institutional processes. Three such influences – behaviourism; cognitive and social constructivism; and the notion of emotional intelligence – provide a means of exploring behaviour management and emotion within these environments. More attention will be given to emotional intelligence, as Chapter 1 provides a more in-depth explanation of the first two influences.

For decades there has been recognition of issues surrounding learner behaviour in schools, with statutory and non-statutory guidance made available to deal with challenges that school leaders and teachers face in day-to-day teaching and learning. A brief sortie into documentation pertaining to the educational system in the UK provides a view of expectations and assumptions about learner behaviour and how it should be managed in educational establishments. A more recent view may be found in the SEND 2015 guidance where the term 'behaviour' has been replaced with 'mental health'.

A critical learner perspective provides a precise means of examining some implications of systemic ideology for the learner experience in such educational institutions. Four critical learner guiding questions provide a plumb line for this exploration. How does the learner engage? How is the learner represented? Is the learner emancipated? How is the learner transformed? Suggestions in response to these questions indicate the significance of adopting a critical learning perspective when seeking to understand behaviour and emotion within educational institutions.

Who is a critical learner?

Critical learning is rooted in critical social theory (CST). CST is a perspective which aims to promote the emancipatory purpose of knowledge, and makes criticism crucial in discourse (Habermas, 1990, 1991; McCarthy, 1978). CST is multidisciplinary, and views an educational environment as a place where a learner finds transformation through engagement with new and unfamiliar ideas. This transformation 'liberates' the learner from possible limitations of their immediate experience which they may have brought to the pedagogical process. CST views the pedagogical relationship between learner and teacher as one which transforms the learner rather than one within which a mere transmission of knowledge takes place.

The notion of critical learning or a critical learner is introduced within this chapter as deduced from CST. Within the dual experience of learning in educational institutions (i.e. what is learned and how learning takes place), a critical learning perspective looks for the extent to which the learner has access to the emancipatory

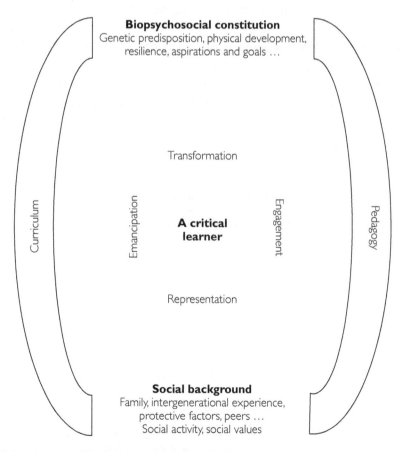

Figure 3.1   A critical learning perspective of influences on emotion and behaviour

function of knowledge and has opportunities to engage in the pedagogic process, resulting in their own transformation and the transformation of others. The critical learner engages with teaching and learning practices which bring about emancipation and transformation within a pedagogic environment which is representative. Representation draws attention to the position of the learner within the learning environment, i.e. how the selection and presentation of knowledge provides a place for the learner within the learning environment or otherwise; and how positions of the diverse groups within society are made explicit.

A critical learner perspective engages a positive view of behaviour and emotion in that choices made by the learner which foster their engagement, representation emancipation and transformation are assumed to be behaviour. These behaviours are indicative of self-knowledge and self-government. A critical learner has a good knowledge of self, i.e. of aspects of their own biopsychosocial constitution; they also know how to manage these aspects and associated facets. A critical learner is resilient (i.e. they engage levels of agency necessary to achieve their objectives), they oscillate between varying levels of autonomy in order to achieve their aims. An illustration is given in Table 3.1.

Resilience is one of the key factors advised in the DfE (2016) guidance as important for learners with social emotional and mental health needs. Critical learning argues that resilience is important for all learners. The individual and their social background are key to resilience. These two areas provide a range of protective factors such as ability, individual disposition, parenting, spiritual development and aspiration, to name a few. Reflections on practice reveal that autonomous learners tend to be more resilient. Learners have varying degrees of autonomy in differing circumstances; a critical learner positions self at differing states of autonomy to build and maintain resilience, i.e. heteronomous, autonomous dependent, heteronomous independent and autonomous.

Table 3.1 A critical learning perspective of social and emotional behaviour

Critical learning factor	Learner's social and emotional behaviours
Engagement	Maintains social connections through resilience. Makes decisions on the basis of self-knowledge and knowledge of others. Makes self-governing choices. Positions self at differing states of autonomy to build and maintain resilience (see Figure 3.2).
Representation	Understands own biopsychosocial constitution and social background, and interprets this effectively within the broader social context.
Emancipation	Uses knowledge gained through understanding of self and others as well as their engagement with the curriculum and pedagogy to make choices which lead to a harmonious existence.
Transformation	Allows new knowledge gained to change secondary aspects of their biopsychosocial constitution and social experience.

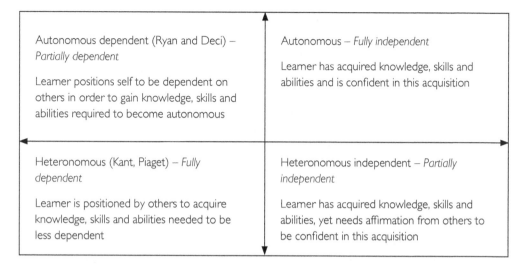

Autonomous dependent (Ryan and Deci) – *Partially dependent*	Autonomous – *Fully independent*
Learner positions self to be dependent on others in order to gain knowledge, skills and abilities required to become autonomous	Learner has acquired knowledge, skills and abilities and is confident in this acquisition
Heteronomous (Kant, Piaget) – *Fully dependent*	Heteronomous independent – *Partially independent*
Learner is positioned by others to acquire knowledge, skills and abilities needed to be less dependent	Learner has acquired knowledge, skills and abilities, yet needs affirmation from others to be confident in this acquisition

Figure 3.2   Building resilience: States of autonomy

In summary, for the critical learner, the learning environment is marked with four main factors: engagement, representation, emancipation and transformation. The nature of and extent to which a learner experiences these factors constitutes an influence on the behavioural choices they make.

Theoretical influences

Behaviourism is one of the earliest perspectives of psychology. Developed from a proposal by Watson (1913) for a purely objective psychology of behaviour, the inception of behaviourism was in response to an unresolved argument among psychologists of the time over the existence and role of the conscious mind and introspection. In Watson's view, the problem was the paradigm prevalent at the time, which he considered antiquated and lacking in experimental rigour. Behaviourism was to follow the rules of positivism, where phenomena were subject to scientific methods of enquiry; psychology was about the study of human action, and the prediction and control of such action. Human states which could not be subject to this process were discountenanced, for example, states such as thought, the mind, emotion, personality and so on. Two main behaviourist approaches are classical conditioning based on the work of Thorndike (1898), Watson (1913) and Pavlov (1927), and operant conditioning (Skinner, 1938).

From an educational perspective, behaviourism assumes a control relationship in between teacher and learner in which a stimulus (S) is provided which elicits a response (R) leading to the formation of S–R bonds. The relationship is maintained as these bonds are strengthened or weakened either through conditioning or positive and negative reinforcements.

Implications of a behaviourist perspective include an inculcation of a predetermined curriculum delivered within a structured pedagogical environment. The curriculum is set; learners are required to go through a process marked by prescribed modes of instruction which should culminate in varying degrees of mastery (Skinner, 1954). Knowledge is viewed as an exhaustive body of facts and skills in specific formats, having a specific language. For learning to take place, the learner needs to acquire this body of knowledge. In the process, the learner is for the most part passive; where the learner is active, it is in making choices guided by reinforcements which may be positive or negative. The teacher is active and in control of the learning environment; learners respond and learn to equate compliance with competence.

Thus behaviour is predicted and controlled, and emotions cannot be observed (and therefore cannot be scientifically investigated) yet could exist alongside behaviours. Emotion bears no direct relation to behaviour (which is purely a response to external stimuli); what people refer to as emotions are actually predispositions to action (Skinner, 1953/1965). Emotions are strengths or weaknesses in particular responses. They are not internal states (as these do not exist).

To apply the principles of behaviourism in the management of behaviour is to create environments controlled by the more dominant individuals. In educational settings, such individuals are usually the teacher, play leader, institutional manager etc. From interactions within the environment, stimulus–response bonds are formed and reinforced with the use of positive and negative reinforcements and sanctions. Assumptions are that all learners will desire rewards and avoid sanctions; that those in control are able to apply reinforcements in a consistent and equitable manner; that there is a shared understanding about what constitutes desired behaviour between key individuals influencing the home environment of the learners, and adults within the educational environment; and that the adults in control of these environments know and model these desired behaviours.

Considering practice: a pause for reflection

Learners whose socially incompatible behaviours are of a physiological aetiology (e.g. Autism) may find the consistency and predictability of the behaviourist environment calming.

How would you meet the needs of this group of children and others?

Observations from practice raise questions about these assumptions; for example, in the day-to-day reality of formal learning environments, there are some learners who repeat behaviours in response to any reinforcement, be it negative or positive. Reflections on work with learners whose behaviours are incompatible with expectations in educational environments indicates that negative reinforcements or punishments often lead to repeats of the undesired behaviour, or have no effect in decreasing these behaviours. Such learners tend to be those whose incompatible behaviours are rooted in social and/or emotional experiences rather than in physiological states.

From a critical learner perspective, the learner within a behaviourist environment engages with the institutional systems and pedagogical practices through interactions with adults and other learners in the classroom. The learner responds to stimuli presented in the learning environment from their position. Their position is governed by factors such as their social background, biopsychosocial constitution, interest/aptitude in the type of knowledge in focus, the teacher narrative, and the extent of influence from other learners.

Their position indicates how they view themselves as represented. Their response may lead to them becoming emancipated and transformed; for example, where their position is congruent with the outcomes controlled by the institutional systems and practices. Where there is incompatibility between the learner response and expected outcomes within a behaviourist environment, controls are increased in a bid to achieve the required response. For example, a typical rewards and sanctions approach to managing behaviour aims at rewarding appropriate behaviours and sanctioning inappropriate ones. It is assumed that all learners will want to earn rewards. Where a learner does not present the desired behaviours, negative reinforcements or punishments are used to extinguish undesired behaviours. However, where the latter proves to be ineffective, a variety of other deterrents are used in a bid to elicit desired behaviours. More often than not, eventually such learners are removed from the environment through a series of fixed term and then permanent exclusion, or 'managed' moves. Moves tend to be to other, similar environments, resulting in such learners attending sometimes up to six or seven schools between the ages of 5 and 16.

A behaviourist perspective is limited in explaining the behaviours of a learner who does not desire a consequence, yet continues to present actions which attract such consequences. A critical learner perspective on the other hand takes into account the individual biopsychosocial make-up of the learner and recognises that learners choose whether or not to be conditioned/reinforced to respond to events, unless there are irregularities which are not of a behavioural or emotional aetiology. Learners consider and interpret their positions within social interactions and make choices to respond to events on the basis of their considerations. This explains why a learner might continue to make certain choices despite the outcomes being unfavourable.

In contrast to a behaviourist approach, a pedagogical environment influenced by a constructivist perspective facilitates the view that all knowledge is constructed from meaning through language (Piaget, 1955; Vygotsky, 1978; Jonassen, 1991). Meaning is found in the discourse produced through symbolic interactions. In cognitive constructivism, meaning is derived by learners through engagement and thought (Piaget, 1955). Such an environment encourages learners to generate their own understanding of knowledge events; to look for patterns and order, and be able to make predictions into the unknown (Von Glasersfeld, 1984). A constructivist learning environment may be social. A social constructivist learning environment recognises the role of others in the construction of meaning (Vygotsky, 1978). Others who are more knowledgeable provide opportunities for a learner to develop by assisting with tasks they can accomplish with help, then progressing to accomplishing the same or similar tasks on their own.

Learner behaviours: a pause for reflection

Make a list of learner behaviours which foster learning.

How does a learner acquire these behaviours?

A critical learner perspective finds that within a constructivist learning environment, a learner may engage and find representation as with a learning environment informed by a behaviourist perspective; however, there is greater scope for learners to harmonise their position as represented by their own experience with the expected outcomes communicated within the organisation. This implies greater scope for emancipation and transformation.

An educational environment influenced by social constructivist ideas is marked by facilitation of the learning experience. Characterised by collaboration between learners and instructors, there is greater shared exploration of knowledge and less transmission of facts. Teachers scaffold learners through knowledge content, and learners model their learning choices on those who in their view have greater ability in the area of focus. It is assumed that there is agreement as to the nature of what is to be learned.

Constructivism helps explain a key limitation to specialist behaviour schools. In these environments all learners have 'knowledge' of social and emotional behaviours incompatible with a positive engagement within mainstream learning environments, i.e. desired cultural expectations. This is evidenced in the required statutory documentation compulsory for admission. Reflections on practice note that many learners in these environments are usually not deterred by reinforcements applied through behaviourist schemes, and the grouping together of such learners is counterproductive as it creates an environment for the modelling and scaffolding of undesired behaviours where these are dominant.

Constructivism views emotion as multifaceted; there are varying views (Kelly, 2003) constructed by researchers involved in scientific or empirical studies. Each view has something important to contribute to knowledge about emotion and may concentrate on differing facets. An example is the Conceptual Act Model proposed by Barrett (2011) and her colleagues. This model views emotions as mental states, i.e. perceptions related to brain states. Proponents hypothesise that emotions are constructed from two main psychological primitives (i.e. psychological ingredients):

a core affect system which includes a range of pleasurable or non-pleasurable mental states that are activated or deactivated, combined with a conceptual system which stores knowledge about these mental states. Both of these systems are mediated by controlled attention – a third psychological primitive. Controlled attention brings into play the executive functioning of neuro-anatomy involving higher order cognitive processes such as language.

In effect, this constructivist view of emotion recognises a relationship between cognition and emotion, and argues that emotions are constructed from neural and psychological states, and are facilitated by language. Other constructivist perspectives view emotion the same as cognition (Kelly, 1963; Cromwell, 2010), and as important for decision making (Schwarz and Clore, 1983).

Emotional intelligence

Something to consider: a pause for reflection

Academic researchers develop a body of knowledge from research within higher education or related institutions.

Research practitioners develop a body of knowledge from research within the practice arena.

Emotional intelligence is a controversial construct. Incepted in Edward Thorndike's notion of social intelligence in 1920, the development of knowledge about emotional intelligence has been (and still is) a difficult journey. Understanding issues surrounding emotional intelligence involves engaging with arguments from three interest groups: academic researchers, research practitioners and both. The former include advocates such as Salovey and Mayer (1990) and Reuven Bar-On (2000), who have theorised and developed measures on emotional intelligence, carrying out exploratory research with a view to an identification as different from other types of intelligence. The latter (e.g. Goleman, 1995) and associates have also theorised and developed measures on emotional intelligence; these have been popularised either by accident or design within the worlds of business and education, where they have been well received; a third category combines both groups – for example, Gardner (1983, 1993, 1995), whose idea of inter- and intrapersonal intelligence is considered similar to emotional intelligence.

It is important to note here a categorisation of emotional intelligence as pure or mixed (Mayer *et al.*, 2000). The pure intelligence typology is found in Salovey and Mayer's model (1990); here, emotional intelligence is viewed as a cognitive ability (Salovey and Mayer, 1990; Goleman, 2001) measured by the Mayer, Salovey-Caruso Emotional Intelligence Test (MSCEIT). Examples of models of mixed typology emotional intelligence include Goleman's emotion in the workplace model which looks at emotion and personality and has a number of measures, one of which is the Emotional Intelligence Appraisal (EIA). Another example is Reuven Bar-On's model which also links emotion and personality and is measured by Bar-On's Emotion Quotient inventory (EQi). This variety in typology is viewed as an inconsistency and contributes to the problem of understanding what precisely emotional intelligence is.

Added to the problem of a lack of clarity is a contention surrounding the basis on which claims are made. On the one hand, some academic researchers argue that the concept of emotional intelligence is in its relatively early stages of investigation (Thorndike and Stein, 1937; Salovey and Mayer, 1990; Mayer *et al.*, 2000, 2004; Landy, 2005, Barrett, 2006) and, although there has been an increase in studies, a great deal of research is still wanting. These researchers call for caution when engaging with related ideas and hypotheses. Some go further and view the conceptual separation of emotional intelligence from other general intelligences as unnecessary, arguing that categorisations of emotional intelligence are already included within other measures of intelligence such as Spearman's general intelligence. Thus the notion of emotional intelligence is a reworking of what already exists and is therefore superfluous.

On the other hand, research practitioners promote emotional intelligence as an ability which can be nurtured within individuals and, therefore, organisations (e.g. Goleman, 2001). They view emotional intelligence as a means of enabling effective self-development, as the individual learns to understand their emotions and those of others, and to take action to foster harmonious relationships.

Consistent among various definitions of emotional intelligence is the ability of a person to be aware of and understand their own emotions as well as the emotions of others, and to carry out decisions and actions on the basis of this awareness which benefit all concerned. According to Salovey and Mayer, emotional intelligence is a part of social intelligence and is 'the ability to monitor one's own and others' feelings and emotions, to discriminate among them and use this information to guide one's thinking and actions' (1990, p. 189). Alongside Meyer *et al.* (2004), they propose a four-branch ability model of EI shown in Table 3.2.

Goleman (2001) defines emotional intelligence as a theory of performance; a person has a natural potential to perform in an emotionally intelligent fashion, yet this potential requires a type of competence in order to be realised. He states that 'an emotional competence is a learned capability based on emotional intelligence that results in outstanding performance at work' (Goleman, 2001, p. 27).

Table 3.2 An illustration of Mayer *et al.*'s (2004) four-branch ability model of Emotional Intelligence

Branch 1	Branch 2	Branch 3	Branch 4
Ability to perceive emotion	Ability to use emotion to facilitate thought	Ability to understand emotions	Ability to manage emotions

Goleman asserts that his claims are based on extensive research in numerous work settings; a limitation to this is that data and research methodology on which these claims are based is proprietary, i.e. commercial intellectual property. Were they to be the proceeds of scientific enquiry within the academic domain of research, researchers would have the necessary access to scientifically replicate and query related procedures and practices to confirm or refute claims. This has resulted in arguments denying the scientific quality of Goleman's claims (Landy, 2005).

A neuro-sociological perspective of emotion may bring some resolution to the array of issues identified above in terms of providing a means of scientific interrogation as well as sociological understanding. Franks (2006) argues for a sociological understanding of emotion which considers findings from neuroscience. This view is congruent with constructivist views of emotion in terms of a close and dependent relationship between emotion and cognition. Studies identify emotion as foundational and causal to cognitive processes (Massey, 2002; Franks, 2006).

Franks' (2006) arguments, based on studies from a number of contributors, (chiefly LeDoux, 1996), include the communal nature of the mind, i.e. the need for the human brain to engage with others in order to work effectively; the human brain being dominated by a collaboration between emotion cognition, which pervades the brain rather than being specifically located. There is also a separation between emotional feelings and emotion, emotion being covert (unconscious) as well as overt (conscious) evidenced in studies on fear.

More to consider: a pause for reflection

Bottom-up and top-down.

Emotion and cognition collaborate.

Emotion provides the basis and influences cognition upward from the bottom.

Through higher processes, cognition regulates emotion downwards from the top.

The close relationship between emotion and cognition from this perspective lends credence to arguments that separating emotional intelligence from general intelligence is superfluous. Reasons for this separation may be that conceptualisations of intelligence placed a greater focus on cognition and appeared to 'side-line' emotion; there was also a failure to recognise the importance of emotion for the development of cognition. Gardner (1995), in reflecting on the response to his ideas, alludes to this when he states that his multiple intelligences (1983) were a critical response to reification of intelligence within the field of psychology at the time. He described his multiple intelligences in the initial stage as 'an ensemble of memes' (1995, p. 200) rather than theoretical constructs.

Emotional intelligence has been accepted as the basis for a curriculum for addressing social behaviour and emotion in schools. Historical programmes such as

Social and Emotional Learning (SEL) in the United States and Social and Emotional Aspects of Learning (SEAL) in the United Kingdom were based largely on Goleman's (1995) view of emotional intelligence. Although SEAL is presently archived following a change in political ideology, it is interesting to see how the notion of emotional intelligence at the time provided a much-needed solution to a gap in the curriculum, i.e. a need for knowledge about emotional and social processes and the implication of this for learner engagement with the curriculum.

Systemic approaches to behaviour and emotion

Filling the gap is guidance on expectations of pupil behaviour and how educational leaders may discipline learners who are non-compliant. The current systemic approach to understanding assumptions about and managing pupil behaviour in the UK may be found in two documents: *Mental Health and Behaviour in Schools* (DfE, 2016) and SEND 2015 (DfE & DoH, 2015). *Mental Health and Behaviour in Schools* adopts a strong behaviourist approach to viewing and managing learner behaviour. There is a clear emphasis on reinforcements and punishment, which may be applied for behaviours judged as inappropriate during and outside school time. Pupils may be disciplined for behaviours which not only affect other individuals, but also the reputation of the organisation.

This systemic guidance is clear about: what teachers' powers are, what is statutorily accepted as punishments, what behaviour and sanctions are, and specific aspects of what teachers can do to control pupil behaviour and provide a safe learning environment. However, what the guidance is completely silent on is what is considered appropriate or acceptable behaviour in schools, be it for students or for teachers. By implication, the term 'behaviour' is assumed to be 'undesirable' behaviour.

SEND 2015 (DfE & DoH, 2015) is a departure from previous special educational needs guidance on learner behaviour, in that previous documents recognised irregularities in learner behaviour as separate categories requiring specialist support. Behaviour Social and Emotional Development was a classification of typologies of behavioural irregularity alongside Cognition and Learning Needs, Communication and Interaction Needs, and Sensory and/or Physical Needs. Behaviour Social and Emotional Development is categorised as Social Emotional and Mental Health Needs in SEND 2015 (DfE & DoH, 2015). This category is further supported with advice from *Mental Health and Behaviour in Schools* (DfE, 2016) which provides non-statutory advice to schools in response to concerns that teachers may have limited knowledge of mental health issues.

Designed to meet mental health needs of a subset of identified learners, the document *Mental Health and Behaviour in Schools* (DfE, 2016) may enable schools to understand issues behind pupil behaviour and encourage school practitioners to look beyond presenting behaviours which may be symptomatic of deeper causes, for which learners will benefit from support rather than discipline and punishment.

Summary

In conclusion, a critical learner perspective provides a holistic means of understanding a learner's experience within an educational environment. Educational environments as agents of cultural reproduction (Bernstein, 2004) need to be representative in the selection of cultural beliefs, values, practices and expectations to be reproduced. This reduces the disconnect between the discourse learners experiences by reason of their biopsychosocial make-up and their social background, and the discourse relating to the curriculum and associated pedagogical practices within the school. Vertical discourses recontextualised from fields of production (Bernstein, 1999) are found in curricular content. Horizontal content constitutes knowledge which comes from the learner's day-to-day experience; for example, cultural expectations of desirable social behaviours. A broader variety of horizontal discourses provides a potential for greater representation.

Behaviourism provides a reductionist view of actions carried out in response to stimuli and is unable to recognise or explain emotion. Constructivism provides a view of actions carried out in relation to significant others. It recognises a relationship between emotion and cognition which is corroborated by findings in neuroscience and neuro-sociology. A relationship which equates emotion with cognition finds that neurologically cognition is by and large dependent on emotional connections.

Educational systems need to recognise the importance of knowledge about emotion and behaviour, and: (1) design policies for the management of behaviour, which aims for all learners to be engaged, represented, emancipated and transformed. (2) Recognise a mutual relationship between emotion and cognition, and to encourage a reflection of this in curricular and pedagogical practice. (3) Aim for greater representation of horizontal discourses, since where there is greater representation there will be greater engagement and congruence between the behavioural choices of learners and institutional expectations.

Lastly, bearing in mind the increase in studies of emotional intelligence across a number of disciplines, engagement is needed from the educational research community for clarity as to what emotional intelligence means for educational systems and practices.

Suggestions for further reading

Franks, D. (2006) The neuroscience of emotions. In J. Stets and J.H. Turner (eds), *Handbook of the Sociology of Emotions*. New York: Springer.

Department for Education (March 2016) *Mental Health and Behaviour in Schools*. DfE-00435-2014. London: Crown Copyright.

Barrett, L.F. (2006) Solving the emotion paradox: Categorization and the experience of emotion. *Personality and Social Psychology Review*, 10(1), 20–46.

Websites to visit

SDT: Self-determination Theory, which includes free articles on theory as well as up-to-date news. Visit http://selfdeterminationtheory.org/

The website of Dr Bill Rogers, a teacher and consultant who writes extensively about behaviour management issues in the classroom. Visit www.billrogers.com.au/

References

Bar-On, R. (2000) Emotional and social intelligence. In R. Bar-On and J.D.A. Parker (eds), *The Handbook of Emotional Intelligence* (pp. 363–88). San Francisco, CA: Jossey-Bass.

Barrett, L.F. (2006) Solving the emotion paradox: Categorization and the experience of emotion. *Personality and Social Psychology Review*, 10(1), 20–46.

Barrett, L.F. (2011) Constructing emotion. *Psychological Topics*, 20(3), pp. 359–80.

Bernstein, B. (1999) Vertical and horizontal discourse: An essay. *British Journal of Sociology of Education,* 20(2), pp. 157–73.

Bernstein, B. (2004) *Class Codes and Control – The Structuring of the Pedagogic Discourse.* e-book ed. s.l.:Routledge.

Cromwell, R.L. (2010) *Being Human: Human Being. Manifesto for a New Psychology.* New York: iUniverse.

Department for Education (DfE) (2016) *Mental Health and Behaviour in Schools: Departmental advice for school staff.* Available from https://www.gov.uk/government/uploads/system/uploads/attachment_data/file/508847/Mental_Health_and_Behaviour_-_advice_for_Schools_160316.pdf (accessed 12 October, 2016).

Department for Education & Department of Health (DfE & DoH) (2015) *Special Educational Needs and Disability code of practice: 0–25 years (SEND).* Available from: https://www.gov.uk/government/uploads/system/uploads/attachment_data/file/398815/SEND_Code_of_Practice_January_2015.pdf (Accessed 12 October 2016).

Franks, D. (2006) The neuroscience of emotions. In J. Stets and J.H. Turner (eds), *Handbook of the Sociology of Emotions.* New York: Springer.

Gardner, H. (1983) *Frames of Mind: The Theory of Multiple Intelligences.* New York: Basic Books.

Gardner, H. (1993) *Multiple Intelligences: The Theory in Practice.* New York: Basic Books.

Gardner, H. (1995) Reflections on multiple intelligences: Myths and messages. *Phi Delta Kappan.* 77, pp. 200–9.

Goleman, D. (1995) *Emotional Intelligence: Why it can Matter More than IQ.* New York: Bantam Books.

Goleman, D. (2001) An EI based theory of performance. In C. Cherniss and D. Goleman (eds), *The Emotionally Intelligent Workplace.* San Francisco: Jossey-Bass.

Habermas, J. (1990) *Moral Consciousness and Communicative Action*, trans. C. Lenhardt and S. Weber Nicholsen. Cambridge, MA: MIT Press.

Habermas, J. (1991) *The Structural Transformation of the Public Sphere: An Inquiry into a Category of Bourgeois Society*, trans. T. Burger and F. Lawrence. Cambridge, MA: MIT Press.

Jonassen, D. (1991) Objectivism versus constructivism: Do we need a new philosophical paradigm? *Journal of Education Research*, 39(3), pp. 5–14.

Kelly, G.A. (1963) *A Theory of Personality*. New York: W.W. Norton.

Kelly, G.A. (2003) A brief introduction to personal construct theory. In F. Fransella (ed.), *International Handbook of Personal Construct Psychology* (pp. 3–20). Chichester, UK: Wiley.

Landy, F. (2005) Some historical and scientific issues related to research on emotional intelligence. *Journal of Organizational Behavior* 26(4), pp. 411–24.

LeDoux, J.E. (1996) *The Emotional Brain*. New York: Simon & Schuster.

McCarthy, T. (1978) *The Critical Theory of Jurgen Habermas*. Cambridge, MA: MIT Press.

Massey, D.S. (2002) A brief history of human society: The origin and role of emotion in social life. *American Sociological Review*, 67, pp. 1–29.

Mayer, J.D., Salovey, P. and Caruso, D. (2000) Models of emotional intelligence. In R. Sternberg, *Handbook of Intelligence*. Cambridge: Cambridge University Press.

Mayer, J.D., Salovey, P. and Caruso, D. (2002) *Mayer-Salovey-Caruso Emotional Intelligence Test* (MSCEIT). Version 2.0. Toronto, Canada: Multi-Health Systems.

Mayer, J.D., Salovey, P. and Caruso, D. (2004) Emotional intelligence: Theory, findings, and implications. *Psychological Inquiry*, 15(3), pp. 197–215.

Pavlov, I.P. (1927) *Classical Conditioning: An Investigation of the Physiological Activity of the Cerebral Cortex*. Oxford: Oxford University Press.

Piaget, J. (1955) Explanation in sociology. In L. Smith (ed.), *Sociological Studies* (pp. 30–96). London: Routledge. (Original work published 1950.)

Rogers, B. (2012) *You Know the Fair Rule*. Harlow: Pearson Education.

Salovey, P. and Mayer, J.D. (1990) Emotional intelligence. *Imagination, Cognition, and Personality*, 9, pp. 185–211.

Schwarz, N. and Clore, G.L. (1983) Mood, misattribution, and judgments of well-being: Informative and directive functions of affective states. *Journal of Personality and Social Psychology*, 45, pp. 513–23.

Skinner, B.F. (1938) *The Behavior of Organisms: An Experimental Analysis*. Oxford: Appleton-Century.

Skinner, B.F. (1953/1965) *Science and Human Behavior*. New York: Free Press.

Skinner, B.F. (1954) The science of learning and the art of teaching. *Harvard Educational Review*, 24(2), pp. 86–97.

Thorndike, E.L. (1898) Animal intelligence: An experimental study of the associative processes in animals. *Psychological Monographs: General and Applied*, 2(4), pp. i–109.

Thorndike, E.L. (1920) Intelligence and its uses. *Harper's Magazine*, 140, pp. 227–35.

Thorndike, R.L. and Stein, S. (1937) An evaluation of the attempts to measure social intelligence. *Psychological Bulletin*, 34(5), pp. 275–85.

Von Glasersfeld, E. (1984) Radical constructivism. In P. Watzlawick (ed.), *The Invented Reality*. Cambridge, MA: Harvard University Press.

Vygotsky, L. (1978) *Mind in Society: The Development of Higher Psychological Processes*. Cambridge, MA: Harvard University Press.

Watson, J.B. (1913) Psychology as the behaviorist views it. *Psychological Review*, 20, pp. 158–77.

4 Creativity
Thinking and innovation for learning and teaching

Diana Strauss and Peter Gregory

Chapter overview

One chapter on creativity cannot do justice to this important topic. Therefore, significant themes are explored to provoke further discussion on how creativity (as a process) can support important learning experiences for both young children and adults. The selected literature includes authors such as Craft (2006), Barnes (2015); Bruner (1972, 1977), Csikszentmihalyi (1990) and Tutchell (2014), because these authors connect children's learning with the process of creativity for critical thinking. Case studies are presented and challenging questions are raised to illustrate how creativity excites, innovates and challenges assumptions. The ensuing debate must continue to push the boundaries that restrict and inhibit learning so that new horizons are more clearly visible. Creativity equips us all to climb our own mountains and reach the highest possible peaks.

Context

Innovation and creativity belong at the centre of learning and teaching activity. This view is connected to the perspective that creativity is indeed 'an inherent part of human nature' (Barnes, 2015, p. 279); play in creativity is the framework for children's self-directed and self-regulated skills for improved cognitive behaviours in social and in learning situations (Singer, 2013, p. 179). This is what quality educational experiences are based upon; and furthermore there are fundamental principles, such as valuing and nurturing a genuine depth and 'dynamism' that fosters 'human abilities of every sort' (Robinson, 2009, p. 250) that should underpin a high-quality education curriculum. Arguably, such principles underpin learning, which is facilitated by adults who are knowledgeable and well equipped to plan experiences (with and for young children) that prioritise opportunities and possibilities for creativity. This is because the purpose of education is to facilitate the development and growth of human beings. Imagining and creating is a prerequisite for creativity; and teaching for creativity promotes collaboration, which has some underlying associated principles such as participation and engagement. These very same principles connect with current Conservative government policy which states that quality education, from birth to age 25, requires high aspiration by teachers for full participation and high engagement to achieve quality provision (Department for Education, 2014, 2015).

Principles guide teachers in their delivery of a curriculum. Underpinning such principles are strong beliefs held by adults. In the context of creativity, these values may include a high regard for children's interests, in terms of what excites and challenges them. Therefore, teachers and adults can use their observational/reflective skills to become active participants in processes such as critical thinking and learning for creativity. It is a truism to say that life can be very complicated for children, and many experiences can make it extremely problematic for adults to discover genuine aspects of children's interests and engagement (Wright, 2010). Just because it is hard work does not mean we should not try and rise to the task in order to cultivate, facilitate and then further develop children's interests, talents and reasons for engagement and deep-level learning (Vygotsky, 1978; Laevers, 2003). In England, teachers and parents are expected to accept and comply with ideological (education) policy changes, which swing from right to left and back again. Regardless of political positioning, in essence children do not change just because government changes. Take just one example; there appears to be a universal fascination in water for many young children. Therefore, despite parents anticipating this and exclaiming, *Stay out of the water*, and *Don't go in that puddle*; on seeing a puddle children just *have* to jump into it. Water is inherently intriguing to children. You can almost see them thinking; *What happens when I throw a stone into this puddle? How hard do I have to jump, with both my feet, to make the water jump?*

The message here is that although teachers and parents face the challenge and the context of relentless and frequent changes to systems and curricula content, what endures is an argument that supports and promotes providing experiences and processes for innovation, critical thinking and creativity that stimulate children to learn and discover, across all curriculum areas and educational provision.

Creative teaching versus creativity for innovation and learning

Terminology associated with school curricula and creativity can be confusing because creative teaching and creativity appear to be used interchangeably. The evolution of this is linked to the legacy of the Department for Culture Media and Sport/Department for Education and Employment (1999) when the National Advisory Committee on Creative and Cultural Education (NACCCE) published ground-breaking recommendations for curriculum design and delivery (see the following section on 'Creativity and imagination').

One perspective on teaching creativity is proposed by the work of Claxton, who in 2003 listed 12 scenarios that *do not* constitute creativity. Third on his list is intriguing: 'Creativity is not necessarily a *good thing*. A lot of very bad inventions have come from very creative people' (Claxton, 2003, p. 1). Barnes (2015, p. 280) also acknowledges that 'Despots, corrupt institutions and self-serving individuals now and throughout history illustrate countless examples of immoral creativity'. In this chapter we advocate positive aspects of both education and creativity, and it is for this reason that we adopt Craft's (2002) interpretation of creativity because she differentiates between the big C and the small c of creativity. This is positive in the context of learning and teaching and creativity with young children aged from 3 to 11 because (although this interpretation has not been adopted universally) it does elevate the creative process, known as *the everyday in the small c of creativity*. Craft's view dispels the myth that only the minority genius types in the population can be identified as *creative*, and this is important for adult educators. In other words, creativity is not necessarily innate, as Claxton highlights: 'Genius may have a very small genetic element to it, but everyday creativity is an acquired art' (ibid., p. 2). The connection between the unattainable genius of big C creativity and the *everyday* small c of creativity is that both require effort and curiosity. Determination and self-belief come to mind, along with positive disposition and persistence. These notions describe process rather than product and are important, regardless of any subjective preference regarding aesthetics. If creativity cannot be taught as a *subject* in the curriculum, then teachers have to find ways to make learning engaging. They must instil habits such as curiosity, questioning, experimenting and making. These habits may be summarised as *participatory* and *active play* (Bruce, 1991; Wood and Attfield, 2005).

Active participation and experimentation through play is connected here with the idea of a positive disposition, which is interpreted as a frame of mind that treats failure as a learning opportunity (Dweck, 2006–2010). In other words, it is an attitude that helps someone *stick at* the *struggle*. It is a feeling of rising to the challenge, because it is worth it, even though it is very hard work. One brilliant example of this is illustrated by the hard work involved in practising scales and repetitive musical exercises or daily drills. A novice, who is learning to play an instrument, has many technical skills to master, and for many this is likely to be a relatively painful and daunting process. It is too time consuming and too repetitive for the novice learner to emulate the proficient teacher. A young child has to devote daily effort and practice to this endeavour. Creativity (in this context) means the music teacher creates patterns, challenges and interesting ways to execute these tasks such as arpeggios. So in this example it seems that creativity can be taught by a role-model who is creative in their approach to becoming a fluent and accomplished musician. The teacher can inspire and motivate the student. This may be described as a top-quality learning experience, and in Froebellian (child-centred education) terms this is *self-discipline*, because the motivation to improve is driven by internal or intrinsic determination. The inherent value base here is enriching teaching. It is at the opposite end of the spectrum in style of teaching to that of *authoritarian teaching,* or learning that is driven by fear of failure or punishment.

Creativity and imagination

Given the varied expectations of education and its processes and outputs by politicians responsible for the system over time, it is not really surprising that different emphases become associated with different eras. Around the close of the twentieth century there was considerable interest in the notion of creativity and the ways in which this could be harnessed to strengthen education for all. In 1999 a major report was jointly published by two government departments with their respective Secretaries of State speaking positively about the need to 'help raise educational standards by boosting a child's self-confidence and self-esteem' and 'express individual creativity' (NACCCE) (DfCMS/DfEE, 1999, Foreword). In 2003, a strategy document was published for schools entitled *Excellence and Enjoyment* (DfES, 2003) which built upon the principles of the former and legitimised more open approaches to curriculum design and activity. Yet, by 2013, the revised version of the National Curriculum (DfE, 2014, updated 2016) prioritised performance in assessment in core subjects of mathematics and English. Despite claiming greater flexibility for teachers in how to reach these targets, the notion of creativity was confined to only a few select subjects (Jeffrey and Troman, 2013). The justification or explanation for the speed of changed emphasis lies outside the scope of this chapter – albeit to acknowledge that those working in schools need to maintain an informed and intelligent approach to developing the pupils in their charge.

Case study I

Sue, a student teacher, arrived on her second placement at the local primary school. She was puzzled to find a strong emphasis on formal learning activities in the Year I classroom as she had assumed that children would follow on from the Early Years approach she had encountered in her first-year placement (in another setting). She found it very difficult to adapt her thinking and turned to the friendly teaching assistant to ask her advice.

Challenge: a pause for reflection

How would you begin to explain the thinking in your school? Would you immediately defend the practice? Or are there ways in which your understanding would allow you to differentiate the expected formalities from the continued creative opportunities still developed in the classroom?

The underlying questions are about what is meant by creativity and how important it is to the learning (and teaching) process. Many – perhaps you included – may be surprised to learn that OFSTED inspectors have appreciated both for some time. In their report *Expecting the Unexpected: Developing Creativity in Primary and Secondary Schools* (OFSTED, 2003), inspectors highlighted the essence of the earlier NACCCE report in their observations in schools. So what features of creativity did they focus on?

> Teachers who inspire creativity have a clear understanding of what it means to be creative. Although they are not always able to put this understanding into words, they can often, if appropriate, model the creative process for pupils; with all the attendant risk-taking this can involve.
>
> (OFSTED, 2003, p.8)

The NACCCE report (DfCMS/DfEE, 1999) differentiated between teaching creatively, (planning and) teaching *for* creativity and also the creative curriculum (although the latter term was not used in the report itself). The implication of the OFSTED report is that the best teachers can utilise all of these aspects when they feel it appropriate to do so. It is perhaps a sad but true reflection that often teaching assistants working in the classrooms alongside the same teachers have their duties regulated to the point that they may not be able to fully participate in these processes and may not grasp the demands on the teacher in teaching in these ways.

Imagination and flow

Very few people, educationalists or otherwise, would suggest that developing the imagination of children is not important. Much has been written about the crucial nature of play and imagination in order to explore (and aid the formation of) identity, investigate the worlds of others as well as enhance the development of empathy and other forms of 'possibility thinking' (Craft, 2002, p. 12). If, as we will see in a moment, human development extends into adulthood as well, it should not be surprising that the adults facilitating this in children might reasonably retain and enjoy the processes for themselves as well. This can be sometimes problematic for adults – whether as training teachers (Barnes and Shirley, 2007) or as qualified teachers (McGill *et al.*, 2007).

Mihaly Csikszentmihalyi identified that people find deep satisfaction during a state of consciousness which he referred to as 'flow' (Csikszentmihalyi, 1990). He stated that in this state people are completely absorbed in an activity, particularly an activity which involves their creative abilities – including their ability to engage with their imagination. He went on to elaborate on nine elements provided by such activity:

- clear goals

- immediate feedback

- balance between challenges and skills

- merging of action and awareness

- elimination of distractions

- lack of fear of failure

- lack of self-consciousness

- distortion of sense of time

- autotelic activity (enjoyment for its own sake).

From these elements, it may be seen that to engage with the imagination and enter a state of flow has many benefits in developing a broad cognitive experience. How then might this be achieved? Let us consider the importance of communication in facilitating such development.

Case study 2

John seemed completely absorbed in building with the construction toys. He had begun to work on a complex spaceship model and was very pleased with his efforts. Not that he looked for reward or recognition by others; he simply spoke his story aloud to himself as he worked. He failed to register that it was time to stop for fruit or playtime and remained working until his teacher interrupted his activity and told him that he had to go out to play. His sense of disbelief was almost audible as he returned to being a quiet, self-conscious individual, put down his model, donned his coat and left the room.

Challenge: a pause for reflection

Reconsider this activity in the light of the above. Was John just 'lost in his own world' or avoiding other school-based activities? Think about the value of his experience from a number of perspectives – John's, his friends, the teacher's – and perhaps your own. What else could an adult have said to him to develop this opportunity?

Multimodal communication and language

The reader may already be aware of the impact of Vygotsky's (1978) work on cultural tools and their relationship to the learning process. Interpretation of his theory is often referred to as 'sociocultural' and is linked to a socio-constructivist understanding of the acquisition of knowledge. Vygotsky himself preferred to describe it as 'cultural-historical', perhaps emphasising the dual focus of this work: the history of human development and the cultural tools that shape this development. Fundamentally Vygotsky believed that human development – that of children as the development of all humankind – results from interactions between people and their social environment. These interactions are not limited to actual people but also involve their cultural artefacts which are often language based (written languages, number systems, various signs, symbols). Many of these serve a two-fold purpose: not only do they make possible the integration of a growing child into the culture but they also transform the very way the child's mind is being formed. Vygotsky (1978) refers to these as special cultural tools, as their acquisition extends one's mental capacities, making individuals the masters of their own behaviour. In the course of child development, a child typically learns how to use these cultural tools through interactions with parents, teachers or more experienced peers. As a result of using these tools – first in cooperation with others and later independently – the child develops higher mental functions: complex mental processes that are intentional, self-regulated, and mediated by language and other sign systems. Examples of these higher mental functions include focused attention, deliberate memory and verbal thinking. According to Vygotsky, although all human beings are capable of developing these functions, the particular structure and content of higher mental functions depend on specific social interactions, as determined by culture in general and by each person's unique social situation of development. Gardner (1990) followed his thinking and also reflected on ways in which the development of our educational systems has emphasised some systems (particularly forms of hard facts, scientific logic) and reduced the importance of others (for example, language, arts, poetry and so forth). He argued that children's experiences of the arts often suffered, as teachers too often reduced the experiences themselves by concentrating on 'a list of dates, a set of definitions, a body of labels … [simply a form of] … disembodied formal knowledge' (ibid., p. 41). His concern needs to be borne in mind as we turn our attention to consider our own classroom and learning opportunities. Although both Vygotsky and Gardner write from a different cultural context to our own, they may have much to aid our consideration of the learning opportunities we offer our own pupils. Before turning to the relatively young field of neuroscience to add to our understanding for the need for creativity, we may also want to contrast human and non-human development.

Kopp and colleagues (2008) analysed the various modes of human language in order to better define multimodal thinking, as this allowed them to develop a 'computational model for the automatic production of combined speech and iconic gesture' (p. 1). In short, their activity allowed them to devise an animated figure on a computer screen which attempted to communicate with human-like gestures in order to convey meaning. Koop et al. (2008) acknowledged the difficulties they encountered, as the cultural variations of human beings made it hard to explain and, they said, even harder to produce a predictive model of combined speech and gesture. From their analysis they described four modes which were particularly problematic: indexing (or classifying), placing (or locating), shaping (or forming) and drawing (or replicating). These modes could also help unlock the challenge of creativity in the classroom.

Case study 3

The Year 6 teacher left her English class, having explained that a hot-seating activity would help develop the children's understanding of characterisation in the book they had been reading together. They were somewhat taken aback a few moments later when the dishevelled and dirty old woman they had just encountered in the text literally fell through the classroom door and addressed them in a coarse, unfamiliar dialect. Within seconds she had sat on the chair at the front of the classroom and began to elicit probing questions from them about herself and her relationship to the other characters in the book.

Challenge: a pause for reflection

How memorable do you think this activity will be in the minds of these 11-year-olds? In the light of your understanding so far, could you describe how the links between imagination, creativity and multimodal communication have been used in both teaching and learning?

Reflect on your own learning experiences as both child and adult. What are the characteristics of the things that you remember best? Or most fondly?

Creativity and neuroscience

The expanding field of cognitive neuroscience is providing further understanding of the ways that creativity might be described, understood and applied. It is known that the brain has extraordinary adaptability, sometimes referred to as 'neuroplasticity'. This is due to the process by which connections between the neurons of the brain are strengthened when they are simultaneously activated and is present throughout life. This is also known as 'experience-dependent plasticity' (Royal Society, 2011, p. 5). This also allows the brain to continuously take account of the environment and to store the results of learning in the form of memories – thus preparing for future events based on experiences.

Using scanning techniques, it has been established that distinct circuits of neurons have been identified which are involved in specific higher brain functions as differing kinds of information are extracted or analysed from the environment. These include, among others, responses to artistic or creative processes (for example, brain imaging studies have found that people with training in those fields process music, art and dance differently to those who have not), and application to generalise and develop cognitive aspects. It has been acknowledged that the neuron activity which generates novelty can occur during two modes of thought (deliberate and spontaneous) and for two types of information (emotional and cognitive) (Dietrich, 2004; Sawyer, 2011).

From such studies of adult human brain activity it is claimed:

> Creativity is the epitome of cognitive flexibility. The ability to break conventional or obvious patterns of thinking, adopt new and/or higher order rules, and think conceptually and abstractly is at the heart of any theory of creativity.
>
> (Dietrich, 2004, p. 1014)

However, as yet, there are very few studies of children's brain activity which leads to some conjecturing from work with adults. Dietrich (2004) suggests that the slow maturation of the human prefrontal cortex (the part of the brain which allows responses to complex and difficult problems) justifies the view that 'children's creativity can perhaps be conceptualised as somewhat limited to the spontaneous processing mode, with the added disadvantage of limited amounts of knowledge stored' (ibid., p. 1021).

The majority of studies have also confirmed the existence of an incubation effect, although the exact nature of the associated unconscious processes remains uncertain (Sawyer, 2011). Another related phenomenon has attracted further attention: that of 'mind wandering' (Sawyer, 2011, p. 146) when a shift is made from the primary task to process other activities or personal goals but in ways that are not obviously related to the first activity and (possibly) not intentional either. This knowledge must be applied and possible implications for schools need to be considered here.

Learning and teaching

Dewey (1997) famously argued that much of what is learned is not taught and there are many examples within institutions (such as schools) that some systems teach children to learn short cuts or unintended consequences that do have the best outcomes. For example, picture this scene: an 8-year-old girl feigns difficulty reading synthetic phonics so that she can leave the classroom where the children are chanting and learning by rote and move to a smaller room to join the special needs groups with Miss Pleasant (a fictitious name) where she can immerse herself in books that have memorable and musical rhymes as well as humorous illustrations that give her a love of books. The learning outcome for this child is underperformance to achieve her goal.

There is little wonder that she chooses to find a space where the joy of reading is brought to life through story-telling. *Immersion* is a common theme that is most cited by creative writers (Michael Rosen and Michael Morpurgo, to name just two renowned children's authors) when they recall the most significant influences upon their own inspiration for their works of fiction. What excites children when they read works by these authors is that they recognise adults who identify children's own capabilities, and their capacity to be creative. As Barnes (2015, p. 282) proposes, 'children are the masters of invention'. One extract by Lee (2015, pp. 98–9) demonstrates this point and it also brings us back to the universal appeal of water, in which he vividly conjures up his childhood as a 4-year-old boy experimenting with water as 'a thousand pleasures'.

> Water is the puddle just big enough for a small boy's boot, the thundering curtains of Niagara Falls, the star in a snowflake, the mist on a cobweb, the protective arm around an ancient city. It is the sting on the lips from a hill-cold spring, the chisel that cut out the shape of Britain, the singing spout of a kettle, the last cry of the man in the desert.
>
> (Lee, 2015, pp. 98–9)

These compelling visual images in Lee's creative writing amplify the point that nature can inspire fantastic language and feed our imagination. Our task is to take note and be observant and therefore immerse ourselves in these gifts from nature. This is an important lesson for teachers, who are learners too (Bruner, 1972, 1977; Wood *et al.*, 1976), because they may need to learn new behaviours and fresh approaches using more flexible thinking; these are their tools for quality teaching. Adult educators have this pivotal responsibility to ignite a passion and a thirst for discovery in child learners (Bruner, 1997, p. 90).

Conditions for learning: theories of critical thinking and creativity

The imperative for teachers and adults is to facilitate children's questioning as the essence of creativity and learning. Positive experiences for adults emerge when they shift their use of language from controlling and from *barking* instructions at children, towards an approach and a model of coaching and socialising children so that they become more confident to ask *why?* questions and articulate phrases including *might be* and *could be* or *I think...* (Bruner, 1972 p. 144). A starting point is for adult talk to become a dialogue that supports children to take notice of what went well. It is much easier to focus upon what went wrong and descend into blame and punishment; much more exciting and educational is to wonder how to make improvements. Unless adult language shifts, children are more likely to learn that adults only notice them or are interested in interacting in order to correct and control. A vivid image is conjured up in this quote attributed to Lefstien (2006, p. 9, cited in Lambirth, 2015, p.171):

> teachers are mandated to limit pupils' movement and speech, assign pupils tasks and determine the quality of pupils' activity (thereby classifying the pupil as 'successful' or 'failing').

The deeds and actions of adults towards and experienced by young children are likely to impact significantly upon the child's self-image. Children tend to try to interpret or make sense of adult intentions by reading what is perceived to be communicated in tone of voice, facial expression and through body language (Trevarthen, 2005; Buchan, 2013). This communication mode is often much more powerful than many words. Furthermore, hollow or empty words and phrases, such as bland and generic comments, even when they sound positive in terms of praise (*Well done! Good!*), are at best meaningless, indifferent and insincere; at worst pupils can even feel embarrassed and/or humiliated (Dweck, 2006–2010). This evidence necessitates genuine talk between teachers and children, so that adults can learn to pose questions for everyone, including the children, to find out answers that they do not already know. A very different scenario is one where teachers ask questions and only one right answer exists, and this answer is inside the teacher's head. My own vivid memories of primary education conjure up such an episode, whereby the entire class avoided making eye contact (with the teacher) hoping they would not be chosen for the inevitable test question. The task merely challenged our powers of guesswork, memory and repetition, rather than equipping us to boldly create questions and personal challenges for more original thinking. Bruner (1972, p. 62) calls this approach to teaching 'transferability of learning'.

> Children like adults need reassurance that it is all right to treat a task as a problem where you invent an answer rather than finding one out there in a book or on the blackboard (e.g. vivid special games, story-making episodes, or construction projects) to re-establish in the child's mind his right not only to have his own private ideas but to express them in the public setting of the classroom.

Challenge: responding to Bruner's 'transferability of learning' (1972, p. 62)

Ensure that children actively experience their own capacity to solve problems. Achieve this by engineering sufficient success (to experience a sense of reward for the exercise of thinking).

Provide opportunities to practise the skill of connecting ideas in problem solving, and practise using the 'tools of the mind'. This includes asking curious questions or hypothesising. Try saying, I am not sure I understand your thinking. This comment provides children with opportunities to test the limits of their predictions and designs.

Even more challenging:

Be active and experiment; make things with children and move about to construct and experiment to test your hypotheses. Action and doing facilitates a greater capacity for experimentation; this is known as Bruner's enactive mode. A process for creativity.

Collaboration, investigation and problem-posing

Many successful innovations across all disciplines necessitate novel processes, fresh connections and, consequently, an element of challenge (even shock) to accepted views. This approach potentially pushes the boundaries of convention, thus challenging the so-called rules. Such ground-breaking ideas of innovation and creation soon become commonplace, and thereafter become accepted and conventional; no longer innovative, just taken for granted (see the section on 'Technology' p. 73). Therefore, imagining new possibilities in disciplines such as engineering and science; technology and mathematics; dance, language and music; art and design all require conditions and processes for learning. Areas of study need not be hierarchical. Increasingly it is evident that to promote creativity is to facilitate greater interconnectivity, as illustrated by the prominence of engineering within great works of conceptual art and design. The message is similar to the argument by Weldon (quoted in Bruner & Gill, 1972, p. 104), stating that:

> There are three kinds of things in the world: there are troubles which we do not know quite how to handle; then there are puzzles with their clear conditions and unique solutions, marvellously elegant; and then there are problems – and these we invent by finding an appropriate puzzle form to impose upon a trouble.

This perspective signals implications for education; a requirement to teach interesting puzzle forms and ways of thinking so that children learn how to convert troubles into problems. Children need to be equipped with the so-called *tools of the mind* to be able to succeed in this approach. The role of the adult is to plan using structured language, to demonstrate with purposeful action and to create opportunities for collaboration. Essential elements include flexible use of physical space, the availability of resources and materials, and extended periods of time and learning in spaces other than the classroom. Discussion and action facilitates deeper understanding and therefore improved chances of success in problem-posing and creative innovation.

Theory makes knowledge useful, compact and accessible, and easier to shape and mould. This should be the aim of teaching rather than teacher-directed instruction, requiring children merely to receive information and process instruction as automata.

Relationships and affective (learning from feelings and emotions) qualities that are unique to human beings promote problem-finding. What some may see as a weakness of the human condition is also the most crucial strength for intellectual growth. Human beings create culture; they create language as the dialogue (written, spoken, performed, created visually) to communicate between the more experienced and the less experienced. Conversation and reciprocal exchange facilitates internalisation of dialogue in thought. The courtesy of conversation may be the major ingredient in the courtesy of teaching. Teaching conversations lead us to explore the significance of imagination and creativity in play (Figure 4.1).

Case study 4: Turner Contemporary (2016) *Art Inspiring Change*

Art Inspiring Change is our most ambitious learning initiative to date. We are working with four primary schools in Margate from January 2016 to July 2017, empowering 80 Young Art Leaders to inspire the whole town to engage with art, transforming Margate through physical and social change.

Primary school children will work with our resident philosopher to develop strong communication and negotiation skills, inspiring adults in their community to engage with culture and make positive change. They will connect with local politicians and council officers, using their new skills to give a voice to their hopes and aspirations for their own town. These 80 children will also recruit and work with artists to transform four neglected sites in their communities, harnessing the help of adults to physically regenerate spaces in their neighbourhood which have potential for positive change.

Empowering children

This project is built around empowering and listening to children, and creating a climate in which to raise aspirations by connecting children, home, school and the wider community. We are working closely with artists as they are creative problem solvers and divergent thinkers. The project has the potential to transform community consultation.

Our experience in developing projects where children and young people take the lead has so far focused on Thanet's secondary school pupils through youth navigators with younger children engaged across Kent through the INSPIRE programme.

Challenge: a pause for reflection

Consider making contact with local museums and galleries because educational outreach is a priority for such organisations. Discover what is available and then network to collaborate with poets, authors, artists, dancers and musicians.

Figure 4.1   Interview day, *Art Inspiring Change*. The primary school children are recruiting and selecting the artists. Here the children are interviewing prospective artists and this selection process is managed by the children alone

Play versus playfulness

Just as the terms 'creativity' and 'creative teaching' are used interchangeably, so are 'play' and 'playfulness'. This means that we need to return to an earlier consideration: is there a difference between play and playfulness? Barnes and Shirley (2007) would suggest that this needs careful consideration. As part of a wider project they tried to facilitate co-created learning with school pupils, their teachers and student teachers. As the project developed, it became very clear that the playfulness required of the adults was difficult to generate and sustain. They did not report this for the pupils. Interestingly, neither did the authors of the wider project which involved another five such projects across England (Downing *et al.*, 2007).

However, it is difficult to entirely separate the concepts of 'play' (which is usually associated with experimentation by children) and 'playfulness' (which may also be extended to include the willingness of adults to engage in similar activities). The measurement of both is also difficult and may include aspects of spontaneity – physical, social and cognitive (Barnett, 1990). Describing children playing in art, Tutchell (2014, p. 17) refers to these dilemmas:

> As children physically and mentally explore a material, they become acquainted with its properties and possibilities. Spooning a dollop of gloopy paint onto a surface, prodding a giant lump of clay ... are all acts of investigative play which allow the child to find out and define their own relationships with these materials *through playful actions*. [Emphasis added]

It is willingness to engage in exploration and investigation which allows the playing to take place. This is perhaps now better understood as we have noted that neuroscience allows the picture of acquiring experience to appreciate the predicament for adults. Anyone who has attempted to entice student teachers to engage in such activities will appreciate that this can be a particularly difficult task. Why is this? The experiences gained in childhood seem to have been classified in such ways as to render it unnecessary to continue to explore the possibilities. As a consequence, the adult learner is less willing to engage in similar ways of investigation. This is a sad situation, as Tutchell (2014, p. 18) continues to explain.

> Playing with art is not simply confined to the realms of childhood, it is something we all do and artists often refer to in it their work ... [it] ... allows for opportunities to find out and explore *and not just to do and finish*. [Emphasis added]

It is easy to see this in young children, as they are much more concerned with the processes involved rather than with the 'products' they produce. Many, many pictures may be painted to explore what happens when certain colours are tried, mixed, blended, removed or painted over. By the time a child leaves primary school they are more likely to believe that they know this information and far fewer pictures will be generated.

Similar situations may be noted outside of the arts, whether playing with concrete materials, 'make-believe'-type activities or just attempting to understand new concepts. (Trevlas and colleagues (2003) observed a correlation between playfulness and aspects of motor development in pre-school children.) Unless challenged and playful behaviours continue to be encouraged, the reluctance of older children becomes risk-avoidance and reinforces attitudes and self-belief about what the individual can accomplish. In Csikszentmihalyi's (1990) terms (see above), the flow is prevented with particularly negative consequences. The 'experience-dependent plasticity' model provided by neuroscience (also see above) would suggest that the brain stops acquiring new knowledge by such exploration on the basis of past experiences.

Case study 5

A family with three children aged 3, 9 and 12 enjoy making things together. Lately the eldest child seems to be only able to participate as 'helping' the youngest.

Challenge: a pause for reflection

Could you explain to the parent or carer why this is the case? Are you able to think of ways in which you are less exploratory now than you were when you were a child? Are you able to identify individuals who continue to maintain a sense of 'playfulness'?

Choreographing creativity for adult play

Possibly one mode which becomes less exploratory is that of physical movement and expressive dance. A recent teaching experience with undergraduate BA Early Childhood students confirmed this view. Within one cohort of 60 students studying creativity (by choice), 40 students sought permission to be excused from the practical dance seminar. The principal lecturer leading the session recognised the participants' anxiety. She provided familiar and safe tasks for the students to complete. To their surprise they were asked to imagine their favourite games and hobbies, and then to demonstrate imagined actions to represent these pastimes. These provocations enabled the young adults to visualise and express movements that felt familiar. This enabled them to relax and concentrate on moving their bodies. They reflected after the session that they had assumed they would be required to listen and respond to music. In the example (Figure 4.2), participants were invited to draw and make continuous moving lines with coloured pens.

Close observation of the flowing lines on paper supported the students in focusing on the reinterpretation of this visual representation and then to move the coloured chiffon scarf, while moving the whole body, to express the movement in the drawing (Figure 4.3).

Figures 4.4, 4.5 and 4.6 (the Turner Contemporary in 2015) illustrate the potential for art to assist both young and old in rediscovering the power of physicality/ movement as modes of learning for creativity. The significance here is to experience sensations and perceptions within stimulating surroundings and physical

Figure 4.2 Continuous flowing moving lines with coloured pens

Figure 4.3 Moving a chiffon scarf to represent the movement in the continuous line on the paper

Figure 4.4 A child encountering artwork

Figure 4.5   The child showing her delight as she wobbles and spins, thus experiencing a new perspective in the gallery

Figure 4.6   A younger child who appears more at ease and 'goes with the flow' in the moving artwork

Challenge: a pause for reflection

How can you plan provocations to stimulate physical investigations (doing, making and dancing)?

environments. This literally gives the family in these photographs the opportunity to *let go* and/or to *go with the flow*. The result is a learning provocation to the body (in terms of proprioception – the sense of feeling where your body is in space), thereby shifting physical/visual perception and (as a result) a viewpoint.

A shift of perception through movement is the basis for the arguments proposed by Matthews (1999), who claims that young children *move* in order to make sense of their experiences. These same movements that consolidate learning for meaning and expression may be observed in the play action of young children. The movements are the basis for children's own mastery of drawing tools that become the tools for communication through abstract writing and drawing. Oussoren (2010) understands this perspective and also recognises that children tune into the language of music. Dancing thus represents forms such as straight lines, rounded shapes and circular movements. The teacher leads the dancing and the music directs the children so that they practise the physical skills of balance, coordination and rhythm. This repeated movement supports development and equips the children to master the necessary fine motor skills for drawing and writing. This is the approach known as *Write Dance*. The research, conducted by Matthews (1999), is convincing because the results are analysed from a longitudinal study showing that children's pen and pencil grip for fluent handwriting is based on their predisposition to move when mastering toy objects. Matthews (1999, p. 51) provides evidence through photographic observations, and demonstrates ways in which young children observe and handle objects to explore the properties of toys (such as vehicles). This is interpreted as a means to express a motivation for sensory discovery. This drive to discover can be facilitated and promoted by listening and dancing to music (Oussoren, 2010). Children move more confidently in this naturalistic mode because verbal instruction is replaced by communication through music.

Very young children (Figure 4.7) respond to musical instruction and the teacher/ leader, which provides the model for slow, melodic dance movements. The children feel the tempo, they hear the melody and copy the teacher, who demonstrates and talks about the flowing, rounded movements; all this as they move around the class or hall space. The teacher plays the same music and the children respond by dancing with the same moves but instead of chiffon scarves the children make movement drawings with chalks, toy cars in paint and shaving foam, water with sponges, and stubby sticks in mud and sand outside.

Figure 4.7 Image of young children dancing with scarves in a *Write Dance* session

---

Challenge: a pause for reflection

Aim to plan more frequent physical experiences that stimulate movement, dance and creativity for critical thinking (Goddard-Blythe, 2010; Ouvery, 2003).

Technology

Having considered the human processes of creativity and ways in which these inform teaching and learning, we now turn our attention to the role that technology might play. Many schools appear to embrace technological developments in the sense that significant investment is made in computing hardware and the various software packages that accompany it. A range of devices, whether hand-held or attached to larger computers, seem to facilitate learning by offering a wide range of games and simulations for pupils to enjoy. But is it all that it seems? And to what extent do these new opportunities aid principles of creativity? Some consider these tensions as 'problematic issues ... putting an education premium on those capacities which have not yet been automated ... [including] ... wisdom' (Craft *et al.*, 2007, p. 6).

Let us consider some historical evidence. By the mid-nineteenth century, the art world had absorbed the idea of using brushes to apply paint to surfaces, whether paper or canvas: they had come to be regarded as essential tools to master and use. Several technological developments took place around the same time, however, which revolutionised art practice and caused intense controversy. First, it became possible to contain paint in metal tubes rather than having to mix the material fresh in the studio. This allowed artists to take their equipment and tubes of paint outside and so paint directly what they saw – rather than make many sketch studies and reinterpret them back in the studio later. The second was the improvements in photographic technologies, meaning that moments in time could be captured photographically rather than by commissioning an artist to construct an image which represented it. The third may appear to have nothing to do with the art world but it explains new sights and experiences of people which affected their willingness to embrace new art forms: the development of the railway. More people were able to travel at speeds which had been unimaginable when relying on horse-drawn transport and they saw the blurred landscape as they did so. The combination of all three technological developments provided an opportune time for what became known as 'impressionism' to be born in France, then explored across most of Europe and the United States of America. Had the artists of that time not been willing to engage in the playfulness we have already described above, almost all of the art movements of the twentieth century would not have taken place.

Over 150 years later, these developments may not seem so challenging to our thinking – but supposing there are similar parallels in our own day and age? Those computing advances have already revolutionised photography and film/audio/music-making to the point that artists are already using the new opportunities to create previously unthinkable works and there seems little sign that the pace of technological development will slow down. Wood (2003) highlighted the reluctance of teachers to approach the technologies with the same playfulness. Instances where scanners were being used to capture unusual images before applying further digital manipulation or experimentation were acknowledged to be rare, and OFSTED (2012) later reinforced this, having inspected a range of schools. Resnick (2006) explored the principle of 'using the familiar in unfamiliar ways' (ibid., p. 9), and highlighted the same principles of playfulness, as we have already noted. He suggested that rather than being overawed by the technology and becoming passive users, we ought to view the computer in the same way as paintbrushes – not outmoded but as adaptive tools – and provided many instances where teachers took risks in supporting their pupils to do just that. The results were not always predictable or expected but significant learning took place in their classrooms.

Case study 6

The subject leaders for computing keenly introduced every new piece of ICT that the school could afford each year. Other teachers relied on their advice so that they could utilise the equipment in their teaching – but no one ever seemed to question whether it could be applied in different ways.

Challenge: a pause for reflection

How many different ways do you apply technology in your day-to-day life? Are you already thinking about how the newer technologies might enter the classroom – or do you avoid them? What is the result for the children's learning opportunities? (To get you started, think about forms of 3D printing, digital animation or using iPads as sketchbooks.)

Planning

So, are we suggesting that learning will just happen and that teachers (and their pupils) should simply approach all new possibilities with joyful abandon? If that is the message you have received, we may have failed in our communication! So far we have presented ways in which children may learn, the opportunities and ways in which teachers may support, extend or indeed block these processes as well as some useful tools they may use. In order to best achieve this development, we now want to consider again the importance of planning.

OFSTED (2003) acknowledged the tensions in teaching for creativity while also being seen to be well organised and planned for the actual lessons. Laurie (2011) states that 'planning is the manifestation of a teacher's thinking about what (and how) she hopes children will achieve and learn by the end of the lesson, week or unit of work' (ibid., p. 126). From this she builds an argument for the degree of care, concern and collaboration that is required to ensure that lesson plans enable creative learning to be developed and avoid constriction of ideas and experiences in the process. One of the important aspects of care to be taken is to ensure that the teacher has developed a good level of subject knowledge and can answer challenging questions from divergent thinkers in their class without fear of either losing sight of the intended outcomes or insisting that all pupils stay on the learning journey together. She further suggests that cross-curricular teaching and imaginative learning can only take place if the adults have a deep level of knowledge and understanding. Even by building on a 'skills-based approach', Laurie (2011, p. 169) identifies the ways in which poorly informed teachers can weaken the experiences and opportunities they offer through topic plans.

There seems little doubt that the best way for teachers to plan for creativity is to allow themselves to work with colleagues, exploring themes, knowledge and activities together. In this way, we do not mean just sitting around a table and talking in order to produce a plan, but rather trying out possibilities, noting how others interpret concepts or instructions and using these as possible variations in the classroom with pupils. In this way, schools can ensure flexibility in planning, encouraging teachers to have confidence to exercise their imagination, take ownership of the statutory curriculum and apply the content to allow creative opportunities for learning according to the needs of their pupils.

Case study 7

The Year 4 team of teachers decide to plan a themed topic for later in the year (over two terms in advance). They construct the topic around a local event, as an ancient building nearby will be celebrating 500 years since it was rebuilt as it stands today. The teachers consider a range of activities, including making cardboard models of the building. After school one day they attempt to build one collaboratively but decide that there is little value in doing this. Instead, they are inspired to visit the building the same week and some take many digital photos which they decide to collage together into a large picture. As the weather is fine the other teachers take some modelling clay and make representations of parts of the building while directly observing it outdoors. Talking on their way back to school, the teachers realise what intensely rich learning experiences they had engaged in.

Challenge: a pause for reflection

How has your own experience of teachers' plans caused you to see them? Many teaching assistants have relied on an extremely brief couple of sentences to summarise an activity. As a result the focus may be on the product rather than the intended learning to be gained through the process. What could you do to ensure that your understanding is improved?

Environments

As Tutchell (2014) reminds us, the notion we hold of the environment will affect all the possibilities for learning which are offered to the pupils. She suggested that the environment is always regarded as part of a triangular relationship: child–adult–space. In fact she prefers the term space to environment (as the latter may have limiting connotations) and applies it to a number of settings: inside, outside, real, imaginary, constructed, found, rich or poor. By so doing, the possibility thinking already encountered earlier in this chapter is utilised and developed for enhancing learning.

This is an important and significant difference to the mindset of many teachers who can list the limitations of the classroom space in which they feel they must deliver their lessons. These individuals are likely to be in awe of the teachers who simply reconceptualise their rooms as a different space, where there are no limitations but for those imagined by the pupils themselves. A room or corridor or hall or playground which can be transformed into a very different place may enthral and captivate the imagination. The associations made in learning, strength of emotional keys and the vividness of the memory can all contribute to the lasting sense of pupils' achievement. It is this surprise and motivation which helps reinforce the underlying message: the environment is not just a room; it is the opportunity or invitation made by the teacher to move further into the learning experience and continue the exploration.

Case study 8

The Year 6 class tiptoed quietly along the corridor towards their classroom. They had been studying the ancient Egyptians and today they were accompanying Howard Carter as he finally broke into Tutankhamun's tomb. Their teacher had constructed this in their classroom when they left the previous afternoon but they weren't sure what would lie ahead of them. Having met them in the playground, their teacher took the morning register while other classes went inside the building. They had been told to examine the corridor for clues as to where they were heading. There were hieroglyphics at intervals and then they had to crawl through a confined space just inside the classroom (created by sacking). The room itself was dark and they forced their way through a stone wall (built of cardboard boxes) before being faced with another wall being displayed on the interactive white board. It was dark, and a few blocks were carefully removed as their teacher read extracts from Carter's diary. For the pupils this was an expedition they would not forget.

Challenge: a pause for reflection

Here was a teacher who was secure in both subject knowledge and reinforcing pedagogy. Had you been working with them, what questions would you have raised in order to build this environment and enhance the pupils' learning? Might you have needed a torch?

Creativity and new perspectives

Rethinking the environment is like shining a metaphorical light on old vantage points to see new perspectives. This philosophy is well documented by the work of Loris Malaguzzi (see 'Recommendations for further reading' at the end of the chapter). The concept of the *environment as the third teacher* derives from this approach. Education settings that identify opportunities to connect the environment with philosophy and learning conversations have the potential to facilitate new and powerful changes that can have a significant impact upon creative processes. Examples and scenarios need to be investigated across localities, regions and within communities. Partnerships and networks can help form connections between modes of creativity such as poetry and the visual arts. Starting points for projects that capture the imagination of communities (of which schools are a significant part) may be found when researching historical and cultural heritage within localities. The challenge is to find more flexible learning opportunities so that time and space can be made for asking questions, such as philosophy for children, in dialogue-friendly spaces, beyond the classroom.

Concluding remarks

It is appropriate to now ask, 'Where does this all lead?'. Throughout the chapter we have considered a range of issues with the express purpose of enabling you to ask questions in and around the learning processes: 'What have you now learned? And what will you do differently next time?'. Have you journeyed with us to this point?

We hope so. We acknowledge that there will be a number of challenges here to your thinking, the provision in your classes, issues around roles and (hopefully) future development opportunities. In each of the sections we have attempted to set out the issues to consider and the links between them. You will need time to read, discuss and reread some of them. We have also set out the references below so that you can dig deeper into them if you wish.

As we close, we will end with a question about your own beliefs, understanding and intention in developing creative minds. It is the same question that Lord Carnarvon asked of Howard Carter as he peered into the darkness of Tutankhamun's tomb: 'Can you see anything?'. We hope that we have enticed you to look further and so make your own connections and associations. We particularly hope that the children and young people who benefit from your understanding and support now and in the future will owe much to your enthusiasm and wonder.

Carter replied to the question with the now famous words: 'Yes, things ... wonderful things!'.

Main points

In this chapter we have provided an overview of the background to understanding what is meant by 'creativity' – including the differences between creative teaching and developing creativity for innovation and learning, and the importance of exploring the imagination by utilising a variety of communication processes. We have also indicated how the developments in neuroscience are challenging assumptions about learning and teaching.

The importance of collaborative activities can enhance play and playfulness in both children and adults, as we have noted above. The new opportunities provided by technology should be embraced in a playful manner. Lastly, we have acknowledged the ways in which planning by adults can affect both the learning opportunities and environments in which creative thinking and innovation can be clearly valued.

Further questions to consider

We would suggest that there are three further questions you may like to consider:

■ Are you inspired, since reading this chapter, to re-examine the learning processes within the educational setting(s) in which you operate?

■ To what extent do adults limit and/or control the boundaries of the creative experiences explored by children?

■ By reflecting on your developing understanding, are there any ways in which you could increase, extend or enhance the playful opportunities they can explore?

Recommendations for further reading

Edwards, C., Gandini, L. and Forman, G. (eds) (1998) *Hundred Languages of Children*. London: Ablex.

Eisner, E.W. (2002) *The Arts and the Creation of Mind*. New Haven, CT: Yale University Press.

Room 13 International, 'An international community of creatives'. Available at http://room13scotland.com/ (accessed 12 February 2016).

Thornton, L. and Brunton, P. (2005) *Understanding the Reggio Approach*. London: David Fulton.

Turner Contemporary (2016) 'Learning Programme Paul Hamlyn: Art Inspiring Change'. Available at www.turnercontemporary.org/news/how-turner-contemporary-is-helping-children-to-take-the-lead (accessed 12 February 2016).

Write Dance Training (2016) Available at www.writedancetraining.com (accessed 19 February 2016).

References

Barnes, J. (2015) 'Towards a creativity-rich curriculum for the well-being of children three to seven years old', in T. David, K. Goouch and S. Powell (eds) *The Routledge International Handbook of Philosophies and Theories of Early Childhood Education and Care*. London: Routledge, pp. 278–89.

Barnes, J. and Shirley, I. (2007) 'Strangely familiar: Cross-curricular and creative thinking in teacher education'. *Improving Schools*, 10(2), pp. 162–79.

Barnett, P. (1990) Definition, design, and measurement. *Play and Culture*, 3, pp. 319–36.

Bruce, T. (1991) *Time to Play in Early Childhood Education*. London: Hodder and Stoughton.

Bruner, J. (1972) *The Relevance of Education*. London: Unwin.

Bruner, J. (1977) *The Process of Education*. London: Harvard University Press.

Bruner, J. and Gill, A. (1972) *The Relevance of Education*. London: Allen and Unwin.

Buchan, T. (2013) *The Social Child: Laying the Foundations of Relationships and Language*. London: Routledge.

Claxton, G. (2003) 'Creativity: A guide for the advanced learner (and teacher)', in *National Association of Head Teachers' Leadership Papers, 2003*. London: NAHT.

Craft, A. (2002) Creativity and possibilities in the Early Years. *TACTYC Association for Professional Development in Early Years*. Available at www.tactyc.org.uk/pdfs/Reflection-craft.pdf (accessed 12 August 2016).

Craft, A. (2006) *Creativity Across the Primary Curriculum*. London: Routledge.

Craft, A., Gardner, H. and Claxton, G. (eds) (2007) *Creativity, Wisdom, and Trusteeship: Exploring the role of education*. London: Sage.

Csikszentmihalyi, M. (1990) *Flow: The Psychology of Optimal Experience*. New York: HarperCollins.

Davies, D., Jindal-Snape, D., Collier, C., Digby, R., Hay, P. and Howe, A. (2013) 'Creative learning environments in education – A systematic literature review'. *Thinking Skills and Creativity*, 8, pp. 80–91.

Department for Culture Media and Sport/Department for Employment and Education (1999) (National Advisory Committee on Creative and Cultural Education) *All Our Futures: Creativity, Culture and Education*. Available at www.creativitycultureeducation.org/all-our-futures-creativity-culture-and-education) (accessed 12 August 2016).

Department for Education (2014, updated 2016) *Schools: Statutory Guidance*. Available at www.gov.uk/government/collections/statutory-guidance-schools (accessed 6 January 2016).

Department for Education and Skills (2003) *Excellence and Enjoyment: A Strategy for Primary Schools*. Available at http://webarchive.nationalarchives.gov.uk/20040722013944/dfes.gov.uk/primarydocument/ (accessed 12 August 2016).

Dewey, J. (1997) *Experience and Education*. New York: Touchstone.

Dietrich, A. (2004) 'The cognitive neuroscience of creativity'. *Psychonomic Bulletin & Review*, 11(6), pp. 1011–26.

Downing, D., Lamont, E. and Newby, M. (2007) *HEARTS: Higher Education, the Arts and Schools – An Experiment in Educating Teachers*. Slough: NFER.

Dweck, C. (2006–2010) *Test Your Mindset*. Available at www.mindsetonline.com/testyourmindset/step1.php (accessed 29 September 2015).

Dweck, C. (2006–2010) *Mindset: How Can You Change from a Fixed Mindset to a Growth Mindset?* Available at www.mindsetonline.com/changeyourmindset/natureofchange/index.html (accessed 29 September 2015).

Gardner, H. (1990) *Art Education and Human Development*. Los Angeles, CA: Paul Getty Trust.

Goddard-Blythe, S. (2010) *The Well Balanced Child: Movement and Early Learning* (2nd edn). Stroud: Hawthorn Press.

Jeffrey, B. and Troman, G. (2013) 'Managing creative teaching and performative practices'. *Thinking Skills and Creativity*, 9, pp. 24–34.

Knoll, M. (2009) 'From Kidd to Dewey: The origin and meaning of "Social Efficiency"'. *Journal of Curriculum Studies*, 41(3), pp. 361–91. DOI: 10.1080/00220270801927362.

Kopp, S., Bergmann, K. and Wachsmuth, I. (2008) 'Multimodal communication from multimodal thinking – Towards an integrated model of speech and gesture production'. *International Journal of Semantic Computing*, 2(1), pp. 115–36.

Laevers, F. (2003) *Involvement of Children and Teacher Style Insights from an International Study on Experiential Education*. Leuven: Leuven University Press.

Lambirth, A. (2015) 'Dialogic space theory', in T. David, K. Goouch and S. Powell (eds) *The Routledge International Handbook of Philosophies and Theories of Early Childhood Education and Care*. London: Routledge, pp. 165–75.

Laurie, J. (2011) 'Curriculum planning and preparation for cross-curricular teaching', in T. Kerry (ed.) *Cross Curricular Teaching in the Primary School: Planning and Facilitating Imaginative Lessons*. Abingdon: Routledge, pp. 125–41.

Lee, L. (2015) *Village Christmas and Other Notes on the English Year*. London: Penguin Classics.

Lieberman, J.N. (2014) *Playfulness: Its Relationship to Imagination and Creativity*. London: Academic Press.

McGill, C., N'Guessan, T. and Rosen, M. (2007) *Exploring Creative Learning: Two Primary Schools and Their Partnerships*. Stoke on Trent: Trentham Books.

Matthews, J. (1999) *The Art of Childhood and Adolescence: The Construction of Meaning*. London: Falmer Press.

Newton, L. and Beverton, S. (2012) 'Pre-service teachers' conceptions of creativity in elementary school English'. *Thinking Skills and Creativity*, 7, pp. 165–76.

Office for Standards in Education (2003) *Expecting the Unexpected: Developing Creativity in Primary and Secondary Schools*. London: OFSTED.

Office for Standards in Education (2012) *Making a Mark*. London: OFSTED.

Oussoren, R. (2010) *Write Dance* (2nd edn). London: Sage.

Ouvery, M. (2003) *Exercising Muscles and Minds: Outdoor Play and the Early Years Curriculum*. London: NCB.

Resnick, M. (2006) 'Computer as paint brush: Technology, play, and the creative society', in D. Singer, R. Golikoff and K. Hirsh-Pasek (eds) *Play = Learning: How Play Motivates and Enhances Children's Cognitive and Social-emotional Growth*. Oxford: Oxford University Press, pp. 192–208.

Robinson, K. (2009) *The Element: How Finding Your Passion Changes Everything*. London: Penguin.

Royal Society (2011) *Brain Waves Module 2: Neuroscience: Implications for Education and Lifelong Learning*. London: The Royal Society.

Sawyer, K. (2011) 'The cognitive neuroscience of creativity: a critical review'. *Creativity Research Journal*, 23(2), pp. 137–54.

Singer, E. (2013) 'Play and playfulness, Basic features of early childhood education'. *European Early Childhood Education Research Journal*, 21(2), pp. 172–84.

Siraj, I., Kingston, D. and Melhuish, E. (2015) *Assessing Quality in EARLY CHILDHOOD EDUCATION AND CARE: Sustained Shared Thinking and Emotional Well-being Scale for 2–5-year-olds provision*. London: IOE Press.

Trevarthen, C. (2005) 'Stepping away from the mirror: Pride and shame in adventures of companionship', in *Reflections on the Nature and Emotional Needs of Infant Intersubjectivity*. Available at http://ddpnetwork.org/backend/wp-content/uploads/2014/02/Trevarthen-Colwyn-2005-Reflections-on-Infant-Intersubjectivity-.pdf (accessed 11 January 2016).

Trevlas, E., Matsouka, O. and Zachopoulou, E. (2003) 'Relationship between playfulness and motor creativity in preschool children'. *Early Child Development and Care*, 173(5), pp. 535–43.

Tutchell, S. (2014) *Young Children as Artists*, Abingdon: Routledge.

Vygotsky, L. (1978) *Mind in Society: Development of Higher Psychological Processes.* Cambridge, MA: Harvard University Press.

Wood, D., Bruner, J. and Ross, G. (1976) The role of tutoring in problem solving. *Journal of Psychology and Psychiatry*, 17, pp. 89–100.

Wood, E. and Attfield, J. (2005) *Play, Learning and the Early Childhood Curriculum* (2nd edn). London: Paul Chapman.

Wood, J. (2003) *A Report on the Use of Information and Communications Technology (ICT) in Art and Design.* London: BECTa.

Wright, T. (2010) 'Learning to laugh: A portrait of risk and resilience in early childhood.' *Harvard Educational Review*, 80(4), pp. 444–63.

5 Assessment
Policies and practice

Gemma van Vuuren-Cassar and Chris Carpenter

Chapter overview

The purpose of this chapter is to provide the reader with an overview of the aims and purposes of educational assessment. In order to do this the principles behind educational assessment will be considered, their relationship with educational policy is examined and then the implications for early years and primary practice will be outlined.

Introduction

There is general consensus that school assessments impact upon the educational achievement and future success of many people across the world and are a significant feature of most modern educational settings. In this chapter we will introduce the reader to issues regarding assessment in Early Years and Primary School settings. Educational assessment can be hard to understand and in part this may be because it serves a number of different purposes. For example, assessment information may be used to give feedback on learning to enable students to get the support they need to improve. It may also be seen to provide evidence about the effectiveness of different educational methods and can act as an indicator of the accomplishments of individual learners. In modern times the assessment of attainment is used as a means to hold teachers to account so as to try to ensure that public money is being spent wisely (Mansell *et al.*, 2009; Black and Wiliam, 2007).

Assessment has been widely acknowledged to be a key element of the learning and teaching cycle (Clarke, 2001; Black *et.al.*, 2003). The intention is that the Early Years and school curriculum provide a common core of knowledge and experiences for young learners across all the settings where they are being educated. An effective curriculum is delivered in an open and transparent manner where students and teachers work together to facilitate learning. Inevitably, assessment risks labelling teachers, learners and institutions as successes or failures especially as in current times, the high levels of political intervention in education means that education policy on assessment is consistently newsworthy. Governments regularly voice their concerns emphasising the need for measurements of progress in schools; 'robust assessments' and controversial online headlines such as 'Tougher primary tests and top teachers in weak schools' (Coughlan, 2015), where an education correspondent for a newspaper went on to report that:

> As well as the 'baseline tests' when pupils start in Reception and national curriculum tests, often known as SATs (Standard Assessment Tests), taken at the age of 11, the government is looking at a tougher approach to tests at the age of seven.

Teachers and early childhood professionals need to be knowledgeable about assessment (Athanasou and Lamprianou, 2002) because they spend a considerable amount of their time each day employing a range of assessment strategies such as observations, asking questions and then using the information to inform the feedback that they give children and to inform their next steps. The fact that children in different situations are so diverse makes assessment such a fascinating topic to study.

As we will see in the third section of this chapter, the policy-making arena is a volatile one and at the time of writing this chapter, teachers are being required to adopt a process of assessment without levels (DfE, 2013). The case for assessment without levels in the UK was prompted by political debate and consultations which revealed that in 2012, fewer than half the pupils who reached the expected standard at the end of primary school in English and mathematics achieved five A*–C GCSEs at age 16, while seven in ten of those with a level 4 at the end of primary school in these subjects achieved this GCSE standard. The Department for Education thus proposed that:

> Teachers will continue to track pupils' progress and provide regular information to parents. How they do so will be for schools to decide, suited to the curriculum they teach. We will not prescribe a single system for ongoing assessment and reporting.
>
> (DfE, 2013, p. 6)

This chapter takes into account the ongoing changes and challenges that the assessment landscape poses for teachers in Primary Schools and Early Years settings as they develop assessments and track progress of learning. With changing National Curriculum expectations in the United Kingdom (UK), teachers need to re-establish confidence in the accuracy of their daily assessment judgements in a context where levels no longer apply.

Assessment

In this section we will offer the reader an overview of the aims and purposes of educational assessment and also present a definition of some key concepts. The terms *assessment*, *test*, *measurement* and *evaluation* are often used interchangeably in the field of education; however, it is important to distinguish between them. Assessment is a generic term defined as a course of action for generating information that is used for making decisions about what learners understand and can do. The Standards for Educational and Psychological Testing[1] define assessment in education as a 'process that integrates test information with information from other sources' (p. 3). Delandshere (2001) defined assessment as a process of forming 'value judgments and interpretations that determine the significance, the importance, and the value of learning and knowing' (p. 132). A test is normally a formal process involving a task, instrument or systematic procedure for generating, observing, describing, computing and recording one or more characteristics, abilities, knowledge or other attributes of a learner. On the other hand, a test has been defined as an 'evaluative device or procedure in which a sample of an examinee's behaviours in a specified domain is obtained and subsequently evaluated and scored using a standardized process' (The Standards for Educational and Psychological Testing, p. 3). Measurement is defined as a procedure for awarding numbers (scores or levels) to a specified quality (e.g. knowledge, skill, competence) in a manner that the numbers/grades describe the degree to which the individual possesses the quality. A numeric measurement is usually linked to a descriptive criterion or set of criteria expanding what that number stands for. A distinction can be made between measurement and testing, in that tests are the instruments by which measurements are made (Hargreaves, 2005).

Normally, a mixture of assessment techniques or modes (Rowntree, 1977) is used in educational settings. Such modes may include, but are not exclusive to, informal, formal, process, product, continuous, terminal, convergent, divergent, coursework, examinations, internal, external, formative and summative assessments. Satterly (1989) points out that these dimensions deal with different aspects of assessments and answer the basic 'what', 'when', 'who', 'why' and 'how' questions of assessment.

Test scores can be pooled together to generate a measurement and information about how a school, region or nation is performing with reference to national and international goals, learning outcomes, standards or benchmarks of such testing procedures. For example, test scores of year groups of pupils are published by the Department for Education[2] online on an official web page entitled 'School and College Performance tables' while newspapers[3] and broadcasters[4] also publish these national scores. The government in the UK claims that information is in the interest of the general public, and acts to hold educational sites to account as it means that parents and other stakeholders have some knowledge about how schools and regions are doing. Many national, regional and local education authorities use benchmarks for testing the success of individual schools at the various stages of schooling from entry to leaving. Other examples of large-scale assessment systems where worldwide test scores for students of the same age are computed and published online include the Progress in International Reading Literacy Study (PIRLS[5]), the Trends in International Mathematics and Science Study (TIMSS[6]) and the Programme for International Student Assessment (PISA[7]) (Black and Wiliam,

2007; Stobart and Eggen, 2012). These worldwide tests result in world rankings of performance of nations, and the results often serve the purpose of improving national education policies and outcomes.

Assessment is a broader term since the scope of a test or measurement is narrower; not all assessments yield measurements. Evaluation is defined as the course of action following the process of assessment. Evaluation of individuals can take place while they are still in the learning process, often referred to as formative or coursework assessment, whereas when evaluation occurs after the educational process has been completed it is often called summative or terminal assessment (Rowntree, 1977; Nitko and Brookhart, 2011). Evaluation is a term which is typically used for schools, programmes and educational material. Formative evaluation is ongoing and occurs after every session in a programme where amendments are often made to session notes. Summative evaluation of schools' programmes and educational materials tend to summarise the strengths and weaknesses, and describe whether the school-implemented programme or educational materials have attained the stated goals. Summative evaluations are usually not intended to provide suggestions for improvements, while formative evaluations are.

There is a consensus that the main purposes of assessment in education are for learning, accountability and certification, while other appropriate purposes include feedback, motivation, diagnosis, goal setting, selecting and screening (Black *et al.*, 2003; Broadfoot, 1979; Gipps, 1990; Satterly, 1989; Wragg, 2001). A significant aspect of assessment in practice that emerged from the literature includes two key concepts: Assessment *for* Learning and Assessment *of* Learning (Black and Wiliam, 1998, 2005, 2009). Assessment for Learning, also referred to as 'formative' or 'informal' ongoing assessment, usually takes place in classrooms and involves the class teachers and professionals who work with the class teacher. It usually refers to assessment procedures involving feedback that improve learning by providing information for teachers and pupils about learning and guides them in planning the next steps in their teaching and learning respectively. What does it look like in the Early Years and primary school settings? Day-to-day school activities that are not graded, such as dialogue, questions and answers among teachers and pupils; sharing of learning outcomes; observing; discussing; comparing; analysing; verbal and written comments; nonverbal gestures; portfolio, and individual education plans become formative assessment when the evidence is actually used to adapt the teaching to meet learning needs (Black *et al.*, 2003). Meanwhile, Assessment of Learning, also called 'summative' or 'formal' assessment, takes place at a fixed predetermined time, and involves marking, grading or recording of a value judgement. Tools that are used for summative assessments include specific tasks of an oral, written and/or practical nature, questions, observations and tests. The focus is on what one has learned and achieved (Wragg, 2001). Furthermore, the links between assessments and inclusion that have arisen from research into effectiveness for all learners (EADSNE, 2009; Bennett, 2011) emphasise that inclusive schools support learners with diverse, linguistic, cultural, educational and cognitive needs.

Nevertheless, assessment is often described as a double-edged sword. On the one hand, the learner is evaluated about the progress of learning or some other criteria, while some teachers might fear testing and assessments since they will be judged about their potential lack of ability to ensure that all learners are successful in achieving their targets. While schools should be held accountable for learning, using assessment findings as a factor of determining whether one teacher is teaching better than another is not appropriate (Gullo, 2005). One may argue that assessment and learning need to be a process integrated with the curriculum in the early years and the primary schooling setting. The purpose of assessment in education is about ongoing learning progress in curricular domains for all learners in a diverse learning setting. Assessment then should be about assessing that which is supposed to be measured, rather than that which is most easily assessable.

The body of literature on the principles of assessments in education such as validity and reliability (Popham, 2011; Osterlind, 2010; Reynolds *et al.*, 2010; Wragg, 2001) provides useful guidelines for those involved in assessments. Validity questions whether an assessment measures what it is supposed to assess and is fit for purpose. Validity is the evaluation of the adequacy and appropriateness of the interpretations and uses of assessment results for a given group of individuals (Miller *et al.*, 2013) and is measured in levels such as high, moderate or low. Content-related validity or face validity refers to the extent to which the programme/learning objectives and the content and methods of teaching and learning are represented in the assessment. This determines how well the sample of assessment tasks represents the domain of tasks. Content validity typically comprises knowledge, skills, competencies, attitudes, behaviours and other relevant components. Meanwhile, construct-related validity evidence is judged by determining how well an assessment can be interpreted as a meaningful measure of some quality or ability. An example would be a written test in maths or science to young learners who are not yet proficient in reading and writing. In this case one will be measuring their achievement in language rather than maths or science. Reliability refers to the consistency of a measurement (Miller *et al.*, 2013) and looks at the similarity of results if different test items are used, if the test was repeated on another occasion, or if a different teacher had graded the test. Unless the results from the assessment are reasonably consistent over different occasions, different markers or different tasks (in the same content domain), confidence in the results will be low and so cannot be useful in improving student learning. Reliability is measured statistically (Popham, 2011; Osterlind, 2010). Assessments with more tasks usually result in higher reliability. Other factors that contribute to higher reliability include clarity of instructions and language in assessment tasks, clear marking criteria, and a common understanding and application of the marking criteria.

A fair assessment provides all learners with an equal opportunity to learn, and to demonstrate what they have learned, without any bias or discrimination related to factors other than what was taught. Therefore, the learning tasks, assessment activities and feedback/marking of performance-based and non-cognitive assessment should be free from bias and disadvantages related to race, religion, gender, ethnic background and special needs (Bradbury, 2013; McMillian, 2013). Fairness is consolidated when learners are knowledgeable about what they are expected to learn and how they will be evaluated. Good teachers assess children regularly to inform teaching, provide feedback to pupils and communicate children's progress to parents.

Assessment: a pause for reflection

- How do you understand the terms assessment, test, measurement and evaluation?

- What do you see as the main purposes of educational assessment? How do they match with your experience as a student?

- What is 'reliability' in assessment? How important do you feel this is?

- What is validity in assessment? How important do you feel this is?

Educational policy and assessment

Introduction

Many of the defining features of the education system we see today can be traced back to the Education Reform Act 1988 (ERA, 1988). This has been widely acknowledged as the most significant single piece of educational legislation in England, Wales and Northern Ireland since the 'Butler' Education Act (1944) (Ball, 2008; Ward and Eden, 2009; Garratt and Forrester, 2012). The changes in state education bought about by the ERA (1988) were part of a wider range of public sector reforms brought in by the Conservative government at the time. These reforms were intended to modernise public services by placing the providers of those services in a free market with the idea that as those providers would have to compete to deliver the services, this would improve efficiency, and drive standards up and prices down.

In this section we will consider the implications for educational assessment when education is placed in a free market. In particular we will look in detail at the implications for teacher assessment and the consequences of the 'high stakes' assessment that the adoption of free-market principles heralded. Finally, we will look at the current recommendations for assessment in the latest policy for the 3–11 stage and draw out the implications for schools.

Education since the Educational Reform Act (1988)

Before the ERA (1988), education had operated very much outside the direct control of central government. Funding for schools had been devolved to local education authorities who then administered schools in their area. Local education authorities

(LEAs) are the local councils that are responsible for education within their jurisdiction. The ERA (1988) gave over 250 new powers to the Secretary of State for Education (Chitty, 2009; Brighouse, 2011) and effectively began a process of dismantling the previous delicate balance of powers that had existed between central government, local authorities, the schools themselves, teachers and, in some instances, the Church. In effect it marked a move towards a process of centralisation and political intervention in all aspects of education that has gathered pace since 1988. The increasing pace of change means that we exist in something of a 'policy frenzy' (Stronach and MacLure, 1997), with new policy initiatives like fireworks bursting into life and then dying away to be quickly replaced by a new one.

Three of the defining features of the ERA (1988) were a National Curriculum, national tests at age 7, 11 and 14, and a new inspection regime for schools. At the heart of this legislation was the need to make education more accountable to its 'users' and central to this was the idea that there had to be an element of choice whereby parents and carers could specify which school was the preferred option for their children's education. This led to education being positioned as a private good rather than as a public responsibility (Whitty, 2002) and marked a shift to neoliberal, free market principles increasingly underpinning educational policy (Ward and Eden, 2009). Of course it may be argued that by treating parents and carers as 'consumers', the state had, to some extent, reneged on its responsibility as a site for education, and children's futures were left to be decided by the market.

Neoliberalism is primarily a theory of political economic practices that is based on the proposition that human well-being can best be advanced by liberating individual entrepreneurial freedoms and skills. This can best occur within an institutional framework characterised by strong private property rights, free markets and free trade. In such an ideology the role of the state is to create and preserve an institutional framework appropriate to such practices (Heywood, 1998; Harvey, 2005).

With parents being constructed as consumers, it followed that they needed to be empowered to make choices, and so visible measures of accountability were required. Two of the solutions to this were found in the development of the Office for Standards in Education (OFSTED) which published their reports in the public domain, and the publication of examination/test results being another. The latter was to have profound implications for assessment which apply to this day, and will be considered in more detail here.

Education in the marketplace: implications for assessment

With education in a marketplace, assessment information became a means by which schools could demonstrate their accountability to the public and enable parents and carers to make decisions about which school to send their children to. Tests and examinations were presented as tangible and quantitative measures which could be used to 'judge' schools. In fact it has been argued that the term 'assessment' was reduced to being synonymous with objective and mechanical processes involving checklists, precision, explicit criteria and incontrovertible facts and figures (Drummond, 2000).

It should be noted at this point that examination and test scores, while often presented as 'true' and 'objective', have limitations. First, at the point of 'allocating' the number to the student's work the teacher is making an interpretation of some kind and this may be seen as a 'construct'. Therefore it may be argued that to some extent what the assessor sees is a 'fabrication in the mind of the beholder' (Rowntree, 1987, p. 84). This is especially true when allocating numbers to more open-ended and subjective 'products' of education such as art and poetry. Second, and related to the first point, is that the process of allocating numbers often erects a pseudo-objective façade on what was a deeply subjective process of interpretation on the part of the assessor (Rowntree, 1987). Third, educational achievements as assessed by grades often serve to *measure* and do little if anything to *create* talent (Dore, 1997). The test is principally a measure of how good the student is at taking the test and this may not necessarily be highly congruent with other aspects of what might be deemed to be worth learning in that subject. Finally, given the unreliability of test scores, it may be seen that if school effectiveness is based on grades then if no attempt is made to obviate them these inaccuracies are actually built upon (Harris and Bennett, 2005).

It should also be remembered that it has been shown that the giving of 'grades', 'marks' or any kind of number can have a negative effect on students' achievement (Black and Wiliam, 2012), the idea being that students will often focus only on the grade and ignore the comments. What seems to make a difference is if the students are given formative comments and, most crucially, are expected to respond to the comments in some way.

The final point to be made here is that when school effectiveness relies on assessment grades this can have a restricting effect on the curriculum. If teachers are accountable for the test scores rather than effective learning (Pollard *et. al.*, 2000), this can mean that the range and depth of learning is compromised. This is because there is a temptation for teachers to 'teach to the test' as doing well in the test becomes the point of education rather than developing a love of the specific content under consideration (Torrance, 1997). Of course in this it should not be assumed that 'teaching to the test' is an unequivocally bad thing but that it can mean that rich learning which might have been possible can be lost to the demands of performing well at the test.

Implications of assessment policy for practice in current times

Earlier in this chapter it was argued that a characteristic of educational policy since the ERA (1988) has been that it tends to be subject to change at a fast pace. This is especially true at the moment where it may be argued that we are in a time of some considerable policy ambiguity as regards assessment. One of the major features of the latest round of reform is that assessment levels have largely been removed from policy directives. Not only that, but the role of assessment appears to have been reconceptualised.

In the United Kingdom the Early Years Foundation Stage (EYFS) is defined as a framework for children up to the age of 5 which sets out six areas for learning. These areas are personal, social and emotional development; communication, language and literacy; problem-solving, reasoning and literacy; knowledge and understanding of the world; physical development and creative development. The recommendation for assessment is summarised below.

> Accurate assessment will depend on contributions from a range of perspectives including the child's. Practitioners should involve children fully in their own assessment by encouraging them to communicate, and review, their own learning. The assessment should build on the insights of all adults who have significant interactions with the child.
>
> Accurate assessment requires a two-way flow of information between setting(s) and home. Reviews of the child's achievements should include those demonstrated at home as assessment without the parents' contribution provides an incomplete picture of a child's learning and development.
>
> (Standards and Testing Agency, 2013, p. 11)

The key points to note here are that it is advised that assessment should come from a range of perspectives while in school and also that there should be knowledge of the children's home setting. This may be seen as having advantages and disadvantages. The advantage is that the staff at school may well have a better appreciation of the child's background and this can be helpful in informing their interactions with the child in school. The disadvantage is that this may be seen as being intrusive.

At the present time primary schools in England are working to the latest version of the National Curriculum which was published in September 2013. In this version the word 'assessment' appears only once on page 8 where in a section on 'Setting suitable challenges' the advice is that 'Teachers should use appropriate assessment to set targets which are deliberately ambitious' (DfE, 2013, p. 8). This marks a departure from the higher levels of prescription that had been a feature of earlier versions of the National Curriculum. In the meantime there had been a widespread consultation carried out in the sector that drew upon responses from 1,187 individuals and organisations, of which 27 per cent were from primary school head teachers and a further 27 per cent from primary teachers, which was published in March 2014. In this it was reported that:

> Good teachers assess children regularly to inform teaching, provide feedback to pupils and to communicate children's progress to parents. This assessment does not need government to prescribe how it should be done.
>
> (DfE, March 2014)

The report also outlined a number of recommendations:

There will be different approaches to assessment through a child's education and development, using the most appropriate approach for capturing children's learning at each stage and to complement ongoing teacher assessment:

- The existing statutory 2-year-old progress check undertaken in Early Years settings.

- A short reception baseline that will sit within the assessments teachers make of children during reception.

- A phonics check near the end of Year 1.

- A teacher assessment at the end of Key Stage 1 in mathematics, reading and writing, informed by pupils' scores in externally set but internally marked tests (writing will be partly informed by the grammar, punctuation and spelling test); and teacher assessment of speaking and listening and science.

- National tests at the end of Key Stage 2 in mathematics, reading, grammar, punctuation and spelling; and a teacher assessment of mathematics, reading, writing and science.

(DfE, 2014)

Thus we can see that the role of assessment is being reformed and that there is a very clear privileging of some areas of the curriculum such as literacy and numeracy. At the same time the government announced the 'Assessment Innovation Fund' which it was said would enable assessment methods developed by schools and expert organisations to be scaled up into 'easy-to-use' packages for other schools to use.

Then, in November 2015, Nicky Morgan, the Secretary of State for Education, announced that there would be a reintroduction of the national tests for 7-year-olds in England, saying that 'robust' assessment was needed to measure progress in schools.

Summary

Thus it may be concluded that we are living in a time of some considerable uncertainty as regards the policy recommendations for educational assessment. The removal of levels may be seen as an opportunity for teachers to move to a more 'comment-only' approach but at the same time it is clear that in some respects there will continue to be 'high stakes' testing.

Policy and assessment: a pause for reflection

■ How do you see the role of government in educational policy in modern times?

■ What do you feel are the possibilities and limitations of using assessment data as a means to judge school effectiveness?

■ What do you feel might be some 'side effects' of educational assessment?

■ What do you feel about assessment without levels? What are the implications for practice?

Assessment in practice

This section attempts to outline briefly what assessment can look like in practice in the Early Years and Primary School settings and classrooms. The discussion will extend to some of the thorny issues of the birthdate effect on assessments and inclusive assessments.

Early Years

In the case of Early Years, the education of and care for young children aged 3 to 5 is often referred to as child care, day care, nursery school, preschool, pre-kindergarten and early education. It can be delivered in a variety of settings: centre based, home based or at local state schools in the community. The learning and assessment activities are often recorded in profiles (STA, 2015a) and activities may also be embodied in a particular philosophy or approach to early childhood education such as Montessori, Reggio Emilia or Waldorf Schools (Edwards, 2002). In the latter settings, parents receive voluminous descriptive and illustrative information about their children's daily life and progress, and share in culminating authentic productions or performances. Meanwhile, in the Early Years settings portfolios and other artefacts of children's individual and group work may be exhibited and sent home at regular intervals and transitions. The most common elements of early childhood education support three key developmental domains: cognitive (language development and problem-solving skills), physical (gross/fine motor development) and social-emotional (interactions with others in a group) to children's overall development (Gordon and Williams Browne, 2016) and academic elements such as numeracy and literacy (Bradbury, 2013). Nevertheless, the Early Years setting promotes a high degree of challenge and enjoyment and personalisation and choice through planned opportunities to explore different activities, materials and contexts. Learners engage with imaginative and creative use of both indoor and outdoor learning tasks and environments (Canning, 2010), while staff in these settings are encouraged to experiment with innovative approaches. Learning tends to occur through a wide range of well-designed activities that are of relevance (relationships with past experience and culture of learners), coherence (connections within and among subject areas) and breadth (a comprehensive range of experiences across a subject area) (Clark, 2015). Assessment is ongoing (continuous) and provides constant feedback (formative), and both experiences (process) and end results (product) are rich sources of evidence of progress of learning. Assessments typically involved teachers and learners building up evidence of learning from a wide range of sources (e.g. observations, records, digital captures of activities, conversations, discussions, models of different textures, self-assessments, rating scales) that ensure monitoring of the progress of learning for each individual, and afford the planning of the next steps in learning. Assessment information is shared and discussed with learners, parents and other stakeholders as appropriate, which then makes learning and assessment objectives transparent. Therefore, the authentic experiences that children engage with in the Early Years settings are captured, recorded digitally, annotated and added to individual hard copies and digital portfolios.

In the United Kingdom, the Early Years Foundation Stage (EYFS) framework sets standards for the learning, development and care of children from birth to 5 years old (Department for Education, 2014). All schools and OFSTED-registered Early Years providers must follow the EYFS, including child minders, preschools, nurseries and school reception classes. This framework supports an integrated approach to early learning and care. It gives all professionals a set of common principles and commitments to deliver quality early education and child care experiences to all children. As well as being the core document for all professionals working in the foundation years, the EYFS framework gives confidence to parents that regardless of where they choose for their child's early education, they can be assured that the same statutory commitments and principles will underpin their child's learning and development experience. A series of downloadable resources are available to support teaching, learning and assessment in the EYFS, including an assessment handbook and a profile template from the gov.uk web page. The areas of learning of the EYFS include communication and language; physical development; personal, social and emotional development; literacy; mathematics; understanding the world; and expressive arts and design (Department for Education, 2014). The introduction to the EYFS Statutory Framework (SF) affirms that the EYFS seeks to provide partnership working between practitioners and with parents and/or carers. Although the EYFS statuary profile assessments data are no longer compulsory as from September 2016, the EYFS itself will continue to be statuary. Nevertheless, learners will benefit if the providers of the Early Years settings send information about the levels of learning and development in each of the areas of learning for individual children, classes and year groups; and the attainment of children born in different months of the year.

Primary schooling setting

In the United Kingdom, the National Curriculum levels for children aged 5 to 16, namely levels 1 to 8, have been removed as from the academic year 2014/15. Schools are therefore empowered with deciding how best to assess, record and communicate the progress of their pupils, and at the time of writing are at very different stages with developing these new systems without levels. It seems likely that issues around consistency, transferability, quality, reporting, accuracy, moderation and inspection will continue to dominate the ongoing development of assessments without levels in schools. The Department for Education in England published the document *Reforming Assessment and Accountability for Primary Schools* where it is stated that the new assessment and accountability system for primary schooling will set a 'higher bar' (DfE, 2014, p. 4), and will reflect the more challenging National Curriculum. Henceforth, it was argued, the more challenging tests will report precise scaled scores (a score where 100 will represent the new expected standard at a stage) at the end of the key stages, rather than a level, to raise expectations. Meanwhile, some of the accountability measures introduced include the introduction of a 'reception baseline' (DfE, 2014, P. 7) as the starting point from which to measure a school's progress. In addition, a new minimum requirement, known as floor standards, will be communicating and reporting the progress made by pupils from reception to the end of primary school. Furthermore, schools will be required to publish information on their websites so that parents can see the progress pupils make and the standards achieved. The new floor standards hold 'schools to account both on the *progress* they make and on how well their pupils *achieve*' (DfE, 2014, p. 10). Meanwhile, in the case of a small minority of low-attaining learners for whom assessments under the new National Curriculum are not deemed appropriate, Performance Scale indicators (P scales),[8] may be used.

The use of educational technology in assessments (e-assessment) brings about new practices such as peer- and self-assessment in the early years and primary school settings; nevertheless, most studies in e-assessment are related to higher and further education. Virtual learning environments (VLEs), including a number of technologies such as Blackboard and Moodle, have emerged as a technology for teaching and learning (Becta ICT Research, 2004; Lazakidou and Retalis, 2010) and may become important tools for e-assessment. Teaching practices with VLE tools facilitate the use of quizzes, multiple-choice activities, portfolios and collaborative writing tools. Meanwhile, there is a growing interest in how e-assessment can foster new educational goals, such as creativity, project work and communication skills. A study conducted by Johannesen (2013) found that tools, like wikis, may be more conducive to processes of collaboration and may be more successfully employed in primary school. The use of a virtual learning environment can promote certain assessment practices, and has the capacity to influence assessment policies at primary and other levels of the educational setting. Meanwhile, in an effort to demonstrate progress of learning, schools are engaging with developing software applications for tracking progress or working with commercial software companies that offer e-profiling and communication platforms (Lilly *et al.*, 2014), often as a management information dashboard and removed from the VLE that supports learning and teaching within the same educational setting.

Informal formative assessment in the primary setting, also known as assessment for learning, is characterised by a strong emphasis on students' active involvement in assessment, especially through processes like peer- and self-assessment (PASA) (Black *et al.*, 2003). PASA can lead to increased student self-regulation and achievement in the primary setting. Nicolaidou (2013) found that fourth-grade students were able to create more complex corrective peer comments on writing tasks with continued practice through an e-portfolio system. Meanwhile the capability of students to offer sophisticated feedback on tasks depended largely on student expertise and ability in the domain. Therefore engaging students in peer- and self-assessment will benefit from training and practice that can potentially help improve the value of their comments. Other typical assessment activities that facilitate learning through teacher–pupil(s) and pupil(s)–pupil(s) interactions during the day-to-day activities in the school setting may include: sharing the learning and assessment objectives; questioning; observing; discussing; analysing; checking children's understanding; engaging children in reviewing progress; teacher- and pupil-generated feedback that helps the learner understand what they have learned and achieved, and what they need to do next to progress their learning and content knowledge.

Some of the most common educational objectives that support learning in the schooling setting have been conceptualised into the holistic nature of transformative learning experience. Transformative learning requires independent, active learners regardless of age (Bracey, 2007). The model for transformative learning emphasised the cognitive domain (head) to critical reflection, the affective domain (emotions) to relational knowing and the psychomotor domain (physical movement) to engagement (Sipos *et al.*, 2008). More detailed information about the definitions of each of these domains has been developed elsewhere (Miller *et al.*, 2013; Krathwohl, 2002) and will not be discussed here. Similarly, information about how these domains can be embedded into the day-to-day and end-of-unit activities and assessments may be found in various sources (Lilly *et al.*, 2014). Thus, Table 5.1 attempts to exemplify the key educational objectives of these domains that inform continuous and terminal; process and product; formal and informal; and formative and summative assessments.

The revised Bloom's Taxonomy developed by Krathwohl (2002) comprised a two-dimensional framework: knowledge and cognitive processes. Table 5.2 provides a clear overview of the classification of learning and assessment objectives. This table is an enhanced 'Table of Specifications' (Ebel and Frisbie, 1991; Miller *et al.*, 2013) whereby a course or curriculum is defined broadly to include both the subject matter and the learning and assessment objectives. The former is concerned with the topics to be learned and the latter with the types of performances students

Table 5.1 The key educational objectives of domains of learning

Learning objectives	Domains of learning objectives to engage the learners		
Cognitive *(head – thinking skills)* (Bloom *et al.*, 1956) (Krathwohl, 2002)	Knowledge /(remembering) Comprehension Application Analysis Synthesis/(evaluation) Evaluation (creating)		
Affective *(heart – social and emotional skills)* (Krathwohl *et al.*, 1964)	Receiving Responding Valuing Organisation Characterisation by a value or a value complex		
Psycho motor *(hands – physical/ kinaesthetic skills)*	1. Reflex movement 2. Basic fundamental movements 3. Perceptual abilities 4. Physical abilities 5. Skilled movements 6. Non-discursive communication (Harrow, 1972)	1. Perception 2. Set 3. Guided response 4. Mechanism 5. Complex overt response 6. Adaptation 7. Origination (Simpson, 1972)	1. Imitate 2. Manipulate 3. Precision 4. Articulation 5. Naturalisation (Dave, 1970)

Table 5.2 The knowledge dimension

The knowledge dimension	1 Remember	2 Understand	3 Apply	4 Analyse	5 Evaluate	6 Create
A *Factual knowledge*	List	Summarise	Classify	Order	Rank	Combine
B *Conceptual knowledge*	Describe	Interpret	Experiment	Explain	Access	Plan
C *Procedural knowledge*	Tabulate	Predict	Calculate	Differentiate	Conclude	Compose
D *Metacognitive knowledge*	Appropriate use	Execute	Construct	Achieve	Action	Actualise

Adapted from Krathwohl (2002).

are expected to demonstrate potentially linked to cognitive, psychomotor and affective learning objectives. Both of these aspects are important and provide a framework for a holistic process for the learning, teaching and assessment continuum.

The function of summative assessments or a terminal assessment at the end of a unit of work, a year or a key stage in the primary school setting is to measure achievement and the progress of learning over a period of time. These assessments are then communicated to pupils and parents. In England, these results are published on school web pages on an annual basis, the idea being that these performance tables enable schools to be judged and held to account in matters of student progress. The publication of these performance tables is controversial because there can be a risk that the low-achieving schools and regions are stigmatised as well as labelling the teachers and pupils in those schools. However, to withhold this data would reduce the access to information which it is argued is of interest to parents, politicians and the general public. Those who argue for the publication of such results believe that this leads to healthy competition that can motivate low-achieving schools to work harder.

One of the reasons why the publication of student and school results is a contentious issue is due to the birthdate effect. There is robust evidence from around the world that, on average, the youngest children in their year group at school perform at a lower level than their older classmates (Daniels *et al.*, 2000). This is a general effect found across large groups of pupils, in particular summer-born pupils. Although they may be progressing well, the strength of the effect for the group as a whole is an issue of very significant concern (Sykes *et al.*, 2009). In the UK, where the school year starts on 1 September, the disadvantage is greatest for children born during the summer months (June, July and August). The effect of being the youngest in the year group prevails in other countries where the school year begins at other times in the calendar year. The birthdate effect is most pronounced during infant and primary school but the magnitude of the effect decreases gradually and continually through secondary school (age 14 to 16) and high school (age 16 to 18). Research by the Institute of Fiscal Studies (Crawford *et al.*, 2013) showed evidence of the disadvantage for August-born children over September-born children in that the expected attainment dropped from an average of 25 per cent at KS 1 (age 7) to 12 per cent at KS 2 (age 11), to 9 per cent at KS 3 (age 14), to 6 per cent at KS 4 (age 16) and to 1 per cent at A level (age 18). Although Sykes and colleagues (2009) believe that the existing research is illuminating in respect of the extent of the birthdate effect and of its causes, work on remedies to alleviate the issues related to birth effect is not sufficiently adequate and robust to formulate a solution. They conclude that, from the work of comprehensive reviews of the quality of primary and Early Years education, it is likely that an acceptable solution will lie in not only development of a strategy regarding when formal schooling should start, but also – at least – in respect of:

> specific balance in respect of curriculum elements devoted to cognitive, emotional and social development; the training requirements of teaching and support staff; curriculum frameworks; inspection foci; pupil grouping strategy; management of differentiation; and the articulation between early years units and compulsory schooling.

Meanwhile, Crawford and colleagues (2013) proposed that assessment feedback be adjusted so as to provide information on attainment at a specific age (rather than at a certain point in time) in one of two ways: first, by adjusting test scores for children born in different months while keeping the same absolute cut-off for levels, including the expected level; second, by adjusting the cut-off at which children born in different months would be deemed to have met each level, including the expected level. The latter approach is favoured because it retains the advantage of preserving an absolute measure of the performance of learners based on test scores, which could be given to teachers and parents if required, while providing an age-appropriate assessment of whether a child is at, above or below the expected level of attainment.

Pause for reflection

- If the main elements of early childhood education are a concern with cognitive, social and emotional dimensions, how do you feel each one might best be assessed?

- What do you think about the 'birthdate effect'?

- What do you feel about the use of assessment data to promote competition between schools? What might the side effects be?

- What do you feel are the educational possibilities of peer assessment?

Conclusions

Recap of main points

What we have argued in this chapter is that educational assessment is a fundamental means by which educational messages are transmitted to children. We have suggested that since 1988 education in the UK has been subjected to high levels of political intervention, and that has served to shape the ways in which assessment is conceptualised and enacted in all settings.

Educational assessment, like any other aspect of education, has developed its own set of conceptual language and what we have tried to do here is to demystify this for the reader. We have also posited the idea that in essence educational assessment serves to act as a means of feedback on learning; as certification and particularly since the Educational Reform Act (1988) it has also been used as a means to make judgements about teacher accountability. These three aims, while being logical in their own right, may actually be in conflict and we hope that knowing the three purposes will help you make sense of both the theory and practices of educational assessment.

Finally, we have also given the reader an overview of how educational assessment activities are employed in Early Years and primary settings, in particular the idea of assessment that serves summative and/or formative purposes. We have also considered the latest government initiative of 'assessment without levels' which at the time of writing is in place in state-maintained schools, the argument being that levels became viewed as 'thresholds' or 'markers' and that quite naturally much teaching became focused on getting pupils to 'pass' the next threshold rather than ensuring deeper knowledge and understanding in the programmes of study.

Points for further reflection

In order to help you take your thinking forward, we have identified some questions for you to reflect on:

- What is your understanding of the terms *assessment*, *test*, *measurement* and *evaluation*?

- How do you see the relationship between teaching and assessment?

- At this point, how do you understand the 'what', 'when', 'who', 'why' and 'how' of assessment?

- What are the differences between *formative* and *summative* assessment?

- What are the challenges and possibilities of assessment without levels?

- To what extent is educational assessment based on theories of learning? Should this be the case?

- Is there a danger that we can end up privileging that which can most easily be assessed? Does that matter?

- To what extent do you feel that children end up being defined by educational assessments?

- How has educational policy shaped educational assessment since 1988?

- In any setting where you are working or placed, what assessment practices have you seen?

- What do you feel technology can offer educational assessment processes?

Notes

1   The Testing Standards are a product of the American Educational Research Association, the American Psychological Association (APA), and the National Council on Measurement in Education (NCME). Published collaboratively by the three organisations since 1966, it represents the gold standard in guidance on testing in the United States and in many other countries. Available at www.aera.net/Publications/Books/StandardsforEducational PsychologicalTesting(2014Edition)/tabid/15578/Default.aspx (accessed 28 January 2016).

2   Available at www.education.gov.uk/schools/performance/ (accessed 5 January 2016).

3   Available at www.telegraph.co.uk/education/primaryeducation/ (accessed 5 January 2016).

4   Available at www.bbc.co.uk/news/education-30422468 (accessed 5 January 2016).

5   The Progress in International Reading Literacy Study (PIRLS) is an international assessment administered every five years that measures trends in students' reading-literacy achievement and in policy and practices related to literacy. Available at http://timssandpirls.bc.edu/ (accessed 5 January 2016).

6   The Trends in International Mathematics and Science Study (TIMSS) is a series of international assessments of the mathematics and science knowledge of students around the world. Available at http://timssandpirls.bc.edu/ (accessed 5 January 2016).

7   The Programme for International Student Assessment (PISA) is a triennial international survey which aims to evaluate education systems worldwide by testing the skills and knowledge of 15-year-old students in reading, mathematics and science. Available at www.oecd.org/pisa/ (accessed 5 January 2016).

8   P scales: attainment targets for pupils with SEN. Available at www.gov.uk/government/publications/p-scales-attainment-targets-for-pupils-with-sen (accessed 28 January 2016).

Recommended reading

In this section we have chosen books on assessment that we feel are worth your consideration for various reasons.

Rowntree, D. (1987) *Assessing Students: How Shall We Know Them?* London: Kogan Page.

In our view this is one of the timeless classics in the field of assessment. While educational policy sets the backdrop and tends to be ever changing, many of the issues at the heart of educational assessment remain the same. In this book Rowntree takes the reader through both the philosophical underpinnings of assessment and also highlights the implications for practice in a way that makes difficult issues easy to appreciate.

Assessment Reform Group (1999) *Assessment for Learning: Beyond the Black Box.* Cambridge: School of Education.

This has come to be seen as a landmark publication. It may be seen as one of the few instances of research informing educational policy. The work is a concise synthesis of research undertaken over a ten-year period by some of the leading thinkers in the field such as Patricia Broadfoot, John Gardner, Caroline Gipps, Wynne Harlen, Mary James and Gordon Stobart.

Black, P., Harrison, C., Lee, C., Marshall, B. and Wiliam, D. (2003) *Assessment for Learning: Putting it into Practice.* Maidenhead: Open University Press.

This is an ideal companion to 'Inside the black Box' as the authors have taken the key ideas and considered how they have played out in practice. To do this they have drawn upon case studies and foregrounded teachers' voices.

Question: When is a comment not worth the paper it's written on? *Answer*: When it's accompanied by a level, grade or mark! Author(s): Simon Butler. Source: Teaching History, No. 115, ASSESSMENT WITHOUT LEVELS? (June 2004), pp. 37–41.

This is a very accessible paper about using assessment without levels. The author develops a rationale and then gives examples of how he has used the principles in a secondary history context.

Harlen, W. (2007) *Assessment of Learning.* London: Sage.

This is a very helpful book written by one of the leading academics in the field and a core member of the assessment reform group. Harlen looks at the philosophical basis for educational assessment and takes the reader through many of the implications. He locates many of the issues in the educational policy landscape and highlights tensions that are not readily visible to the reader such as the 'uses' and 'abuses' of assessment information.

Gardner, J. (2012) *Assessment and Learning.* London: Sage.

This book consists of chapters written by eminent academics in the field of educational assessment. It is both an ideal first stop for newcomers to the field and also offers the more experienced valuable insights into many aspects of assessment. The chapters are organised into themes of purpose and practice of assessment; impact; theory of assessment; and validity and reliability.

Miller, D., Linn, R. and Gronland, N. (2013) *Measurement and Assessment in Teaching* (11th edn). Boston, MA: Pearson Education.

This is a book written by North American academics and this is reflected in the tone of the chapters which tend to focus on the practical issues related to implementing assessment and do not really address the philosophical considerations. The authors tend to approach this with the assumption that assessment is principally a matter of 'measurement' rather than 'interpretation'. However, the reader is taken through the processes of assessment methods in great detail and, especially for newcomers to the field or for teachers who are charged with implementing assessment processes, this book has much to offer.

References

Athanasou, J. and Lamprianou, I. (2002) *A Teacher's Guide to Assessment.* Tuggerah, NSW: Social Science Press.

Ball, S. (2008) *The Education Debate.* Bristol: Policy Press.

Becta ICT Research (2004) *What the Research Says about Virtual Learning Environments in Teaching and Learning.* British Educational Communications and Technology Agency.

Bennett, R.E. (2011) Formative assessment: A critical review. *Assessment in Education: Principles, Policy and Practice*, 18(1), pp. 5–25.

Bernstein, B. (1971) On the classification and framing of educational knowledge. In M. Young (ed.), *Knowledge and Control.* London: Collier Macmillan (pp. 47–69).

Black, P., Harrison, C., Lee, C., Marshall, B. and Wiliam, D. (2003) *Assessment for Learning: Putting it into Practice.* Maidenhead: Open University Press.

Black, P. and Wiliam, D. (1998) Assessment and classroom learning. *Assessment in Education: Principles, Policy & Practice*, 5(1), pp. 7–71.

Black, P. and Wiliam, D. (2005) Lessons from around the world: How policies, politics and cultures constrain and afford assessment practices. *The Curriculum Journal*, 16(2), pp. 249–61.

Black, P. and Wiliam, D. (2007) Large-scale assessment systems: Design principles drawn from international comparisons. *Measurement: Interdisciplinary Research and Perspectives*, 5(1), pp. 1–53.

Black, P. and Wiliam, D. (2009) Developing the theory of formative assessment. *Educational Assessment, Evaluation and Accountability*, 21(1), p. 531.

Black, P. and Wiliam, D. (2012) Assessment for learning in the classroom. In J. Gardner (ed.), *Assessment and Learning*. London: Sage (pp. 11–32).

Bloom, B., Englehart, M., Furst, E., Hill, W. and Krathwohl, D. (1956) *Taxonomy of Educational Objectives: The Classification of Educational Goals. Handbook I: Cognitive Domain*. New York, Toronto: Longman.

Bracey, G.W. (2007) How does school influence out-of-school experience? *Principal Leadership*, 8(4), pp. 54–6.

Bradbury, A. (2013) *Understanding Early Years Inequality Policy, Assessment and Young Children's Identities*. London: Routledge.

Brighouse, T. (2011) *Decline and Fall; Are State Schools and Universities on the Point of Collapse?* Speech at Oxford Education Society.

Broadfoot, P. (1979) *Assessment, Schools and Society*. London: Methuen.

Broadfoot, P. (1996) Liberating the learner through assessment. In Claxton *et al.* (eds), *Liberating the Learner: Lessons for Professional Development*. London: Routledge (pp. 32–44).

Butler, R. (1987) Task-involving and ego-involving properties of evaluation: Effects of different feedback conditions on motivational perceptions, interest and performance. *Journal of Educational Psychology*, 79(4), pp. 474–82.

Canning, N. (2010) The influence of the outdoor environment: Den-making in three different contexts. *European Early Childhood Education Research Journal*, 18(4), pp. 555–66.

Carr, W. and Kemmis, S. (1986) *Becoming Critical: Education, Knowledge and Action Research*. London: Routledge-Falmer.

Chitty, C. (2009) *Education Policy in Britain*. London: Palgrave Macmillan.

Clark, I. (2015) Formative assessment: Translating high-level curriculum principles into classroom practice. *The Curriculum Journal*, 26 (1), pp. 91–114.

Clarke, S. (2001) *Unlocking Formative Assessment: Practical Strategies for Enhancing Pupils' Learning in the Primary Classroom*. London: Hodder and Stoughton.

Coughlan, S, (2015) Tougher primary tests and top teachers in weak schools. *BBC News*, 3 November. Available at www.bbc.co.uk/news/education-34700911 (accessed 15 December 2015).

Crawford, C., Dearden, L. and Greaves, E. (2013) *When You Are Born Matters: Evidence for England*. Institute for Fiscal Studies (IFS), Report R80. Available at www.ifs.org.uk/comms/r80.pdf (accessed 26 December 2015).

Daniels, S., Shorrocks-Taylor, D. and Redfern, E. (2000) Can starting summer-born children earlier at infant school improve their National Curriculum results? *Oxford Review of Education*, 26(2), pp. 207–20.

Dave, R.H. (1970) Psychomotor levels. In R.J. Armstrong (ed.), *Developing and Writing Behavioural Objectives*. Tucson, Arizona: Educational Innovators Press.

Delandshere, G. (2001) Implicit theories, unexamined assumptions and the status quo of educational assessment. *Assessment in Education: Principles, Policy and Practice*, 8(2), pp. 113–33.

Department for Education (2013) *Primary Assessment and Accountability under the New National Curriculum*. Available at www.gov.uk/government/uploads/system/uploads/attachment_data/file/298568/Primary_assessment_and_accountability_under_the_new_curriculum_consultation_document.pdf (accessed 5 January 2016).

Department for Education (2014) *Reforming Assessment and Accountability for Primary Schools.* Available at www.gov.uk/government/uploads/system/uploads/attachment_data/file/335504/EYF_framework_from_1_September_2014__with_clarification_note.pdf (accessed 26 January 2016).

Dore, R. (1997) *The Diploma Disease.* Southend on Sea: Formara.

Drummond, M. (2000) *Assessing Children's Learning.* London: David Fulton.

Ebel, R.L. and Frisbie, D.A. (1991) *Essentials of Educational Measurement* (5th edn). Englewood Cliffs, NJ: Prentice Hall.

Education Reform Act 1988 (ERA) (1988). Available at http://www.legislation.gov.uk/ukpga/1988/40/contents (accessed 12 October 2016).

Edwards, C. (2002) Three approaches from Europe: Waldorf, Montessori and Reggio Emilia. *Early Childhood Research*, 4(1). Available at http://ecrp.uiuc.edu/v4n1/edwards.html (accessed 26 January 2016).

European Agency for Development in Special Needs Education (EADSNE) (2009) Assessment for learning and pupils with special educational needs. Available at www.europeanagency.org/sites/default/files/assessment-for-learning-and-pupils-with-special-educational needs_assessment-for-learning-graphic-en.pdf (accessed 8 January 2016).

Garratt, D. and Forrester, G. (2012) *Educational Policy Unravelled.* London: Continuum.

Gipps, C. (1990) *Assessment: A Teacher's Guide to the Issues.* London: Hodder and Stoughton.

Gordon, A.M. and Williams Browne, K. (2016) *Beginning Essentials in Early Childhood Education* (3rd edn). Boston, MA: Cengage Learning. Available at gov.uk/government/publications (2015) Final report of the Commission on Assessment without Levels. Available at www.gov.uk/government/uploads/system/uploads/attachment_data/file/483058/Commission_on_Assessment_Without_Levels_-_report.pdf (accessed 9 February 2016).

Gullo, D.F. (2005) *Understanding Assessment and Evaluation in Early Childhood Education* (2nd edn). New York: Teachers College Columbia University.

Hargreaves, E. (2005) Assessment for learning? Thinking outside the (black) box. *Cambridge Journal of Education,* 35(2), pp. 213–24.

Harlen, W. (2007) *Assessment of Learning.* London: Sage.

Harris, A. and Bennett, N. (2005) *School Effectiveness and School Improvement.* London: Continuum.

Harrow, A. (1972) *A Taxonomy of the Psychomotor Domain: A Guide for Developing Behavioural Objectives.* New York: David McKay.

Harvey, D. (2005) *A Brief History of Neoliberalism.* Oxford: Oxford University Press.

Heywood, A. (1998). *Political Ideologies: An Introduction.* Basingstoke: Palgrave.

Johannesen, M. (2013) The role of virtual learning environments in a primary school context. An analysis of inscription of assessment practices. *British Journal of Educational Technology*, 44(2), pp. 302–13.

Krathwohl, D.R. (2002) A revision of Bloom's Taxonomy: An overview [electronic version]. *Theory into Practice*, 41(4), pp. 212–18. Available at www.unco.edu/cetl/sir/stating_outcome/documents/Krathwohl.pdf (accessed 15 December 2015).

Krathwohl, D., Bloom, B. and Masia, B. (1964) *Taxonomy of Educational Objectives. Handbook II: Affective Domain.* New York: David McKay.

Lazakidou, G. and Retalis, S. (2010) Using computer supported collaborative learning strategies for helping students acquire self-regulated problem-solving skills in mathematics. *Computers & Education*, 54(1), pp. 3–13.

Lilly, J., Peacock, A., Shoveller, S. and Struthers, d'R. (2014) *Beyond Levels: Alternative Assessment Approaches Developed by Teaching Schools* (DfE Research Report 375A). London: DfE. Available at http://bit.ly/1ptsnRq (Report) http://bit.ly/1xGb0os (Outcomes and Impact) [October, 2014]. Website: GOV.UK (DfE).

Mansell, W., James, M. and the Assessment Reform Group (2009) *Assessment in Schools. Fit for Purpose? A Commentary by the Teaching and Learning Research Programme.* London: Economic and Social Research Council, Teaching and Learning Research Programme. Available at www.tlrp.org/pub/documents/assessment.pdf (accessed 15 December 2015).

McMillian, J.H. (2013) *Classroom Assessment: Principles and Practice for Effective Standards-based Instruction* (6th edn). Boston, MA: Pearson Education.

Miller, M.D., Linn, D.L. and Gronlund, N.E. (2013) *Measurement and Assessment in Teaching* (11th edn). Boston, MA: Pearson Education.

Nicolaidou, I. (2013) E-portfolios supporting primary students' writing performance and peer feedback. *Computers & Education*, 68, 404–15.

Nitko, A.J. and Brookhart, S.M. (2011) *Education Assessment of Students: International Edition* (6th edn). Boston, MA: Pearson Education.

Osterlind, S.J. (2010) *Modern Measurement: Theory, Principles, and Applications of Mental Appraisal* (2nd edn). Upper Saddle River, NJ: Pearson Education.

Pollard, A., Triggs, P., Broadfoot, P., McNess, E. and Osborn, M. (2000) *What Pupils Say: Changing Policy and Practice in Primary Education.* London: Continuum.

Popham, W.J. (2011) *Classroom Assessment: What Teachers Need to Know* (6th edn). Boston, MA: Pearson Education.

Ravet, J. (2013) Delving deeper into the black box: Formative assessment, inclusion and learners on the autism spectrum. *International Journal of Inclusive Education*, 17(9), pp. 948–64.

Reynolds, C.R., Livingston, R.B. and Willson, V.I. (2010) *Measurement and Assessment in Education* (2nd edn). New York and Cambridge: Pearson.

Rowntree, D. (1977) *Assessing Students, How Shall We Know Them?* London: Harper and Row.

Rowntree, D. (1987) *Assessing Students: How Shall We Know Them?* London: Kogan Page.

Satterly, D. (1989) *Assessment in Schools: Theory and Practice in Education.* Oxford: Wiley-Blackwell.

Simpson, E. (1972) *The Classification of Educational Objectives in the Psychomotor Domain: The Psychomotor Domain.* Vol. 3. Washington, DC: Gryphon House.

Singleton, J. (2015) Head, heart and hands model for transformative learning: Place as context for changing sustainability values. *Journal of Sustainability Education.* Available at www.jsedimensions.org/wordpress/content/head-heart-and-hands-model-for-transforma tive-learning-place-as-context-for-changing-sustainability-values_2015_03/ (accessed 15 December 2015).

Sipos, Y., Battisti, B. and Grimm, K. (2008) Achieving transformative sustainability learning: Engaging head, hands and heart. *International Journal of Sustainability in Higher Education*, 9(1), pp. 68–86.

STA (Standards and Testing Agency) (2013) *Early Years Foundation Stage Profile.* Available at www.gov.uk/government/uploads/system/uploads/attachment_data/file/301256/2014_EYFS_handbook.pdf- (accessed 14 December 2015).

STA (Standards and Testing Agency, UK) (2015a) *2016 Early Years Foundation Stage Assessment and Reporting Arrangements (ARA)*. Available at www.gov.uk/government/uploads/system/uploads/attachment_data/file/472680/2016_EYFS_Assessment_and_reporting_arrangements__ARA__PDFA.pdf (accessed 2 December 2015).

STA (Standards and Testing Agency, UK) (2015b) *2016 KS1 Access and Reporting Arrangements (ARA)*. Available at www.gov.uk/government/uploads/system/uploads/attachment_data/file/488559/2016_KS1_Assessment_and_reporting_arrangements__ARA__23122015_PDFA.pdf (accessed 2 December 2015).

STA (Standards and Testing Agency, UK) (2015c) *2016 KS2 Assessment and Reporting Arrangements (ARA)*. Available at www.gov.uk/government/uploads/system/uploads/attachment_data/file/512097/2016_KS2_Assessment_and_reporting_arrangements__ARA__22122015-_PDFA.pdf (accessed 2 December 2015).

Stobart, G. and Eggen, T. (2012) High-stakes testing – Value, fairness and consequences. *Assessment in Education: Principles, Policy & Practice*, 19(1), pp. 1–6.

Stronach, I. and MacLure, M. (1997) *Educational Research Undone: The Post-modern Embrace*. Buckingham: Open University Press.

Sykes, E.D.A., Bell, J.F. and Rodeiro, C.V. (2009) *Birthdate Effects: A Review of the Literature from 1990 on*. Cambridge: Cambridge Assessment.

Torrance, H. (1997) Assessment, accountability and standards: Using assessment to control the reform of schooling. In A. Halsey, H. Lauder, P. Brown and A. Stuart-Wells (eds), *Education: Culture, Economy and Society*. Oxford: Oxford University Press.

Ward, S. and Eden, C. (2009) *Key Issues in Educational Policy*. London: Sage.

Whitty, G. (2002) *Making Sense of Educational Policy*. London: Paul Chapman.

Wragg, T. (2001) *Assessment and Learning in the Primary School*. London: Routledge Falmer.

6

Supporting individual learners: working with Deaf learners
The role of the communication support worker (CSW)

Andrew Owen, Jill Bussien and Gary Callahan-Ferris

Chapter overview

The role of the CSW working with Deaf learners in educational institutions and beyond is discrete. The CSW role is distinct from the interpreter role, and charts a contested journey over many years, towards a first foundation degree pathway. This chapter considers how Deaf children develop language, and how that deafness impacts upon reading, cognition and writing. Those born Deaf may have differing needs to a learner who became Deaf later, after some language acquisition, and this impacts upon the work of the CSW. For this reason, the chapter has a theoretical starting point for language modification for Deaf learners. There is great value in planning with understanding, from initial individual assessment, through learning, examination assessment, and before and after transitions, and on the language of examinations and its evolving regulations. There are a range of professionals involved in the Deaf learner's educational journey, from Early Years screening, through each transition to university or employment. There is a finely balanced tension between support and independence, and the CSW must be armed with the theories and have the skill-sets to facilitate this. The range of Deaf learners is discussed in this chapter, incorporating those who do not sign, those with cochlear implants, emerging users of sign language, culturally Deaf learners and others. We start with a discussion of what the role of a CSW is.

The role of the CSW. Historical perspective: a personal experience

When Gary was aged 5 in 1977, he and his brother found themselves placed in the care of an aunt and uncle in Bury St Edmunds. Their aunt and her daughter were both Deaf.

Because Gary was the same age as his cousin they were sent to the same mainstream school and placed in the same class. That was when Gary realised how different his cousin was; at home they used sign language and speech, although outside in public they exclusively used speech. At school, Gary's cousin was fitted with radio aids, which were big and cumbersome. Signing was discouraged and on more than one occasion when caught, both Gary and his cousin were punished for signing in class. For most of her lessons she had an adult with her who repeated instructions very loudly to her. Gary did not realise at the time but that was his first encounter with what is termed today a 'Language Support Professional'. Because it was in an educational setting it could be argued that this professional was a precursor to the modern CSW.

This true story highlights the differences in educational support in 1977 compared to today. In 1977 oralism was the popular method in mainstream education. The prevailing thinking around this time was focused on integrating Deaf children into society. Signing was frowned upon except inside the home. The language professionals in 1977 focused on Gary's cousin's speech. The view was that a child with clear speech would do better in society as a whole. This view was not confined to Britain (Gregory and Swanwick, 2007).

Eventually they were split up and placed in different classes. This was because it was felt that signing was disruptive to the class and could prevent Gary's cousin from acquiring normal speech. Even Gary's aunt was told to keep her sign language at home to a minimum.

According to Green and Nickerson, the role of the communicator was defined and developed during the mid-1980s at a series of National Association for Tertiary Education for Deaf People (NATED) workshops, the last of which met in Coventry in 1985. One major outcome of that final workshop was a report, which listed the sources and types of support that it was believed were required by Deaf students entering post-compulsory education. The list included: interpreter; lip-speaker; social worker; Teacher of the Deaf; note-taker; personal tutor; and counsellor, among others (Green and Nickerson, 1992, p. 65).

In 2010, in conversation, Gary's cousin summed up her educational experience thus: 'Learning to act like a hearing person through hours and hours of speaking and language therapy.' She commented on what happened later, when she was provided with a signing support worker:

> At first I thought the idea was great but it wasn't a good experience. I felt that my form of communication, although really nice (which by then was very 'Oral' with some signs for clarification), frustrated the person. She kept telling me my signs were wrong and suddenly after so many years of being told not to sign, this is all this person wanted me to do. I could sense her frustration with me and when she was off sick I was relieved. Sometimes to save time she would even do my work for me! She eventually left when she got her stage 3 [sign language] to be an interpreter I think.

This betrays the mindset that a CSW is simply an interpreter in the making. This view and other wrong views are pervasive, so we must consider just who a CSW is.

The role of support staff: a pause for reflection

If it is true that the role of those who support Deaf learners is decided by educators and professionals, and responds to current educational trends and paradigms, should not Deaf people themselves be consulted about what the role entails? If so, how can this consultation be expedited?

Who is a CSW?

The acronym CSW (communication support worker) is well known, but the discrete role may not be universally understood. Indeed, many CSWs are unsure of their own role, partly because employers are not sure, and regard the acronym as a general umbrella term to apply to all staff working with Deaf learners. It is therefore important to be able to identify the role, so this chapter addresses that issue. It is also important to identify a discrete CSW role because there are other discrete roles working with Deaf people, such as interpreter, lip-speaker, manual and electronic note-taker, etc., each currently having a category within the National Registers for Communication Professionals working with Deaf and Deafblind People (NRCPD). Perhaps one reason why the CSW's role is not universally understood is because there is no category there for CSWs, despite discussions and formal representation (Bailey and Owen, 2012).

What the CSW's role is not

An explanation of the discrete role of the CSW may benefit from a description of what the CSW's role is not, because we will then begin to narrow down the field to address what the role actually is. There are several mistaken views of the role of the CSW and it would be useful to consider these views. Three are briefly discussed here.

The 'CSWs have too many roles' view

Many people hold the view that the role of the CSW is difficult to identify because it has many parts. Many believe that it is impossible to become qualified and proficient in all parts and use the figure of speech 'Jack of all trades, master of none' to describe a person who is competent in many skills, but not necessarily outstanding in any particular one. Frank Harrington expounded this view in his document, 'The rise, fall and re-invention of the communicator: Re-defining roles and responsibilities in educational interpreting' (2001). Harrington says: 'I am not convinced that the roles carried out by CSWs can appropriately remain the responsibility of one individual or that the training available to them at present adequately prepares them for all of the tasks they undertake.' It could be that this view has been a sticking point for CSWs becoming registered, because those who hold this view, and/or those who have been influenced by this view, find it difficult to pin down just what the CSW's role is. It means that other roles have been assigned to the CSW, such as note-taker, lip-speaker or interpreter, in an attempt to understand or identify just what the role is. But this intellectual re-assigning of roles has served to perpetuate the confusion and has laid CSWs open to criticism that they are not qualified to undertake the roles that have been re-assigned to them.

It is true that in the search for developing personal skills, many CSWs have been able to achieve qualifications in other areas, such as note-taking, qualified teacher status, plus a range of other roles not intrinsic but complementary to the CSW's role. Those qualifications have not served to change the role – rather they have enhanced it. As Peter Llewellyn-Jones commented (Bailey and Owen, 2012), he has 'no argument at all with the breadth of role that the CSW has' because he argues that 'any competent interpreter needs that breadth of role also'. It is important, therefore, that the discrete role of the CSW should not be dependent upon nor conflict with the skills or qualifications assigned to the roles of other professionals working with Deaf or Deafblind people, but rather it should depend upon the National Occupation Standards for CSWs, expanded in the Standards Application Guide (see also Lifelong Learning, 2010), in much the same way that the discrete interpreter role depends on the National Occupational Standards in Interpreting (CILT, 2006).

The 'CSWs are not teachers' view

This view is that CSWs should not be performing a teaching function without appropriate qualifications, which most do not have. This view is that a Teacher of the Deaf (ToD), support tutor or similar specialist must undertake any literacy work. Some provisions propose this model that CSWs simply go into the classroom to provide access to the curriculum, usually through BSL, then report back to the ToD, who meets with the learner from time to time to work on literacy. These provisions view CSWs as 'interpreters-in-waiting', and those CSWs who pass through and become qualified interpreters may not fully grasp the value and breadth of their role.

Other provisions, however, hold the view that the CSW is at the 'chalk face' in the classroom, and therefore in a much better position to make immediate judgements without delay and to make full use of the concepts and skills gained from CSW courses. At the direction of the ToD, who may well be peripatetic and whose time is limited, the CSW performs aspects of literary support, documents events, feeds back and discusses issues with the ToD, who works with the CSW and others in the team to achieve educational outcomes. This view is held by at least one Head of Service (Bailey and Owen, 2012) who says of his team: 'Staff therefore need to take those students from where they currently are and move them onto the next appropriate emotional and cognitive phase. I see my team of CSWs being directly involved in that process.'

The 'CSWs are not teachers' belief is instrumental in promoting a view of the CSW's role as a stepping-stone to interpreter status, because it limits the CSW's role to an interpreting function, of necessity requiring constant improvement, and marginalises many facets of the CSW's role as identified in the National Occupation Standards for CSWs, expanded in the Standards Application Guide. It denies oral Deaf learners the opportunity to make use of qualified CSWs who have the appropriate skills to steer them through the educational pathway, and misleads those who eventually become interpreters into thinking they performed the proper role of the CSW.

The 'CSWs should not interpret' view

This view is that CSWs should not be performing an interpreting function without interpreting qualifications, which most do not have. This view states that most CSWs have inadequate BSL skills, let alone those required for interpreting. CSWs are perceived as less qualified and less skilled people, who therefore should not be supporting Deaf students.

This is both a developmental and a domain-specific issue. It is a developmental issue because a growing number of CSWs hold BSL/English interpreting qualifications. It is a domain-specific issue because individual CSWs should be assigned to domains that match their skill-set. That is, to match the specific skills of each CSW to specific age groups of learners, subjects, or the communication/personal needs of individual learners.

The claim that the main role of the CSW is to interpret between BSL and English requires constant appraisal, because the communication requirements of Deaf students are constantly shifting. In 2015, the Consortium for Research into Deaf Education (CRIDE) conducted a UK-wide survey on educational staffing and service provision for Deaf children in the 2014/15 financial year. The report states that there are at least 41,377 Deaf children in England, but only 10 per cent use sign language to some extent to communicate. These findings do not contain data for those who no longer have an educational statement, having progressed to further education, but the findings do show that the preferred communication method used by a majority of Deaf learners is not BSL. Therefore, many CSWs work with Deaf students who do not sign, and those who prefer to speech-read requiring the occasional sign or note to keep them on track, and some prefer to have notes only. An increasing number are cochlear implant users who require speech, Sign Supported English, or simply some curriculum support with their written work. These requirements have few or no features of interpreting.

The 'CSWs are not interpreters' view is instrumental in promoting a view of the CSW's role as a stepping-stone to interpreter status (Signature, 2008). This view also propounds the suspicion that CSWs are not concerned about professional development. The mistake, however, lies in two misconceptions: (1) that all CSWs want to be interpreters; and (2) that interpreting is what CSWs mainly do. It is important, therefore, that the discrete role of the CSW should not be founded on interpreting skills or interpreting qualifications, but rather, it should be founded on the National Occupation Standards, expanded in the Standards Application Guide. Therefore, we must now turn to these documents.

National Occupational Standards

The discrete role of the CSW must spring from and mirror the occupational standards of the role itself. This is especially important within a register such as the NRCPD where roles may overlap. Overlapping takes place because all the roles have a mutual occupation, namely of 'communication professionals'. In addition, all the roles operate within the remit of communication with Deaf and Deafblind people. As has been stated above, it is important that the discrete role of the CSW should not be founded on the skills or qualifications assigned to the roles of other categories in the NRCPD, but rather, the role should depend on the National Occupational Standards and the Application Guide for CSWs.

Standards Application Guide

The National Occupational Standards Application Guide (NOSAG) is a guidance document that applies the National Occupational Standards for learning support practitioners to the role of the CSW. An application guidance document like this provides more detail for occupation standards and can be written for any suite of standards and for a particular context such as offender learning, for a particular subject such as literacy and numeracy or for a particular group of people such as CSWs working with Deaf learners.

This NOSAG for CSWs was produced by Signature in association with NATED, ACSW and Lifelong Learning UK, in response to the government-funded I-Sign Project. One of the strands within the project was to develop a qualification for CSWs supporting Deaf students in education. That qualification sprang from the NOSAG, which means that it was a three-step process: the National Occupation Standards, the Application Guide, and the Qualification. It was therefore a robust and thorough consultative process that charts and details the discrete role of the CSW. There should therefore be no confusion as to the role of the CSW.

What quality of person is a CSW?

Any discussion of a discrete CSW role that springs from Occupational Standards and Application Guides will be the bare bones. The CSW Code of Practice (ADEPT, 2014), held historically by NATED, now ADEPT, adds some more understanding, but we can flesh out the role and discuss what sort of person takes on the role of CSW.

The stability of the CSW

A watchword in education is 'continuity', which is an issue when students go through transitions between primary and secondary, and between secondary and tertiary settings. It is an issue when parents are posted regularly to different geographical locations (armed forces personnel), or when children leave home to attend boarding school. Continuity is also an issue when a teacher leaves and another joins during a course. As a measure to promote continuity, a teacher's typical/standard contract of employment states that, should they wish to leave their institution/position or end their contract, one term's notice must be given. Many CSWs have a similar contract and, like teachers, are not able to take leave off work during term time except for illness or some other serious event, and certainly not for a holiday. Working in education therefore requires a commitment that is accepted as integral to the ethos of education. The majority of CSWs accept that commitment as part of the role. Crucially, this has an impact on assessment. In an examination situation, the CSW often performs the function of an Oral Language Modifier, which is an access provision that includes Deaf candidates, regulated by the Joint Council for Qualifications (JCQ). Their regulations (2011/12) state:

> 2.11.3 The provision of an Oral Language Modifier should reflect the candidate's normal way of working within the Centre and should be appropriate to the needs of the candidate. The candidate should be familiar with the Oral Language Modifier. Where this is not the case, the candidate must have the opportunity to familiarise him/herself with the Oral Language Modifier using a trial presentation. The candidate must be comfortable with the method of communication.

The CSW who has been working with a Deaf learner through a course will know the content, structure and vocabulary of the course and will be in a better position to work with the learner when he or she becomes a candidate in an examination. Moreover, the CSW will be working towards this end as the course proceeds, identifying subject-specific vocabulary, training the learner to identify the English vocabulary independently (not just the BSL) and working with the learner to expect a different sort of support in the examination room. The CSW will also work with subject staff to have in place appropriate provisions such as extra time in mock examinations, so that the learner can pace him or herself and be aware of the different convention of support so that there are no surprises in the examination room. A freelance interpreter (or indeed a CSW) used for a one-off booking to interpret for a Deaf candidate in an examination is therefore inappropriate.

The outlook of the CSW

It has been argued (see Chapter 9) that all adults working in a classroom situation should have the outlook: 'educator'. For those who work in education – teacher, teaching assistant, CSW or interpreter – the outlook of 'educator' is shared by the whole team. The role of teacher is a specialism that may not be shared by the CSW (except in the case of the CSW also holding a teaching qualification) but the CSW supports the aim of the teacher, which is to educate. This is supported by at least one head of service (Bailey and Owen, 2012) who pondered whether CSWs should be described as educators or perhaps actually as teachers, albeit on the unqualified teachers' pay scale. For many interpreters however, the outlook often remains 'interpreter'. In contrast, those who perform the role of CSW require an outlook that addresses other important educational issues, such as those that are taught within CSW training courses. But that is not all: because the outlook of the CSW is to promote education, it follows that it is also instrumental, together with the role of teacher (Brooks, 2008; Segal, 1988) in fostering resilience and self-esteem in Deaf children and young people. The role not only aims to provide access to curricula, but also aims to develop the individual Deaf learner holistically. This demands a multitude of duties that a CSW is accustomed to performing: cleaning juvenile clients' hearing aids, testing and changing batteries, rearranging a room to become acoustically appropriate, building long-term reciprocal relationships with teaching staff and students, modifying teaching resources to match appropriate levels of English for Deaf students, promoting Deaf awareness by organising events for staff and students, being flexible and willing to use SSE (Sign Supported English), BSL (British Sign Language), note-taking or whatever is required for understanding to take place. These are accepted functions and the personal attitudes of CSWs reflect the need for these functions to be performed.

How to become a CSW

The routes to becoming a qualified CSW are various; experienced in general classroom support work or the Deaf community and sign language, a parent of a Deaf child, or a child of a Deaf adult (CODA), but the long-term aim is to obtain the required standards to be a qualified CSW. These are laid out in more detail in the Code of Practice (ADEPT). A CSW will only work within an educational setting with learners in various ways and on differing levels, with the aim of supporting the learner's requirements.

The accepted basic criteria to be a qualified CSW are GCSE at C in English and maths, British Sign Language Level 2, a Level 3 Certification in Communication support for Deaf Learners (QCF) (6259-07) or a previous version of this course with a genuine interest in Deaf people and their education. However, in practice, the nature of the work demands that the CSW holds higher personal academic qualifications such as A levels or a degree and various skills qualifications such as note-taking, lip-speaking, MSI communication, language modification, translation or BSL Level 6. There is a Foundation Degree in CSW work available from Canterbury Christ Church University with the option to complete to a full degree. Some CSWs continue to work in education, even though they may have qualified as a BSL/ English interpreter, as they enjoy the variety and nature of the work.

Considering the Deaf learner: a pause for reflection

Given the obvious tension between the discrete interpreting function of BSL interpreters, and the wider remit of CSWs, where do the rights and preferences of the Deaf learner sit within this tension?

Audiology and communication methods

The early detection and identification of a hearing loss is vital for the progression of the Deaf learner's education, and any delay will impact on the child's acquisition of language and ability to communicate. In the UK, Newborn Hearing Screening Programme (NHSP) identifies and diagnoses deafness as early as possible, thus leading to early intervention. Paediatric audiology departments assess the child's hearing and responses to sounds. Audiologists and ear, nose and throat (ENT) consultants work with other professionals (e.g. Teachers of the Deaf), Speech and Language Therapist (SLT), Educational Audiologists and CSWs. The family and child are supported through this journey of developing listening, communication and language skills. The consultants/audiologists investigate the cause(s) of the hearing loss and offer advice about the type, level of hearing loss and treatment. The ToD offers advice and support to the parents, the learner and the educators from diagnosis until leaving education.

The early fitting of hearing aids encourages the development of language. ToDs and SLTs work with the family to develop communication skills such as turn-taking and vocalisation. Signs from BSL may be introduced to assist learning; this does not mean that the child will later go on to accept BSL as their first language. Children born into a family where BSL is the first language will naturally learn BSL, and in this situation the professionals will encourage the development of listening skills and speech.

There are alternatives to hearing aids such as cochlear implants or bone-anchored hearing aids; it is the responsibility of the medical professionals to advise the family regarding the best option for the child.

Various communication methods encourage the child's language and communication skills to develop and the selection depends on the medical diagnosis, family circumstances and outside influences. Communication modes can be divided into auditory/oral or signing approaches: the Natural Aural approach, Auditory Verbal Therapy, The Maternal Reflective or Graphic Oral method, Structured Oral approaches, Cued Speech, Total Communication (TC), Sign Supported English or Signs Supporting English (SSE), Signed English (British), Fingerspelling, Makaton, Signalong Paget-Gorman Signed Speech (Previously Paget-Gorman Systematic Sign Language [PGSS]), Augmentative and Alternative Communication (AAC) or Sign Bilingualism. In contrast, BSL is a full language with grammatical structures and is different from the other approaches, which are tools to assist communication. The issues around Deaf learners in hearing classrooms are expertly developed by Hopwood (2003).

Making decisions? A pause for reflection

If it is true that Deaf adults can arm themselves with an array of communication preferences and methods, what of the Deaf child, where the decision is made by another? Could a wrong decision be a potential time bomb? (See Crowe et al., 2014.)

Language modification

Why should we modify text for Deaf people?

CSWs regularly modify teaching resources for Deaf learners. In addition, note-taking, either manual or electronic, are methods of working with Deaf learners in class. This task must be approached in specific learner-sensitive ways, because for Deaf people, levels of English understanding often depend on when an individual has become Deaf. Those who became Deaf later in life will typically have the same relative literacy skills as the general population, diverse as that may be. However, some people who were born Deaf or became Deaf as children (before the opportunity of acquiring sophisticated aspects of the English language) may have difficulties with some specific aspects of grammar and vocabulary, much the same as those non-Deaf people who have a weaker second language that they use rarely. An understanding of how these Deaf children learn is therefore of vital importance (Marschark and Hauser, 2011). Issues may include the following:

- Slower and delayed vocabulary attainment, presenting in an under-developed vocabulary range.

- Unconventional perception of English grammatical rules.

- Slower and delayed reading skills.

- Writing that is grammatically unorthodox, particularly the use of verbs, prepositions and tenses.

For some, the meaning of different words that appear the same can be difficult to identify, such as *fountain* and *foundation*. This is because, when learning English, non-Deaf toddlers will attempt words, hear themselves saying them and pick up the morphemes (or irreducible sounds contained within them). Adults correct the childish pronunciations, the child repeats the words and reinforcement takes place. Without being able to hear, all this cannot take place. Indeed, non-Deaf adults, when learning a new complex term, will verbalise (audibly or mentally) and apply existing rules of how these sound in order to guess at a pronunciation. Deaf people, however, typically see a jumble of letters, and some will ask a non-Deaf person to say the word in order to see how it shapes the lips. Many Deaf learners are therefore advised to access the printed word, partly because educational resources are in that format, and also because they cannot take notes as the lesson gets under way, and because, for many, a CSW or even a sign language interpreter is not enough for access to be complete. That is why a note-taker becomes an important link. In a class where two language professionals are working; one for interpreting and the other for note-taking, often the gaze of the Deaf learner will leave the interpreting and search the text on a monitor (electronic) or paper (manual) for clarification.

English-language skills are not a measure of intelligence

We must be careful not to make assumptions about a Deaf person based on English-language skills. Never automatically equate English-language skills with intelligence. In addition, do not assume that a Deaf person who uses BSL will have more difficulty with English than a Deaf person who uses speech. All are different.

Many Deaf readers have difficulty with complex sentence structures, and therefore miss the meaning contained within them. Deaf readers often process complex sentences very slowly. This means that they have less working memory to focus on features of cohesion or comprehension. Therefore, they may need more time in which to gain an understanding of what they read. The aim should not be to type or write as fast as possible to get everything in, but rather to get the meaning into simple, deliberate, short sentences. We must not, however, simply supply summarised notes or leave out some detail deemed as having low priority in the interest of speed (although this may occur as a coping strategy) but rather the overarching aim should be to 'interpret' the source message. That is, to pick out the meaning, step back, drop the source syntax and reformulate into a new 'language' that is simplified English, but with another aspect: simplified English for Deaf people. It is important to consider that those Deaf people whose first language is sign language, and whose second language is written (English), may require text to be presented in a specific way in order to facilitate understanding. In our consideration, there are a number of language conventions we must think carefully about.

Identify and define educational terms

Deaf people need to understand subject-specific educational terms in order to access concepts. We should not take these out, but we should consider defining them so that Deaf learners understand the meaning of the terms. We should try to keep definitions simple, and even consider doing some preparation work on creating a glossary of good, clear definitions, bearing in mind that the vocabulary in definitions should be kept as simple as possible.

Choose frequent words whenever possible

As well as identifying the subject-specific terms, other difficult words need to be considered. Some of these will be infrequently used words that may be outside the vocabulary of a weak reader. They can be changed to more frequently used words, provided that the meaning is maintained. Replace them with words that are synonyms, or equivalents. The sentence structure will probably need to change at the same time to accommodate the easier, everyday words.

Cohesion

Cohesion may be described as the features of text that help stick it together, achieved in English by two main types of cohesion: grammatical, referring to the structural content, and lexical, referring to the language content. A cohesive text is created in many different ways. Halliday and Hasan (1976) identify five general categories of cohesive devices that create coherence in textual matter: reference, ellipses, substitution, lexical cohesion and conjunction. These features of cohesion should be made as simple as possible without the glue becoming too weak.

Ellipses

Ellipses are missing words in a sentence. Speakers and writers often miss out words because the context provides the meaning and renders the words superfluous. For example: *The beginning of the book is hard-going. If you read to the end it is very entertaining.* For weak readers, sentences are often easier to understand when the missing words are included; here, *'of the book'* is missing in the second sentence and should be included, as in: *If you read to the end of the book it is very entertaining.*

Reference words and connectives

Reference words are pronouns (e.g. *him, them, they, she, this, that, these, it*). These words should be kept simple. Connectives can be words such as *but, and, if, though.* Some of these connectives will be hard to understand for Deaf readers, so, if used, they must be kept simple. This also applies to signposting between sentences and paragraphs: *first, second, on the other hand, now we will look at, in conclusion.* These should be kept simple, or bullet points may be considered.

Complex sentences

A simple sentence has one clause, but a complex sentence contains one or more subordinate clauses. In complex sentences a main clause is a group of words that can stand on its own, usually containing a subject and a verb. A subordinate clause is a group of words including a verb that is attached to the main clause.

Not all complex sentences will be difficult to understand. People who became Deaf at a young age often have difficulty in understanding relative and defining clauses. They may not understand some of the words used to signal finite adverbial clauses, such as *although, awhile, once, as, just as, unless, provided that.* Therefore, complex sentences can be split into separate sentences or simpler coordinating words used, such as *but, then, so,* to signal the connection between the clauses. In some instances, the meaning between the clauses in the original spoken sentence has changed in the modified text, so great care should be taken. The CSW needs to decide if the connection is required, and, if it is considered unnecessary, it should be left out. In these examples below the complex sentences are also lengthy sentences, so they should be modified.

- **Finite adverbial clause:** Just as the dog arrived at speed around the corner, the cat took fright and sped off through a hole in the fence.

- **Noun clause:** Juliet the booking clerk didn't know if Romeo the security guard was coming in that day to pay back the £5 he had borrowed from her.

- **Relative clause:** Mark and Grace gave me a beautifully illustrated book they bought in a second-hand shop in a little street near the castle.

- **Non-finite clause:** The police found a small child who was crying pitifully, walking around the park looking for his auntie.

- **Defining clause:** Rachel is the kneeling police officer who is comforting the small child sitting over there on the park bench.

- **Non-defining clause:** After half an hour's work I found the answer to the immediate problem, which served to throw up many more confusing questions.

When typing or writing notes from speech as a source, it is almost impossible to mentally classify complex sentences into these groups in order to simplify them.

A more attainable aim is simply to judge when a sentence is becoming over-long or complex and potentially difficult for a weak reader to process, and start a new sentence.

Passives

Passives are sentences or parts of sentences rendered typically in the third person, widely used because, for example, the focus is on the process, not on the person who did something. Good readers can identify who (or what group, party) did something and interpret the verb phrases correctly. However, less skilled readers often cannot work out what has happened. Examples of passive sentences with their active equivalents are as follows:

- **Passive:** I've been asked to help in school assembly.

- **Active:** The head teacher asked me to help in school assembly.

- **Passive:** The school assembly was badly organised.

- **Active:** They organised the school assembly badly.

One danger in changing all passives to actives is that the speaker or writer's chosen emphasis is lost. The passive is often used when it is not the speaker's main focus, or when the speaker does not know who caused the action. It is therefore sometimes difficult to change a passive into an active without departing too far from the source. Some Deaf people have learned about passives in English classes, so we must match the task to the person. However, in a group there will be differing needs, so we must aim for as wide an understanding as possible. Sometimes, when people are referred to as passive, it is clearer to nominate oneself and work in the first person.

Idioms

Idioms are used frequently in spoken English. The reason people use them in written text is typically to make the text more informal. This is successful with some groups of readers, but for Deaf people the text becomes more difficult. However, if we are interpreting a lesson it is an oral presentation, so there may be a great number of idioms to process. Some examples are as follows:

- **Idiom: Pigs might fly:** Something will never happen or succeed.

- **Idiom: Eat your words:** Accept publicly that you were wrong about something you said.

Idioms are used as a method of abbreviating a concept in terms that have a shared meaning for speaker and listener, but when the meaning is not shared, the idiom must be explained. However, unpacking and explaining can typically take time, and the explanation often looks comical to the casual reader. If there is a danger of losing the overall meaning and thrust of the message, the CSW may consider dropping the idiom. This decision is the CSW's alone, but rather than use this coping strategy as a last resort, they should begin their work positively looking for material to drop, because often an attempt to get everything in can obscure the real meaning.

Phrasal verbs

Phrasal verbs are particularly hard for Deaf people to access. The reason they are difficult is that the verb phrases look very similar and the meaning of each one has to be learned; the meaning is not apparent from its parts. Examples are: *put off (delay), ran into (unexpectedly), run up (debt), look over (glance at), look into (think about), get over (forget), get on (start work), get around to (do later), slip in (mention in passing), get out of (not have to do), slip down (quickly visit), carry out (do).* Consider using an alternative verb with the same meaning as the phrasal verb. But consider how frequent your new verb is, because a weak reader may not know it either.

Double meanings

Weak readers may not know that words have more than one meaning, or the other meanings of words. Usually they know the most frequent meanings of a word, but not always. For example, Deaf people may know the word for the animal *bear*, but may not know the less frequent use of the word, meaning to carry.

Rules of thumb for interpreting into plain English

- Keep sentences short.

- Use frequent 'everyday' vocabulary.

- Do not use words with more than three syllables.

- Consider carefully when to use passives.

- Avoid complex sentences and idioms, or simply explain the meaning behind the idiom.

- Retain simple features of cohesion.

- Use clear textual layout.

- Use bullet points and space well.

- Use capitalisation, but infrequently to preserve relative importance.

- Words that have more than one meaning: be aware and use with care.

- Do not use ellipses: aim for stand-alone sentences.

- Use frequent paragraphs with double returns.

After the event, check with someone else: Has the meaning been retained? Can a Deaf learner understand?

Do we give enough time to consider the meaning of words? A pause for reflection

The Deaf learner is faced with not only learning the content of a curriculum, but is also forced to attend much more closely to English, the carrier language, than his or her 'hearing' peers. Is there sufficient consideration for this added level of work within a mainstream structure and a tight timetable?

Deaf transition from 0 to 25 years

Transition, whether it is from home to preschool, to primary school, to secondary school, to further education, to higher education or into employment, is an important time for all concerned, whether learners, parents or professionals, as it marks a point in time when the existing situation is reviewed and changes made, if required. Therefore it is important that all the facts and opinions are obtained before a decision is made. The Educational, Health and Care Plan (EHCP) records the process with annual reviews and the transition between institutions. Local authorities, schools and services along with professional bodies and charities provide advice, guidance with paperwork (i.e. templates/forms/passports) to assist in the transition process, all of which are valuable resources.

However, it is important to remember the practical and personal aspects of this process. It is the almost unrecordable activities that are perhaps the most valuable, namely by talking with parents and children, to learn their opinions, likes and dislikes, so that this practical information becomes available and valuable. By letting the new CSW/TA visit the child in their present setting to learn about the 'trivial' but important details such as the games and toys they like, hobbies, preferred colour, etc. and by allowing the time for this communication and planning, practical problems can be avoided and will therefore make the transition process less stressful. The advantage of this aspect of the process and honesty is that confidence and trust will grow for the people involved. Alongside these educational changes there are also changes in the audiological support and type provided, especially from local service to cochlear implant or from paediatric to adult hearing services.

Transition planning: a pause for reflection

In the quest for appropriate transition, a Deaf learner's natural feeling is to be with those of a shared language and shared understanding. This may prompt Deaf learners to go where other Deaf people are, rather than where the best course of study/ employment is. How can this concept be appropriately rolled into transition planning?

Drawing the threads together

It is clear that the role of the CSW is a discrete role, encompassing much more than 'support', and a role that explores learning with the student in a holistic way. There is confusion over the role, and professionals in other domains perpetuate this. The role is young; it crystallised in the late 1980s and has developed over recent years. Medical, audiological and acoustic issues impact on the work of the CSW, who is very much part of a team of professionals. The CSW's role is sensitive to Deaf learners and their preferred learning styles, and is not only aware of typical English levels and understanding of Deaf learners' English acquisition, but also when and how they started to acquire English. That is why there is so much material in this chapter to aid an understanding of 'Deaf-friendly' English and how to modify 'standard' English for Deaf learners. The transition of Deaf learners is much more complex and joined up than non-Deaf learners, and, if done well, enhances the learning exploration. But we have only scratched the surface: there is far more study to be done in order to fully understand the CSW's role, and the overarching aim of providing access to the curriculum for Deaf learners.

Suggested further reading

Burns, A. and Gordon, M. (2014) Sound advice. *Special Educational Needs (SEN) Magazine*. January/February, Issue 68.

Holmans, A. (2005) Early intervention – The new challenges when supporting families with babies identified through NHSP. *BATOD Association Magazine*. September, pp. 8–9.

Kitchen, R., Swanwick, R.A. and Clarke, P.J. (2012) Practitioner talk on Deaf children's reading comprehension: Analysing multiple voices. *Deafness and Education International*, 14(2), pp. 100–20.

Maltby, M. (2000) *Audiology: An Introduction for Teachers and Other Professionals*. London: David Fulton.

Maltby, M. (2013) *A Dictionary of Hearing*. New York: Thieme Medical Publishers.

Segal, J. (1988) Teachers have enormous power in affecting a child's self-esteem. *The Brown University Child Behavior and Development Newsletter*, 4, pp. 1–3.

Signature (2008) Report prepared by Signature (www.signature.org.uk) on behalf of the LSC in the North West and the North West Partnership. Research findings from the 'Bridging the Access Gap Conference', 22 November.

Swanwick, R. and Tsverik, I. (2007) The role of sign language for Deaf children with cochlear implants: Good practice in sign bilingual settings. *Deafness and Education International*, 9(4), pp. 214–31.

Underwood, A. (ed.) (2009) Audiology refreshers. *BATOD Association Magazine*, 16(2), pp. 61–85.

Online resources to explore

1. The British Association of Teachers of the Deaf (BATOD) have a wide range of resources and information available on their website, www.batod.org.uk. Visit here to view their magazine articles, read about the history of education for the Deaf and generally browse their resources.
2. Association of Deaf Education Professionals and Trainees (ADEPT) also have a website at www.adeptuk.co.uk, which offers useful documents, such as the CSW Code of Practice and advice for those wishing to access training for the role of CSW.
3. The website for the National Deaf Children's Society (NDCS) at www.ndcs.org.uk contains useful information about transition as well as other support documents for families and individuals.
4. The City and Guilds website at www.cityandguilds.com has information regarding qualifications and apprenticeships for those interested in pursuing the Learning Support role.
5. The National Sensory Impairment Partnership (NatSIP) is dedicated to improving the outcomes for children and young people with sensory impairment, and a visit to their website at www.natsip.org.uk will provide you with a wealth of information.
6. Signature is an organisation that prides itself on improving communication between Deaf, Deafblind and hearing people. Visit its website at www.signature.org.uk to find out more.
7. Finally, many universities have programmes of study that include elements of training for those learning to teach, as well as support services for students who are Deaf. For example, check out what is available at Canterbury Christ Church University website, www.canterbury.ac.uk/home.aspx.

References

The references include texts cited within the chapter and references that have influenced the thinking of the authors of the chapter but have not been directly cited.

ADEPT (2014) *CSW Code of Practice for Communication Support Workers for Deaf Learners.* Available from http://adeptuk.co.uk/GalleryEntries/Adept_Documents/Documents/CSW_Code_of_Practice.pdf (accessed 5 April 2016).

Andrews, E. (2009) The climate of change. *BATOD Association Magazine.* January, pp. 4–6.

Archbold, S.M. (2010) *Deaf Education: Changed by Cochlear Implantation?* Nijmegen: Holland. Thesis Radboud University Nijmegen.

Bailey, M. and Owen, A. (2012) *History of CSWs: Communication Support Workers.* Gloucestershire: Talk With Sign Books Ltd.

Brooks, R. (2008) The mindset of teachers capable of fostering resilience in students. *Canadian Journal of School Psychology*, 23(1), pp. 114–26.

CILT (National Centre for Languages) (2006) *National Occupational Standards in Interpreting (revised)*. Available from www.cilt.org.uk/home/standards_and_qualifications/uk_occupational_standards/interpreting.aspx (accessed 5 April 2016).

Crowe, K., Fordham, L., McLeod, S. and Ching, T.Y.C. (2014) 'Part of our world': Influences on caregiver decisions about communication choices for children with hearing loss. *Deafness & Education International*, 16(2), pp. 61–85.

Ewing, A. and Ewing, E.C. (1964) *Teaching Deaf Children to Talk*. Manchester: Manchester University Press.

Green, C. and Nickerson, W. (1992) *The Rise of the Communicator: A Perspective on Post-16 Education and Training for Deaf People*. England: Moonshine Books.

Gregory, S. and Swanwick, R. (2007) Deafness and Education International Special Issue. *Sign Language and Deaf Education*, 9(4), pp. 214–31.

Gregory, S. and Swanwick, R. (2012) The Sign Bilingual Movement. *BATOD Association Magazine,* March, pp. 11–13.

Halliday, M.A.K. and Hasan, R. (1976) *Cohesion in English*. Harlow: Pearson Education.

Harrington, F.J. (2001) The rise, fall and re-invention of the communicator: Re-defining roles and responsibilities in educational interpreting. In F.H. Harrington and G.H. Turner (eds), *Interpreting Interpreting: Studies and Reflections on Sign Language Interpreting*. Coleford: Douglas McLean, pp. 89–101.

Hopwood, V. (2003) Deaf children in hearing classrooms. In C. Gallaway and A. Young (eds), *Deafness and Education in the UK: Research Perspectives*. Gateshead: Athenaeum Press, pp. 75–91.

Iantaffi, A., Jarvis, J. and Sinka, I. (2003) Deaf pupils' views of inclusion in mainstream schools. *Deafness and Education International*, 5(3), pp. 144–56.

Kumsang, M. and Moore, T. (1998) Policy and practice in the education of deaf children and young people. In S. Gregory, P. Knight, W. McCracken, P. Powers and L. Watson (eds), *Issues in Deaf Education*. London: David Fulton.

Lane, H. (1988) *When the Mind Hears*. London: Penguin Books.

Leigh, G. (2008) Changing parameters in deafness and Deaf education. In M. Marschark and P.C. Hauser (eds), *Deaf Cognition: Foundations and Outcomes*. Oxford: Oxford University Press.

Lifelong Learning UK (2010) *Communication Support Workers for D/deaf Learners: An Application of the National Occupational Standards for Learning Support Staff who Provide Communication Support*. London: Alliance Sector Skills Councils. Available from http://repository.excellencegateway.org.uk/fedora/objects/import-pdf:17175/datastreams/PDF/content (accessed 5 April 2016).

Marschark, M. and Hauser, P.C. (2011) *How Deaf Children Learn: What Parents and Teachers Need to Know (Perspectives on Deafness)*. Oxford: Oxford University Press.

Signature (2008) *Conference Proceedings "Bridging the Access Gap" 22 November 2008*. Available at http://www.cacdp.org.uk/accessgap/ (accessed 12 October 2016).

Wheeler, A., Archbold, S., Gregory, S. and Skipp, A. (2007) Cochlear implants: The young people's perspective. *Journal of Deaf Studies and Deaf Education,* 12(3), pp. 303–16.

7 Learning to be literate

Polly Bolshaw

Chapter overview

Although literacy may traditionally be considered as reading, writing and communicating, there are other ways whereby children can become 'literate', which this chapter will consider. It will begin by considering how literacy may traditionally be interpreted as 'the ability to read and write' and from that move away from conventional interpretations of literacy towards three other crucial understandings. First, it will explore what is meant by emotional literacy, then consider how children can become digitally literate, and then discuss what is suggested by ecoliteracy. We will then explore how these themes are interrelated and our willingness, knowledge and pedagogical skills to ensure a connected approach is a significant element in children's successful literacy development.

Traditional interpretations of literacy

We begin by considering what may best be described as 'traditional interpretations of literacy'. The National Literacy Trust (2016) describes literacy as 'the ability to read, write, speak and listen well'. This corresponds with the Department for Education's (2013, p.13) aims for English within Key Stages 1 and 2 of the National Curriculum, which intend to (among other elements) ensure the ability of children to 'acquire a wide vocabulary, an understanding of grammar and knowledge of linguistic conventions for reading, writing and spoken language'. These aims build upon the two Literacy Early Learning Goals for reading and writing in the Early Years Foundation Stage (Department for Education, 2014) – showing the importance of exploring literacy learning strategies for children from 3 to 11 years.

How children learn to be literate may be linked to Bruner's (1966) modes of representation. Bruner cites six rules to describe human growth and one of his rules is that 'growth depends upon internalising events into a "storage system" that corresponds to the environment' (1966, p. 5). Essentially, Bruner is suggesting that to grow, human beings need to develop a way to store information. He proposes that this happens through three modes of representation – that is, three advancing stages of how we process information. The first of these is *enactive representation* – learning through action. For instance, Bruner (1966) illustrates this by explaining the difficulty one may have in teaching someone in words or pictures how to ride a bike, despite the fact that it could be demonstrated with ease through action. Second, he describes *iconic representation*, whereby by the time a child is 3 years old, they are able to store information using a powerful visual memory, but rely on images to process information. Finally, Bruner suggests that following these two stages, from the age of 7 children develop *symbolic representation,* which is the ability to store information clearly in words or language. It is within this stage that the concept of learning to be literate comes into play, because this is where children begin to learn that symbols like letters and numbers stand for something they can understand, read and replicate.

This knowledge, that letters and numbers stand for something that children can understand, and also reproduce so that others can understand, fits with Corden's (2000, p. 41) definition of literacy which incorporates the ability to 'decode text (in its various forms) in order to read fluently and independently'. However, a distinction must be made between the difference between 'reading' and 'decoding'. Parvin (2014) notes that although, in simple terms, reading may be seen as decoding words so that meaning can be drawn from them, there is more to reading than being able to 'differentiate, segment and blend sounds in order to decode' (Parvin, 2014, p. 174), which are the foundations for phonological awareness. When children are phonologically aware, they are able to note the sound structures that make up spoken language. Cohen and Cowen (2008, p. 79) suggest that this includes being aware of:

- *Phonemes*: the smallest parts of sound that make one word different from another word.

- *Rhymes*: how two words may agree with their sound in some parts.

- *Syllables*: a part of a word which has a vowel sound.

- *Onsets and rimes*: these are parts of words.

By breaking down phonological awareness in this way, we can see how a child's phonological awareness can be measured in different ways. For instance, this may be on a syllable level (e.g. 'Say popcorn without saying "pop"') or on an onset level (e.g. 'Which word rhymes with *house? Mouse* or *friend*?') (McBride, 2016, p. 28).

There are a variety of skills and strategies that those working with children can do to support children's phonological awareness, which will in turn assist children in acquiring traditional literacy skills. Whitehead (2009) speaks of the importance of playing with language to develop rhythms and repeated sound patterns through nursery rhymes and alliterative tongue-twisters. This is echoed by McDonald (2014) who notes the musicality of picture books in particular for developing early literacy. Rhyming stories can help children develop their recognition of sound streams and also build their confidence in reading and decoding meaning, as rhyming texts can have a reassuring predictability to them.

However, when we think of picture books and texts for older children that foster traditional literacy skills, we may think of them holding physical books, learning which way up they go and how to turn the pages. Certainly this is important, and may instil in young children a sense of how to behave like a reader, as well as develop fine motor skills and promote positive relationships with literacy (Makin and Whitehead, 2004). However, e-books may also be used to develop an awareness of print, vocabulary and phonological awareness. Ihmeideh (2014) conducted a study in Jordan in which he split 92 children aged 4 and 5 into two groups. The first group had exposure to e-books and the second group had access to traditional printed books of the same story, and he tested emergent literacy skills beforehand and afterwards. The children who had completed e-book activities had developed slightly higher emergent literacy skills than those who had traditional texts. This may be because of the novel nature of e-books in schools and Early Years settings, but it may also be because e-books have features that traditional texts don't – for instance, sound, music, narration and animation. These interactive features help children focus on the text and vocabulary, which aids development in all features of emergent literacy (which Ihmeideh (2014, p. 47) notes as 'vocabulary, print awareness, phonological awareness, and alphabetical knowledge').

Electronic technology: a pause for reflection

Ihmeideh (2014, p. 42) suggests that electronic technology in education 'can no longer be considered a luxury but is rather an important and a real learning tool'. With this in mind, how could schools and settings develop their use of electronic technology to foster traditional literacy skills?

We can think about how, if we want to develop children's ability to 'read, write, speak and listen well' (National Literacy Trust, 2016), an understanding of how children go through stages of storing information and the components of phonological awareness is important. However, we can also think about other ways in which children need to develop capabilities in certain areas of knowledge, including that of their emotions and the emotions of others.

Emotional literacy

While leading the learning of language, reading and writing may be one aspect of fostering literate children, another key characteristic to consider is how we create learning opportunities for children to develop emotional literacy. In the simplest sense, being emotionally literate is being able to understand one's own emotions as well as the feelings of others. Weare (2004) breaks this down into key competencies in (1) understanding the self, (2) understanding and managing emotions, and (3) understanding other people and making relationships. Supporting children to understand themselves and the people around them is important because it will create children who are more resilient and motivated in their learning, and who are more able to form positive bonds with their teachers and peers. In this way, we can draw upon Maslow's (1943) Theory of Human Motivation, and acknowledge that giving children the emotional literacy skills that promote a stronger sense of belonging and feelings of self-confidence and self-esteem can act as a powerful tool in equipping them to achieve the maximum of their potential.

The concept of emotional literacy links to the idea of emotional intelligence. One of the people who is most commonly associated with emotional intelligence is Daniel Goleman (1996). He argued that the ability to have a high level of emotional intelligence may be more important than having a high IQ. This is because an ability to understand your own emotions and those of other people, and to be able to form positive bonds and relationships with them, may be more fruitful when it comes to achieving success in both a personal and professional capacity than having solely high levels of what Gardner (1999) would consider to be traditional indications of aptitude. In brief, Goleman (1996, cited in Sharp, 2001) describes the key competencies of emotional intelligence as being self-aware, being able to self-regulate, being motivated, having empathy and having social skills. These attributes link seamlessly to the Personal, Social and Emotional Development prime area of the EYFS (DfE, 2014) in terms of making relationships, self-confidence and self-awareness, and managing feelings and behaviour. However, within the National Curriculum, although 'all schools should make provision for personal, social, health and economic education (PSHE)' (DfE, 2013, p. 5), there are no statutory requirements for the development of skills that may be considered emotional literacy. Although the Education Select Committee recommended in 2015 that PSHE should be a statutory subject both at a primary and secondary level, the Education Secretary confirmed in February 2016 that it would be remaining non-statutory for the time being. Nonetheless, as the majority of schools do incorporate PSHE into their curriculum, which the PSHE Association (2016) defines part of PSHE as 'developing self-understanding, empathy and the ability to work with others', this is arguably evidence to suggest that schools are providing the foundations for children to become emotionally literate.

To foster emotional literacy in children learning within the Early Years Foundation Stage, an enabling environment is one where spaces are created that give opportunities for children to make relationships with their peers, for instance, in the form of a 'snug den or cosy space' (Early Education, 2012, p. 9). For older children, Bruce (2010) observes the different types of space that a practitioner or teacher may need to consider when creating a classroom environment with emotional literacy in mind. This requires thought to be given to a communal quiet space, in which children can relax or calm down, spaces for documenting thinking and personal successes, and a clear and tidy communal teaching space (for instance, a carpeted area) where organised daily routines promote consistency and a feeling of belonging. All of these spaces would benefit children both in Early Years settings and across Key Stages 1 and 2. Bruce (2010) above all promotes creating a sense of belonging as the key criterion in creating an inclusive environment which supports children with social, emotional and behavioural needs. Fostering a sense of belonging is something that those working with children do as part of their role implicitly every day; however, perhaps it should be considered more explicitly as a facet in 'fostering the emotionally literate child', which is gaining increasing sway in educational contexts.

For children who may have emotional and behavioural difficulties, there are strategies that incorporate emotional literacy with traditional approaches to literacy learning. For instance, Waters (2004) uses therapeutic story writing as a tool to help develop emotional literacy, but acknowledges that academic literacy skills may also be expanded in this way. She focuses on the use of story metaphors to support children in articulating their internal emotions and feelings to express their internal world, which she advocates explicitly for children with emotional and behavioural difficulties owing to the additional complexities they may have encountered in their life experiences. Similarly, there are other ways to combine emotional and traditional literacy approaches; for example, through the use of stories and books. As we have considered, a key feature in emotional literacy is developing an understanding of other people's emotions, and observing characters in picture books is a way to do this. The emotions that young children may have observed in other people may have been restricted due to their short life experiences, but through picture books children are able to assess emotions in other people and begin to explore how to understand these emotions and empathise with other people (Nikolajeva, 2013). Picture books may also give opportunities for children to learn to manage emotions that they may be less familiar with – such as a feeling of fear when encountering the one shiny wet nose, two big furry ears and two big goggly eyes of Rosen's (1993) titular character of *We're Going on a Bear Hunt*.

Emotional literacy: a pause for reflection

Weare (2004) breaks down emotional literacy into three areas. What strategies and methods could you use to help children:

1 Understand themselves?

2 Understand and manage their emotions?

3 Understand how other people feel?

Overall, developing aspects of emotional literacy will lead towards children having a better view of themselves, being more able to manage their emotions and occupying a stronger position to communicate and form relationships with others. Many of the strategies that may be used are transferable for children across age ranges, and can be differentiated to support children with additional needs. Becoming emotionally literate is vital for children to achieve academic success, not only in terms of traditional approaches to literacy, but also in terms of ecoliteracy and digital literacy.

Digital literacy

Within a twenty-first-century context, it is particularly pertinent to consider the role that digital technologies play in creating literate learners. Ofcom (2015) notes that in terms of access to digital technologies, in 2015 over half of 3- and 4-year-olds used a tablet, with 15 per cent having their own. This figure increases for children aged between 5 and 15, with three-quarters having access to a tablet and 40 per cent having their own. Access to digital information may come from smart phones, tablets, games consoles, PCs, laptops, netbooks, MP3 players and cameras. Effective educators will seek to explore and use the wide range of new approaches to accessing text and modes of communication, rather than seek to ignore them. This is supported by Carrington and Robinson (2009, p. 2) who describe how the digital technologies that can give children a feeling of competence, knowledge and understanding are in some instances viewed by teachers as 'irrelevant' or even 'dangerous'. We must, therefore, take into account how we can ensure the digital literacy of children, especially due to the fact that both the breadth of types of technology that may transmit the written word, spoken word or visual images (or a combination thereof) is increasing, alongside the amount of time children are engaging with these media. You may be familiar with the now-viral online video from 2011, *A Magazine Is an iPad That Does Not Work*, which shows a 1-year-old effortlessly using an iPad to swipe, zoom in and press buttons. When faced with a magazine, she displays what Piaget (1952) may refer to as cognitive disequilibrium, when she attempts to scroll across magazine pages, pinch to enlarge the images and tap printed text, yet nothing happens. Having purposefully pushed her finger onto one page several times with no effect, she resorts to pushing her finger onto her knee, presumably to check that her finger can still apply pressure. This anecdotal evidence shows that children's digital literacy abilities may be overtaking their traditional literacy skills from a very young age. Wohlwend (2015) describes this particular child's ability to operate a touchscreen tablet as some evidence of a digital literacy practice, which does not transfer to what we may consider traditional forms of literacy practice in the shape of a magazine. She lists other digital literacy practices as those incorporating the mouse and keyboard on a computer, as well as touchscreen and voice recognition technologies on a tablet.

The range of digital literacy practices outlined by Wohlwend (2015) demonstrates how the concept of digital literacy has developed. One of the first definitions of digital literacy comes from Glister (1997, p. 1), who describes it as 'the ability to understand and use information in multiple formats from a wide range of sources when it is presented via computers'. Yet we may now consider this explanation to be somewhat outdated, as it does not take into account the other types of screens that children may employ. JISC (2015) describe it as six elements which incorporate 'the capabilities which fit someone for living, learning and working in a digital society'. Two elements of particular relevance for children aged between 3 and 11 are ICT proficiency and information, data and media literacies. For instance, Ofcom (2015, p. 86) found that although children are accessing information from an ever-growing range of digital technologies, their ability to evaluate and critique these sources of information is somewhat limited. While 86 per cent of 8- to 11-year-olds say that part or all of the reason they go online is for support with their homework or classwork, almost one-third of these children believe that all the information they find on websites is true. We as educators know not to take everything we read on the Internet as truth, but children need more support in evaluating sources of information to be able to identify the ones that can be trusted.

An ability to discern digital content is a notion which should be taught as part of the National Curriculum Key Stage 2 Computing area of study (DfE, 2013, p. 179). Through learning to evaluate information in this way, teachers and educators are supporting the Primary National Curriculum aim to ensure that pupils become digitally literate by being 'able to use, and express themselves and develop their ideas through, information and communication technology' (DfE, 2013, p. 178). This builds on the characteristics of an effective environment suggested within the EYFS (Early Education, 2012, p. 29) which considers ICT to be a key feature in the development of reading skills within the specific area of literacy. Several strategies can be employed to support children in considering whether a website is likely to be reliable, so that they can build up their ability to evaluate information. Encouraging children to consider how clearly online information is presented, the timeliness of the information, whether they are familiar with the author, or whether they think the author may have a particular bias, will help children develop an ability to look at online sources with a critical eye.

However, alongside a part of being digitally literate as encompassing information literacy, another element incorporates media literacy, as 'the ability to use, understand and create media and communications in a variety of contexts' (Ofcom, 2013). In this sense we must consider the role of children not only as the consumers of electronic sources of information, but also as the producers of them. Through embracing digital technologies, children are able to show their literacy competencies on an ever-expanding range of platforms. These may include blogs, tweets, status updates, text messages, emails, vlogs, podcasts and animations. For instance, one idea that may be used in practice in the classroom is academic blogging. Chamberlain (2015) worked with a class of 10- and 11-year-olds in Australia to consider how facilitating opportunities of children to write weekly blogs could support in developing children's comprehension skills in metacognition and reflective thinking. She found that the children's critical literacies developed considerably, in part as children could virtually contribute to online discussions about blog entries, but also because reading their classmates' entries facilitated a greater appreciation that other people may have different viewpoints. Activities for children to create their own media content may also link to the notion of emotional literacy in promoting self-esteem and self-confidence by providing children with a feeling of having their voices heard. Academic blogs may be tailored around different curricular areas both inside and outside the classroom; for example, to develop ecoliteracy skills too.

Children and technology: a pause for reflection

Wohlwend (2015) considers the vast range of electronic technology to which children have access, both in the home but also in Early Years settings and schools. Think about the following:

1   How could children be supported to evaluate the information to which they have access on these devices?

2   How could children be given opportunities to create their own online media to support their traditional literacy skills?

Seeing digital literacy as a dual aspect of both learning how to access and evaluate electronic information, and also learning how to create it and contribute to online communities, will equip children with vital skills necessary for the twenty-first-century world. However, to make a child truly literate in a contemporary context, in addition to considering their traditional, emotional and digital literacies, it is also necessary to consider their ability to be ecoliterate.

Ecoliteracy

If we consider traditional literacy to be driven by the desire to seek out new knowledge, Orr (1989, p. 334) suggests that ecological literacy is 'driven by the sense of wonder'. He adds that it 'begins in childhood' (1992, p. 86), which stresses the importance of considering a literate child equipped with skills and knowledge to be ecologically intelligent. We live in a world that is increasingly aware of the current unsustainability of both local and global practices, and in which a global climate agreement was signed in Paris at the end of 2015 to attempt to curb the rise in global temperature and the amount of greenhouse gases emitted. In this way we can see that equipping children to be digitally literate may be seen as more important than ever before in the twenty-first century, and the same is true for ecoliteracy.

Goleman *et al.* (2012, p. 2) suggest that developing children to be ecoliterate is a 'critical need for the 21st century' owing to, they suggest, the four major concerns of food, water, oil and coal. Earlier in this chapter we considered that one facet of creating a literate child may be their emotional literacy, strongly advocated by Goleman. Alongside this, Goleman (2009) has since introduced the notion of ecological intelligence. He suggests that just as by using emotional and social intelligence we are able to develop a greater degree of empathy for others alongside a greater understanding of others' perspectives (a skill that you will remember Chamberlain (2015) has developed digitally in children by encouraging the use of blogging), developing ecological intelligence may increase one's capacity to care about and understand the natural world.

To create ecoliterate children, Goleman *et al.* (2012, p. 10) promote the integration of social, emotional and ecological intelligence, and give five key practices for this:

1. Developing empathy for all forms of life.

2. Embracing sustainability as a community practice.

3. Making the invisible visible.

4. Anticipating unintended consequences.

5. Understanding how nature sustains life.

All of these principles can be fostered when working with children aged between 3 and 11, and all of them may be applied to English education policy. For instance, the EYFS's *Development Matters* (Early Education, 2012) suggests that children should have opportunities to explore their setting's locality to build on an awareness of both natural and manmade features of their neighbourhood as part of the understanding the world-specific area of development. Similarly, the Primary National Curriculum (DfE, 2013) notes that primary school children should be given the opportunity to explore the local environment to develop a scientific awareness of plants, animals and habitats. In this way, children are able to develop a greater understanding about both the connection between the nature and manmade world and how natural systems support the Earth's processes, which is key knowledge to becoming ecoliterate. This may be built upon by fostering positive partnerships with parents who can give access to sites of environmental or ecological interest, and also access to specialist skills and resources that create opportunities for ecoliteracy (Peacock, 2004, p. 106).

Goleman *et al.*'s (2012) principles link to a wider agenda of Education for Sustainable Development (ESD), which is the promotion of fundamental attitudes, beliefs and values about sustainable practices. In order for ESD to have the best possible impact, it should be introduced as early in a child's life as possible (Siraj-Blatchford *et al.*, 2010). There are ways in which ESD can link developing traditional literacy with building an awareness of the natural environment, thus both can be promoted in Early Years settings and schools simultaneously. For instance, Ramos and Ramos (2011) note examples of wordless picture books that attempt to foster both ecoliteracy and emergent traditional literacy skills, called proto-literacy. Proto-literacy is very early literacy development, and being proto-literate focuses on knowing that there is a link between letters and their names and also letters and their sounds, which can be fostered through an exposure to print (Barron, 1991). Being proto-literate supports children in developing their phonological awareness, and, later on, their ability to read and write. Although wordless picture books have no text or letters to examine, Ramos and Ramos (2011) suggest that developing an ability to interpret the message or story that a sequence of pictures may be trying to transmit will support in decoding skills that are useful later on when considering the printed word. However, they also highlight advantages that wordless picture books may have over traditional texts in promoting ecoliteracy, because visual images are able to display elements of the natural environment in a way that text cannot. In addition to this, if a vital element of ecoliteracy is an active notion of developing empathy for all forms of life and anticipating unintended consequences, as Goleman *et al.* (2012) believe, then drawing out meaning from picture books without the 'right answer' that supporting text may provide offers this opportunity.

Progressing from picture books, there are many written sources of literature that may expand primary school children's ecological awareness. Peacock (2004) recommends that teachers and educators use not only prose but also poetry such as by English poet John Clare (1793–1864). Clare has been credited with raising notions of ecological instability into the public consciousness since the nineteenth century (Paul, 2011), and his texts are accessible to an upper primary audience. Primary school children will be able to relate to Clare's concepts, such as an affinity with nature and the destruction of natural habitats, which will be relevant to and resonate with a contemporary reader.

Reflective, critical question

Ramos and Ramos (2011) explore wordless picture books that promote ecological awareness for younger children, while Peacock (2004) considers texts for older children that focus on sustainable issues. Think about the following:

1 What books or stories can you think of that give opportunities for exploring sustainable practices?

2 What strategies could be developed for children to create their own stories that show empathy for the natural world?

There are, therefore, ways in which ecoliteracy may be considered in a broader sense of promoting education for sustainable development, but also ways in which ecoliteracy practices can be linked more directly to practices around traditional literacy development. These means could be for younger children in the form of picture books, but also through the exploration of poetry and prose that considers ecological issues. In a similar way, we can link traditional, digital, emotional and ecological literacy elements together to make a comprehensively literate child, as the following section of this chapter will explore.

The interrelationship between literacies

So far we have considered how, when thinking about what a literate child looks like, this encompasses more than we may understand as 'traditional literacy' skills in terms of reading and writing. Children also need to be emotionally literate, so that they are able to understand and manage their own feelings and the emotions of those around them. They should also be well versed in digital literacy, which incorporates being able to use electronic technologies, access and evaluate information from digital sources, and also to create their own online media sources. Finally, a literate child is one who is ecoliterate, so that they can empathise with and care for not only human beings, but for the natural world as well.

Some of the ways in which these literacies interlink have already been reflected upon, such as ways in which writing stories might support children's ability to manage their feelings, how examining wordless picture books can afford a greater

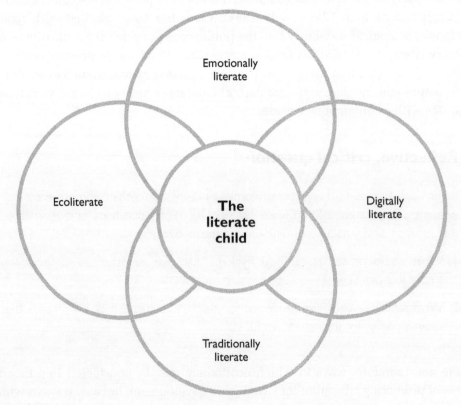

Figure 7.1 The interrelationship among literacies for the literate child

ability to empathise with the natural environment and how writing and reading blog posts can build a child's perspective to understand other people's perspectives. There are other strategies, too, for drawing connections between these literacies. For instance, iPad applications like the *Our Story* app allow opportunities for children to create personal digital stories using texts, audio and images, which may facilitate positive parent–child interactions as well as act as an innovative story-writing and sharing medium (Kucirkova *et al.,* 2013). Using tablets like iPads may also give support in ecoliteracy, as using portable technology that children are familiar with may make them more comfortable in new environments where they may feel less secure (Baker, 2014). Digital cameras or other electronic devices that take photographs may be used to support children's positive self-esteem, sense of belonging, language and literacy with strategies that can be differentiated for both younger and older children (Good, 2005).

As access to digital technologies and online media is increasing, so is the importance placed upon education for sustainable development and emotional intelligence. We will be doing children a disservice if we do not consider that these types of literacy are interrelated, and we will need to consider all of them holistically if we are to effectively equip children to be literate in a twenty-first-century context. To do this, we must ensure that children have opportunities to develop their traditional, emotional, digital and ecological literacies, ideally when also viewing these aspects as interwoven and entwined.

Final thoughts: a pause for reflection

This chapter has considered many ways for children to build up their ability to become literate in more than one way, which may be differentiated for children of different ages. For children working within the EYFS, Key Stage 1 or Key Stage 2, what activities can you think of that allow children the opportunity to build their:

1 Emotional literacy and ecoliteracy?

2 Traditional literacy and digital literacy?

3 Digital literacy and ecoliteracy?

Further reading

These readings will provide you with a sound basis for considering elements of children's literacy in greater depth.

Peacock, A. (2004) *Eco-literacy for Primary Schools.* Stoke-on-Trent: Trentham Books.

Weare, K. (2004) *Developing the Emotionally Literate School.* London: Paul Chapman.

Whitehead, M. (2007) *Developing Language and Literacy with Young Children* (3rd edn). London: Paul Chapman.

Wiseman, C. and Taylor, L. (2015) Digital harmony or digital dissonance? Developing literacy skills in the new technological age. In C. Ritchie (ed.) *Challenge and Change for the Early Years Workforce.* Abingdon, Oxon: Routledge, pp.99–109.

References

Baker, E. (2014) Developing an aptitude for learning in the outdoors. *Primary Science*, 135, pp. 19–21.

Barron, R.W. (1991) Proto-literacy, literacy and the acquisition of phonological awareness. *Learning and Individual Differences*, 3(3), pp. 243–55.

Bruce, C. (2010) *Emotional Literacy in the Early Years.* London: Sage.

Bruner, J.S. (1966) *Toward a Theory of Instruction.* Cambridge, MA: Belknap Press.

Carrington, V. and Robinson, M. (2009) *Digital Literacies: Social Learning and Classroom Practices.* London: Sage.

Chamberlain, E. (2015) Extending the classroom walls: Using academic blogging as an intervention strategy to improve critical literacy skills with elementary students. *Education 3–13.* Available at http://dx.doi.org/10.1080/03004279.2015.1078831.

Cohen, V.L. and Cowen, J.E. (2008) *Literacy for Children in an Information Age.* Belmont, VN: Thomson Wadsworth.

Corden, R. (2000) *Literacy and Learning through Talk: Strategies for the Primary Classroom.* Buckingham: Open University Press.

Department for Education (2013) *The National Curriculum in England.* Available at www.gov.uk/government/uploads/system/uploads/attachment_data/file/425601/PRIMARY_national_curriculum.pdf (accessed 19 February 2016).

Department for Education (2014) *Statutory Framework for the Early Years Foundation Stage.* Available at www.foundationyears.org.uk/files/2014/07/EYFS_framework_from_1_September_2014__with_clarification_note.pdf (accessed 19 February 2016).

Early Education (2012) *Development Matters in the Early Years Foundation Stage.* Available at www.foundationyears.org.uk/files/2012/03/Development-Matters-FINAL-PRINT-AMENDED.pdf (accessed 19 February 2016).

Gardner, H. (1999) *Intelligence Reframed: Multiple Intelligences for the 21st Century.* New York: Basic Books.

Glister, P. (1997) *Digital Literacy.* New York: Wiley.

Goleman, D. (1996) *Emotional Intelligence: Why it Can Matter More Than IQ.* London: Bloomsbury.

Goleman, D. (2009) *Ecological Intelligence: How Knowing the Hidden Impacts of What We Buy can Change Everything.* New York: Broadway Books.

Goleman, D., Bennett, L. and Barlow, Z. (2012) *Ecoliterate.* San Francisco, CA: Jossey-Bass.

Good, L. (2005) Snap it up!: Using digital photography in early childhood. *Childhood Education*, 82(2), pp. 79–85.

Ihmeideh, F. (2014) The effect of electronic books on enhancing emergent literacy skills of pre-school children. *Computers & Education*, 79, pp. 40–8.

JISC (2015) *Developing Students' Digital Literacy.* Available at www.jisc.ac.uk/guides/developing-students-digital-literacy (accessed 15 February 2016).

Kucirkova, N., Messer, D., Sheehy, K. and Flewitt, R. (2013) Sharing personalised stories on iPads: A close look at one parent–child interaction. *Literacy*, 43(3), pp. 115–22.

Makin, L. and Whitehead, M. (2004) *How to Develop Children's Early Literacy*. London: Sage.

Maslow, A. (1943) A theory of human motivation. *Psychological Review*, 50(4), pp. 370–96.

McBride, C. (2016) *Children's Literacy Development: A Cross-cultural Perspective on Learning to Read and Write*. Abingdon, Oxon: Routledge.

McDonald, R. (2014) Picture books. In V. Bower (ed.), *Developing Early Literacy 0–8 from Theory to Practice*. London: Sage, pp. 153–68.

National Literacy Trust (2016) *FAQs: What is Literacy?* Available at www.literacytrust.org.uk/about/faqs/4432_what_is_literacy (accessed 19 February 2016).

Nikolajeva, M. (2013) Picturebooks and emotional literacy. *The Reading Teacher,* 67(4), pp. 249–54.

Ofcom (2013) *Media Literacy Data: Consultation on the National Curriculum for Computing*. Available at http://stakeholders.ofcom.org.uk/binaries/research/media-literacy/october-2013/DfES_consultation_data.pdf (accessed 19 February 2016).

Ofcom (2015) *Children and Parents: Media Use and Attitudes Report 2015*. Available at http://stakeholders.ofcom.org.uk/binaries/research/media-literacy/children-parents-nov-15/childrens_parents_nov2015.pdf (accessed 19 February 2016).

Orr, D. (1989) Ecological literacy. *Conservation Biology,* 3(4), pp. 33–5.

Orr, D. (1992) *Ecological Literacy: Education and the Transition to a Postmodern World*. Albany: State University of New York Press.

Parvin, T. (2014) 'This is how we teach reading in our school.' In V. Bower (ed.), *Developing Early Literacy 0–8 from Theory to Practice*. London: Sage, pp. 169–83.

Paul, R. (2011) 'A language that is ever green': The poetry and ecology of John Clare. *Moderna Sprak*, 105(2), pp. 23–35.

PSHE Association (2016) *What is PSHE and Why is it Important?* Available at www.pshe-association.org.uk/content.aspx?CategoryID=1043 (accessed 19 February 2016).

Piaget, J. (1952) *The Origins of Intelligence in Children*. Translated by M. Cook. New York: International Universities Press.

Ramos, A.M. and Ramos, R. (2011) Ecoliteracy through imagery: A close reading of two wordless picture books. *Children's Literature in Education*, 42(325), pp. 325–39.

Rosen, M. (1993) *We're Going on a Bear Hunt*. London: Walker Books.

Sharp, P. (2001) *Nurturing Emotional Literacy*. London: David Fulton.

Siraj-Blatchford, J., Smith, K.C. and Samuelsson, P. (2010) *Education for Sustainable Development in the Early Years*. Available at www.327matters.org/Docs/ESD%20Book%20Master.pdf (accessed 19 February 2016).

Waters, T. (2004) *Therapeutic Storywriting*. London: David Fulton.

Weare, K. (2004) *Developing the Emotionally Literate School*. London: Paul Chapman.

Whitehead, M. (2009) *Supporting Language and Literacy Development in the Early Years*. Berkshire: Open University Press.

Wohlwend, K.E. (2015) One screen, many fingers: Young children's collaborative literacy play with digital puppetry apps and touchscreen technologies. *Theory into Practice*, 52(2), pp. 154–62.

8

Learning mathematics

Clare Wiseman

Chapter overview

This chapter examines the way in which children learn mathematics and looks at how children's early experiences of the world provide them with opportunities to begin to explore the mathematical ideas and concepts inherent in that world. The way in which a child may develop understanding related to mathematical concepts is also explored and the role of the practitioner in supporting such development is discussed. The chapter also considers how young children can make the transition between their early explorations with mathematical ideas to the more formalised learning of mathematics in the educational setting.

Mathematics is a vital part of all our lives and a part of human endeavour at many levels (Pound and Lee, 2011). Understanding, applying and being creative with mathematics allows us not only to solve problems, discover, understand the natural world and create new meanings and new technologies, but also to find beauty, fascination and satisfaction from looking at the world in a mathematical way. Speaking recently on national radio, broadcaster and writer Alex Bellos shared his view on the importance of the subject: 'The only way we can understand the world and life is through numbers and mathematics' (*Inside Science*, 2015).

Mathematics has always been important to all of us; the development of culture, art, science and technology in contemporary society is all built on the early thinking and theories of those such as Pythagoras, Euclid, Fibonacci and Archimedes, to name but a few. It may be argued that our increasingly technologically driven world makes the case for the development of mathematical ideas stronger than ever (Vorderman, 2011). We need competent, creative and enthusiastic mathematicians for the future development of the economy, culture and understanding of the world. The challenge for those working alongside young children is how best to nurture and support the innate and intuitive mathematical abilities of young children and allow them to explore the subject; this chapter considers how this may be achieved, examining in particular:

- The importance of early learning experiences.

- Linking 'informal' and 'formal' mathematics.

- An enabling environment.

The importance of early learning experiences

Research (Butterworth, 1999, 2005; Devlin, 2000; Montague-Smith and Price, 2012) has suggested that all human beings are born with a faculty for learning mathematics and a range of mathematical competences. Gardner's (1983) theory of 'multiple intelligences' was founded on empirical evidence that the human mind processes different symbolic systems separately and that human minds are capable of seven (later expanded to nine) forms of thinking, including 'Logicalmathematical' intelligence, which is manifested by 'sensitivity to, and capacity to discern, logical or numerical patterns; ability to handle long chains of reasoning' (Gardner and Hatch, 1989, p. 4). Recognising this human capacity for the *learning* of mathematics, it is then imperative to think about how the *teaching* of mathematics can complement this innate ability. Lately, advances in neuroscience have allowed us to understand more about the complexity of the human brain and highlighted the importance of early opportunities to ensure that the significant or 'sensitive' periods of brain development that occur in the early years are nurtured (Durell, 2015). Early opportunities for learning about mathematical concepts will occur naturally through the young child's everyday experiences. Children are born into a culture and society where they are immersed in the mathematical concepts, symbols and language that have evolved to discuss and record such ideas. The natural inquisitiveness and curiosity of the young child means that there are multiple opportunities for them to begin to explore and understand mathematics, before being introduced to a formal mathematics curriculum.

The notion of young children as learners has been considered by theorists, and many of these can be related to the learning of mathematics. Particularly useful in relation to how children learn mathematics are the theories of Piaget, Vygotsky and Bruner, all of whom emphasise the child as an active and inquisitive constructor of knowledge and meaning, and these theories will be briefly considered in this section. Much of the subsequent understanding of how children learn has been built on the foundations of these theorists, but this subject is too extensive to discuss within this chapter.

Piaget (in Halfpenny and Petterson, 2014) and Vygotsky (in Smidt, 2009) both believed that children construct their own knowledge by *interacting with and exploring* the environment around them (as opposed to being passive learners who *respond* to implicit or explicit teaching). Piaget proffered 'stages of development', which, although questioned today, provide a solid foundation for thinking about how young children learn. The first stage of development suggested by Piaget is the 'sensory motor' stage. During this stage children learn through exploration with their senses and through movement; the baby who wants to pick up a toy from beyond the edge of the play mat will explore mathematical concepts such as distance, size, weight and balance. Although not cognitively aware of such concepts and, as yet, lacking the language to describe them, the baby is nonetheless assimilating and accommodating new knowledge and will repeat the actions and behaviour once successful and adapt the behaviour if not. According to Piaget (in Halfpenny and Petterson, 2014), subsequent learning continues to develop in response to explorative and active learning until the child is able, around the age of 11, as they reach the stage of 'formal operations', to think abstractly. This staged pattern of the development of thinking can be helpful when considering how children may develop an understanding of mathematics but, most importantly, Piaget's assertion that children are active and curious learners should alert us to the need to allow children plenty of opportunities to explore and discuss their surroundings and experiences. This active and exploratory approach to learning is relevant to learning about mathematics; Worthington and Carruthers (2006, p. 205) highlight 'the importance of a play-based environment that promotes independence and challenge for children to successfully engage in mathematics'. How this type of environment can be developed will be discussed later in the chapter.

Vygotsky (in Smidt, 2009) supported the theory of the child as an active learner, but emphasised the 'social' aspect of learning. He proposed that learning is most effective when engaged in with others, and developed the idea of the 'more knowledgeable other' who could offer guidance, support and appropriate challenge in learning. He suggested that when children work and learn alongside more knowledgeable others they are able to achieve more than they would if working alone. He called the gap between what the child can achieve alone and what they can achieve with the support of another 'the Zone of Proximal Development'. The following case study demonstrates how mathematical learning can occur when children are allowed to actively explore their own interests, reflect upon them and discuss them with others.

Case study 1: the see-saw

Rosie (aged 5) had spent the weekend with her grandparents. They had taken her and a neighbour's grandchild to the local park where the two children had much enjoyed playing on the see-saw and the swings. When Rosie returned home, she drew a picture of herself and her friend at the park on the see-saw (see Figure 8.1). Grandma sat and talked with Rosie about her picture, gently asking her questions and helping her to clarify her thinking. They discussed how the two children had made the see-saw move and how one of them had been 'higher' than the other. Many of the concepts and vocabulary used during this relatively short and informal exchange were mathematical: 'higher'; 'lower'; 'up'; 'down'; 'heavier than', 'lighter than'; 'underneath'; 'bigger than'; 'smaller than'. Rosie was also introduced to new ideas and associated vocabulary: 'equal'; 'balance' and 'the same as'. This short

Figure 8.1   Rosie and the see-saw

episode not only illustrates the theory of Siraj-Blatchford and colleagues (2002) related to 'sustained shared thinking', but also that children can learn about mathematics through self-directed exploratory activities. It highlights Vygotsky's (in Smidt, 2009) ideas related to the importance of learning in a social situation where there is sensitive support and guidance offered to challenge and promote the child's thinking and understanding.

Bruner (in Smidt, 2011) was highly influenced by the work of Vygotsky and posited the theory of the 'spiral curriculum', suggesting that children can begin to learn about any subject at any age if it is presented to them in an appropriate form and matches their interests; an appropriate and interesting form for very young children to learn mathematics is through experience and dialogue, with playful, multi-sensory activities offering rich opportunities for discovery. For example, children's sand and water play is an appropriate, playful introduction to ideas related to capacity and conservation of volume, an area of mathematics which children will later encounter in a more formal way in the mathematics curriculum. Likewise, this case study illustrates children learning at the 'level' which is appropriate for their development; Rosie was able to understand some sophisticated mathematical concepts in a way that is appropriate to her age, experience and cognitive ability. Haylock (2006) and Liebeck (1990) argue that early experiences of sorting, naming, classifying and identifying similarities and differences are crucial for laying the foundations for the genuine mathematical thinking and reasoning that children will be required to master later on. When Rosie revisits mathematical concepts relating to comparison, equivalence and measurement in a more formal way later in the curriculum, she will have the opportunity to refine and develop her existing thinking around them.

Theories about how children learn can indeed help us think more deeply about how children may begin to understand the body of knowledge that we call 'mathematics'. Common to these theories is the proposition that young children learn most effectively when they have opportunities to explore, investigate and participate in activities that are relevant and important to them. Play, planned or unplanned, is a crucial vehicle for such learning. (For more on mathematics and play, see 'Further reading' at the end of this chapter.) Liebeck (1990) proposed the ELPS approach to supporting children to learn mathematics; E stands for Experience – children need hands-on experience of the idea; L stands for Language – children need the language of mathematics to talk about ideas; P stands for Pictures – children should have opportunities to represent their mathematical ideas diagrammatically and pictorially. Finally, S stands for symbols – the formal recording and representation of mathematics through the particular and recognised mathematical symbols developed by our culture. It may be seen in this case study that Rosie is afforded the opportunity for Experience, Language and Pictures; it is not yet appropriate or necessary for her to be introduced to the symbols that might demonstrate the mathematical concepts involved; this can be developed later on. The following section addresses the question of how we can support children from their very early exploratory mathematical learning experiences and discussions to progress to more complex mathematical concepts and to the formalisation of the application and representation of these ideas.

Bridging the gap between 'informal' and 'formal' mathematics

Young children need to be sensitively moved from their 'informal' understanding of mathematics, to the more formal and abstract mathematics required by the school curriculum and beyond. However, to make this step too rapidly not only means that opportunities for building on the mathematical knowledge that children bring to school with them can be lost (Hughes, 1986), but also that children may become confused about the relationship between what they understand and how this is represented mathematically (Carruthers and Worthington, 2006).

Concept development

It is essential that young children are secure in early mathematical concepts such as sorting, matching, pairing and classifying (through practical and meaningful activities) before being moved on to more abstract secondary, tertiary and fourth-degree concepts such as number, counting and calculation. Liebeck (1990, p. 15) explains that mathematics involves a 'hierarchy of abstractions'; the understanding of a concept lower in the hierarchy is fundamental for building the connections that will provide a 'chain' through to understanding key mathematical concepts at the more complex level. Skemp (1971) proposes that learning mathematical concepts is first about learning 'primary concepts', which prepare us for the later learning of higher order concepts. Primary concepts are those learned through direct sensory and motor experiences on to which understanding of higher order concepts can be built. For example, he suggests that 'three' is a secondary concept which cannot be grasped until the primary understanding of three objects, grouped together, has been recognised. Understanding number, to include everything that is more and less than three (see the example illustrated in Table 8.1) is, according to Skemp (1971), a tertiary concept; addition, for example, being the next level of the hierarchy of concept development, is a 'fourth-degree' concept. This hierarchical building of concepts continues until children are able to cope with highly complex and abstract mathematical ideas, such as fractions, decimals and negative numbers.

This suggestion about concept development is indeed helpful when aiming to create a curriculum or programme of study for mathematical learning for children; much of the current curricula for the teaching of mathematics are based on the progressive learning of increasingly abstract and higher order concepts. However, it does not tell us *how* children might learn such concepts, which is where it is useful to think about theories about how children learn and the factors which might affect this learning (opportunity, motivation, aspiration, ability, attitude, learning style, appropriate challenge and practice). Sensitivity, skill and good pedagogical practice are important factors in supporting children to progress through the 'hierarchy of concepts'. Practitioners need to find ways to help children move from the informal mathematical learning encountered in early learning environments to the more formal learning required for the understanding of abstract and complex mathematical ideas.

Case study 2 provides an example of good practice in supporting children to progress to more complex concepts in mathematics.

Table 8.1 Understanding the basic concepts of number

	**Primary concepts:** learned through the multi-sensory experiences.
3/three	**Secondary concepts:** cumulative and built on previous learning, repetition and practice.
Other numbers	**Tertiary concepts:** linking of related ideas (e.g. that numbers greater and lesser than three also exist).
2+1=3 1+1+1=3 3=1+2	**Fourth-degree concepts:** simple application and manipulation of the concept.

Case study 2: the sand tray

Mikesh (aged 4 years) and Frankie (aged 4.5 years) are playing in the sand tray, looking for toy dinosaurs buried by some other children in the nursery. As they unearth the toys, both of the boys can organise and count their own items successfully; Mikesh finds five dinosaurs and Frankie finds three. The boys want to know 'how many have we both found?'. The practitioner demonstrates to the boys how to combine the two sets and use a 'count all or counting continuously' strategy to add the two sets together and find a total (see Carruthers and Worthington, 2010, p. 108). Mikesh and Frankie observe and then imitate the actions and the language of the practitioner counting and recounting the two sets together, until they are completely satisfied with the total of eight toys. They are keen to explore and practice this new learning further and continue gathering their own separate sets of objects and combining them together. The boys are demonstrating that, secure in the more simple concepts related to number (ordering, counting, cardinality of sets), they are ready to explore and accommodate more complex, higher order concepts, such as addition.

Moving to standard representation of mathematical thinking

Case study 2 may demonstrate how experience, language, repetition and motivation can help support children to develop understanding of mathematical concepts. However, it is necessary at some stage for children to move from the enactive stage of representation (for example, lining up a set of toy dinosaurs to be counted) to the iconic stage (using pictures and diagrams) and finally to the symbolic stage of representation (using the accepted notation of numerals and mathematical signs) (Bruner, 1966). Supporting children in the exploration of how to use pictures, and later symbols, to represent and record mathematical thinking is a crucial step in moving to 'formal' mathematics and to meeting the expectations of the mathematics curriculum and assessment requirements.

Research carried out by Hughes (1986) suggested that very young children can begin to use their own invented pictures and symbols to represent their mathematical understanding. Although some of the marks made by the children were personal and idiosyncratic in nature, they were meaningful to the individual child and showed an understanding of mathematical concepts such as one-to-one correspondence and children's ability to visualise and remember small quantities of objects. Moreover, the children were still able to interpret their own mark making successfully up to one week later, suggesting a depth of learning and understanding. Carruthers and Worthington (2010) similarly argue that this stage of exploratory mathematical mark making, where children use their own invented symbols and pictures to represent their mathematical thinking, is an important step towards grasping the somewhat arbitrary, formal symbolisation used by our culture to record mathematics. If the formal methods for recording mathematical algorithms are

Figure 8.2 Maths stories and meaning: drawing of a dog

forced upon young children too early, there is a danger that confusion is created and the connections to be made with what the symbols actually represent are lost, resulting in partial learning, or misconceptions. Therefore, as practitioners, it is important that opportunities are afforded for children to experiment with different methods of recording their mathematical ideas and so begin to build up both visual and permanent pictures and diagrams of the concept learned. In the same way that children might be supported in their efforts of learning to read and write with the use of picture books and emergent writing, so too can children be encouraged to represent and communicate their mathematical thinking. Gradually, through the introduction of models and images such as number lines, hundred squares and place value cards, and by encouraging children to write and retell 'maths stories' (with accompanying pictures and appropriate mathematical language), the conventional mathematical symbols required for the communication of mathematical ideas in an accepted form will begin to have meaning and make sense alongside the developing understanding of mathematical concepts.

An enabling environment

If we accept that young children can develop mathematical understanding through the physical exploration of the environment, leading to the construction and application of ideas related to shape, space, measure, number and data handling (Piaget, in Halfpenny and Petterson, 2014) and that this development can be aided by the sensitive intervention of a 'more knowledgeable other' (Vygotsky, in Smidt, 2009), then attention needs to be paid to how to create an environment that encourages this type of learning to happen. There are two key aspects to consider when thinking about an 'enabling environment' for mathematics learning: physical resources and human resources. These are explored in the following section.

Physical resources

Resources for mathematical learning need to be available and relevant to children of all ages to assist them in developing an understanding of mathematical concepts. To maximise opportunities for learning, these resources need to be both inside and outside of the classroom, and may be 'structured' (designed to teach a particular mathematical concept, such as Diennes apparatus, Cuisenaire Rods, geared analogue clocks, number fans, calculators, etc.) or 'unstructured' (not necessarily designed to teach a mathematical concept, but very useful for aiding thinking, such as cooking utensils, board games, construction toys, etc.). Many of these resources are naturally part of any contemporary learning environment, but consideration needs to be made in relation to how accessible the resources are for the children and what opportunities are afforded to the children to explore, experiment and learn from them. It is also necessary to think about the choices of resources that may be available to assist children's mathematical thinking; older children will not feel comfortable using resources that are routinely used in the classrooms of the younger children. However, although engagement with concrete resources (structured or unstructured) is undoubtedly critical in supporting children's developing understanding, they do not, in themselves, teach the mathematics; demonstration, modelling, dialogue and explanation all have their place.

The environment outside of the classroom, including other inside spaces, such as corridors, hall space and office space, as well as the outside environment within and outside of the immediate setting, provides a stimulating and realistic context in which exploration of mathematical concepts can be developed. Learning outside of the confines of the classroom is particularly useful when supporting children to understand mathematical concepts on a larger scale and for helping them to see the purpose and relevance of mathematics to their own lives. In addition, many traditional 'playground games' (e.g. 'What's the time Mr Wolf?'; Hopscotch; skipping games) and their accompanying rhymes are mathematically based and rely on an understanding and application of some fundamental mathematical concepts.

The practitioner will not only need to think about the concrete resources provided to aid or prompt mathematical thinking, but also to consider how the visual resources in the environment, such as labels, posters, number lines, number tracks, etc. are displayed to encourage children to develop an understanding of the pictorial and symbolic representation of mathematical ideas. Such resources need to be updated regularly to stimulate and maintain interest, and should also include displays of children's own mathematical thinking and recording. A 'working wall', or interactive display to which children can contribute, encourages children to physically explore and develop mathematical thinking in a more spontaneous way, developing independence, contextual thinking and ownership (Price, 2014).

Opportunities for learning through other curriculum subjects should also be considered; many stories and poems are an excellent starting point for encouraging children to think about mathematical concepts and to support them in developing an accurate and full mathematical vocabulary. Nursery rhymes provide an engaging and practical way for young children to learn about counting principles, especially the 'stable-order' principle (Gelman and Gallistel, 1978, in Thompson, 2008). (For further ideas for teaching mathematics through literature, see 'Further reading' at the end of the chapter.) Projects undertaken in design and technology studies can provide meaningful and relevant opportunities for children to explore and develop many of the concepts related to measurement; physical Education activities can support children in exploring and applying many mathematical ideas also related to measurement and data collection. All curriculum subjects can afford opportunities for relevant and applied mathematical learning and help children to make the connection between different mathematical ideas, other areas of learning and application to real life.

Human resources: the role of the adult/practitioner

The role of the supportive adult or practitioner in encouraging children's learning has been variously considered over the years. Those with a constructivist view of teaching and learning consider the role of the adult/practitioner to be one of a facilitator; opportunities for learning are planned and provided, but the child explores and experiments without intervention to construct knowledge, skills and understanding. Those who take a socio-constructivist stance towards teaching and learning would argue that the role of the adult is more involved; the adult/ practitioner should not only plan and prepare learning opportunities for the child but should also work alongside the child in the role of a guide, sharing previously gained knowledge and understanding with the child in a way which supports and sensitively challenges thinking. In relation to the teaching and learning of mathematics, it is perhaps most useful to use a combination of both approaches, so that children have some autonomy and independence to discover mathematical concepts for themselves, but also that there is appropriate and planned support for children to help them recognise and apply what they are learning in relation to mathematics, but also to address any misconceptions that may arise.

Askew (2012, p. 28) proposes that an important role for the adult/practitioner in supporting children in learning mathematics is accepting that the child has significant contributions to bring to the 'topic' and that negotiation and shaping of the mathematical 'conversation' is 'jointly owned'. If children are learning through play and open-ended activities, there may need to be sensitive intervention by the adult or practitioner to make the inherent mathematical learning explicit, so that opportunities for learning are not missed, and children can begin to appreciate and understand the centrality of mathematics in understanding the world around them. For example, watching children pretend playing at 'show-jumping horses' highlights how readily children can be naturally engaged in applying and developing ideas and vocabulary related to estimation, distance, speed, counting and ordinal number. Sometimes it is serendipitous opportunities for mathematical learning such as these that can be powerful if 'exploited' and developed, or 'lost' if ignored. The professionalism of the adult or practitioner will be paramount in knowing when and how to intervene in such situations or not.

However, it is well documented that many adults lack confidence in their own mathematical abilities (see e.g. Askew, 2010; Boaler, 2009; Eastaway; Haylock and Thangata, 2010 and Pound and Lee, 2011). The Vorderman Report (2011, p. 11) suggested that 'one in four economically active adults is functionally innumerate' and that many parents have a 'fear of mathematics' (p. 16). However, it is not suggested that such innumeracy or anxiety is the fault of those affected, rather that it is due to many factors beyond their control and that 'many young people have a fear and little understanding of mathematics' (p. 19). The possible reasons for such a situation among our young people are not for discussion here, but it is necessary to be aware that the anxieties that exist around mathematics can be easily and unwittingly transmitted to children. Providing a confident attitude and role model to the young child to encourage a positive image of mathematics (and mathematicians) is an equally important role for the practitioner and sound subject knowledge is essential.

The ethos of the learning environment and the attitudes of those working in it should aim to develop confidence and a 'can do' attitude towards mathematics, where all those involved believe they can achieve, and are given opportunities to do so. The dialogue that develops around mathematics teaching and learning is of paramount importance, and children need to be confident that their thinking and exploration of mathematical ideas are valued and developed; misconceptions and mistakes are equally to be seen as an opportunity for reflection and reconsideration of thinking. Askew (2012) draws on the work of Robin Alexander (Alexander, 2006) to explain an important distinction between 'dialogue' for mathematics teaching and learning, and 'discussion' for mathematics teaching and learning. He suggests that while 'discussion' may tend more towards predetermined positions and 'point-scoring', 'dialogue' is more centred around a back-and-forth exchange of ideas, a willingness to listen and to genuinely understand alternative ideas, and to 'risk one's more cherished prejudgments' (Askew, 2012, p. 130). To promote such dialogue in mathematics teaching and learning is indeed a challenge, and depends on practitioners'/adults' confidence in allowing for, or planning for, opportunities for children to explore mathematical ideas and engage with the associated dialogue, questioning, practical resources, pictures, diagrams and language, words and mathematical symbols that support the thinking. This is where consideration of the physical environment in which the children are exploring mathematical ideas and those who are supporting them in such endeavours are crucial in being mutually supportive both physically and psychologically.

Conclusion

In conclusion, this chapter has aimed to demonstrate how the everyday encounters and explorations that children have with mathematics and mathematical ideas are the most natural medium for helping them develop the increasing knowledge, skills, models and ways of mathematical thinking which they can use to interpret their experiences and to solve problems. These fundamental life skills will allow for success in everyday tasks, more formalised learning and, ultimately, in adulthood. The understanding that exists around the way in which children learn can help us promote and plan for exploration and learning in mathematics which is characterised by opportunities for both self-direction and support in developing thinking , but, most importantly, an environment and ethos that values the child as a mathematician and problem-solver.

Final questions to consider and reflect upon

How can you develop the learning environment in which you work to ensure that children have ample opportunities to explore mathematical ideas?

How can you ensure that the young children in your care have extensive practice of early mathematical concepts such as sorting, matching, classifying and grouping objects?

How can you support your colleagues and parents in nurturing and developing a positive attitude towards mathematics?

Further reading

Montague-Smith, A. and Price, A. (1997) *Mathematics in Early Years Education* (3rd edn). London: David Fulton.
This book incorporates research and thinking related to the early teaching and learning of a range of mathematical areas, including ideas for observation and questioning, how attitudes can influence learning and suggestions for language development.

Taylor, H. and Harris, A. (eds) (2014) *Learning and Teaching Mathematics 0–8*. London: Sage.
This edited volume offers both mathematical subject knowledge and teaching ideas on a range of mathematical concepts. There is clear guidance on how to support young children's learning in an effective way.

Carruthers, E. and Worthington, M. (2006) *Children's Mathematic: Making Marks, Making Meaning*. London: Sage.
This book combines theory and practice to help explain how children's own mathematical marks and drawings reveal deep levels of mathematical thinking. The book also considers how children's mathematical mark making can enable practitioners and parents to help their children achieve success in mathematics at school.

Pound, L. and Lee, T. (2011) *Teaching Mathematics Creatively*. London: Routledge.
This book includes a range of innovative ideas to encourage practitioners to think about how mathematics can be taught in a creative way to inspire and enrich learning. The book includes ideas on using story-telling, play and music to bring mathematics alive for children.

References

Alexander, R. (2006) *Towards Dialogic Teaching: Rethinking Classroom Talk*. Cambridge: Dialogos.
Askew, M. (2012) *Transforming Primary Mathematics*. London: Routledge.
Boaler, J. (2009) *The Elephant in the Classroom*. London: Souvenir Press.
Bruner, J. (1966) *Toward a Theory of Instruction*. Cambridge, MA: Belknap Press.
Butterworth, B. (1999) *The Mathematical Brain*. London: Macmillan.
Butterworth, B. (2005) The development of arithmetical abilities. *Journal of Child Psychology and Psychiatry,* 46, pp. 1003–18.
Carruthers, E. and Worthington, M. (2006) *Children's Mathematics*. London: Sage.
Carruthers, E. and Worthington, M. (2010) *Children's Mathematics: Making Marks, Making Meaning*. London: Sage.
Devlin, K. (2000) *The Maths Gene*. London: Weidenfeld and Nicolson.
Durell, B. (2015) Neuroscience and young children's learning. In C. Ritchie (ed.), *Challenges and Change for the Early Years Workforce*. London: Routledge.
Eastaway, R. and Askew, M. (2010) *Maths for Mums and Dads*. London: Random House.
Gardner, H. (1983) *Frames of Mind*. New York: Basic Books.
Gardner, H. and Hatch, T. (1989) Multiple intelligences go to school: Implications for the Theory of Multiple Intelligences. *American Educational Research Association,* 18(8), pp. 4–10.
Halfpenny, A. and Petterson, J. (2014) *Introducing Piaget*. London: Routledge.
Haylock, D. (2006) *Mathematics Explained for Primary Teachers* (3rd edn). London: Sage.
Haylock, D. and Thangata, F. (2010) *Key Concepts in Teaching Primary Mathematics*. London: Sage.
Hughes, M. (1986) *Children and Number: Difficulties in Learning Mathematics*. Oxford: Blackwell.
Inside Science (2015) BBC Radio 4, 27 August.
Liebeck, P. (1990) *How Children Learn Mathematics*. London: Penguin.
Montague-Smith, A. and Price, A. (2012) *Mathematics in Early Years Education* (3rd edn). London: Routledge.
Pound, L. and Lee, T. (2011) *Teaching Mathematics Creatively*. London: Routledge.
Price, B. (2014) Mathematics and display. In H. Taylor and A. Harris (eds) *Learning and Teaching Mathematics 0–8*. London: Sage.
Siraj-Blatchford, I., Sylva, K., Muttock, S., Gilden, R. and Bell, D. (2002) *Researching Effective Pedagogy in the Early Years (REPEY) (Research Project 365)*. London: DfES.
Skemp, R. (1971) *The Psychology of Learning Mathematics*. London: Penguin Books.
Smidt, S. (2009) *Introducing Vygotsky*. London: Routledge.
Smidt, S. (2011) *Introducing Bruner*. London: Routledge.

Thompson, I. (2008) *Teaching and Learning Early Number* (2nd edn). Maidenhead: Open University Press.

Vorderman, C. (2011) *A World Class Mathematics Education for all our Young People.* Available at www.tsm-resources.com/pdf/VordermanMathsReport.pdf (accessed 21 December 2015).

Worthington, M. and Carruthers, E. (2006) Key Stage 1 Mathematics. in T. Bruce (ed.), *Early Childhood.* London: Sage.

9 Science trends in education

Lin Shaw

Chapter overview

A historical overview of science in Early Years and primary education demonstrates how steps have been taken to introduce children to what is now a core curriculum subject. The status of science and the attitudes to the subject have, however, become less popular. Children appear to like science less than their predecessors and in England attitudes towards science fall below those of our European neighbours. Science is the foundation of our enlightened universe and the value of scientific literacy is growing in all aspects of modern culture. To ensure that children develop prerequisites for lifelong learning and employability in our rapidly evolving environment, understanding scientific concepts is essential.

The Enlightenment

I have always been fascinated by science and during my teaching career I have promoted science within Early Years and primary schools, and also taught GCSE science equivalencies and the application of science within wider concepts. During this time I have frequently heard students of all ages making the statement 'I don't like science', often accompanied by the stereotypical assumption that anyone interested in science is 'weird'. I have also noted that the majority of students who say this are female. The apparent negativity towards scientific knowledge is certainly not due to any differences between the ability of men and women to study science; therefore it raises the question of cultural perceptions and dialogue relating to the status of science within our society. These observations are supported by Solomon (1993), who investigated children's images of science and scientists, and found that while idiocies were decreasing, gender stereotyping was more difficult to counteract.

Science is an integral part of everyday life but the unique language used and the knowledge required to understand scientific laws and principles has shrouded all science disciplines in mystery. Past social conformities viewed science as a masculine domain and the sciences were founded and controlled by men. Throughout Western culture it is gender, a set of socially constructed stereotyping of male and female characteristics, that remains a force in perpetuating the male-dominated science industry. The Organization for Economic Cooperation and Development (OECD) (2014) reported that data from the UK highlighted that secondary school girls still fair particularly badly in science compared with boys, with a much wider attainment gap than most countries. They conceded that the gap in attainment may indicate cultural genderisation promoting the perception of what subjects boys and girls would be good at. In the twenty-first century the scientific workforce remains a male-dominated domain (UNESCO, 2015), with women averaging only 12.8 per cent of the science, engineering and technology (SET) workforce (Kirkup *et al.*, 2010). The reasons behind the gender divide and the current deficit in young UK scientists is in part due to the historical cultural perceptions of the value of science within society.

Views of science: a pause for reflection

What are your views of scientists and science? Do you find the language used, a barrier?

Do you think children believe that science is an occupation more suited to men than to women? Perhaps you can ask some children what they think a scientist looks like – do they describe a scientist as a 'weird man in a white coat'? Why/why not?

The beginnings of the scientific world

The discipline and discourse of science was not always as socially accepted as it is now. Since ancient cultures, science has fallen in and out of favour as a way of knowing. Historically, the most significant event followed the fall of the Roman Empire which gave rise to Christianity as the new ruling power in the Western world. The strict adherence to the concept of creationism saw the rise of the so-called Dark Ages. Throughout this period science was denounced as heresy and to question divine knowing was deemed a crime so severe that it carried the death sentence, often burning at the stake. It was not until the 1620s to the 1780s that social attitudes began to change and a cultural revolution took place that questioned the philosophical and spiritual governance of the Church. The Age of Enlightenment followed, displacing traditional lines of religious authority with an emphasis on reason, analysis and individualism. This coincided with the scientific revolution that sought the rigorous pursuit of scientific truth that still exists today.

In Victorian England, new scientific discoveries swept through Western culture and the relevance of teaching the subject of science in primary school was influenced by the rise in demand for scientists. Dewey (1910) advocated improving science education for young children to ensure a widening of scientific thought processes through inquiry rather than rigid scientific method. This began the progressive education movement which advocated child-centred and social re-constructionist approaches in education. Traditional teaching methods were replaced by 'learning by doing', using everyday activities to implement scientific knowledge, respect diversity and develop critical, socially engaged intelligence. However, this vision was hampered by the introduction of the three 'R's (reading, writing and arithmetic) as part of the selection process for transfer to secondary schools, leaving science to virtually disappear from the curriculum.

In the 1920s science lessons in primary schools were based mainly on the study of nature, with a move towards including physical science and experiential learning being introduced during the 1930s. The Hadow Reports of 1926 and 1931 recommended further science education for young children but this was not implemented until the mid-1940s, when the demand for scientists and technologists following the Second World War was hampered by the lack of science teaching in schools. In the 1960s when science was introduced as a curriculum topic in primary schools (Isaacs, 1962), it was met with resistance, as the common belief among scientists was that the subject of science had to be taught in a laboratory (Barrow, 2006). However, as Isaacs (1962) of the Frobel Institute asserted, the rationale behind teaching science to young children was not to study science but to develop scientific ways of knowing. This would allow children to develop a scientific approach to all problem-solving tasks.

Implementing the theory of childhood development

The 1960s saw the introduction of an educational policy in which scientific and technological advances were to be embraced and the golden era of discovery celebrated. However, a conflicting pedagogy of how to teach science soon became apparent and it was not until the Plowden Report (1967) that a constructivist approach towards learning in science was developed. This was supported by Piaget (1952) who believed children acquired knowledge by using their own interactions within their environment to construct understanding, making them 'natural born scientists'. The constructivist approach also included Vygotsky's (1986) concept of the zone of proximinal development in which a child operating independently in cognitive development may be assisted by a knowledgeable other to expand their knowledge. However, most primary teachers were not trained as science specialists and were therefore limited in their role as the knowledgeable other. This was evidenced by the Department of Education and Science (1978), which recognised that progress in the teaching of science within primary schools was extremely disappointing. The role of the teacher was seen as crucial, and as Dewey (1910) had observed at the beginning of the century, the teacher's greater knowledge and understanding was a vital component in helping children make sense of their world.

The strict Piagetian perspective was soon superseded by pedagogy that recognised the value and importance of language, social factors and cultural influences for children to become more confident in specific discourses. Instead of viewing a child's concept as wrong due to limited cognitive skills, the child is viewed as inexperienced in the use of scientific language. In the teaching of scientific inquiry, language discourse may be embedded in a wider framework of social situations rather than purely applied to a science lesson. Bruner (1997) believes that sense making of everyday life may be viewed as a narrative. This may be expanded to the study of science by applying logical or categorical means to the narrative, and this different way of knowing will allow a child to prepare for cultural and subject differences within their society. Säljö (2000) emphasised that the teaching of science in early childhood is predominately through the discourse of natural science. For the child to become knowledgeable in this, the teacher must facilitate exposure to situations that familiarise the child to frameworks of practice. This is done through working together to explore, participate and discuss the nature of science and embedding historically developed scientific knowledge. By broadening the concept of natural science within the framework, it encourages a child to apply knowledge within everyday social activities and enhances spontaneous learning alongside a sense of social participation (Pramling and Samuelsson, 2001).

Contemporary national trends in Early Years and primary science education

Methods of teaching and modes of testing science subjects have been based on core curriculum work. The introduction of the National Curriculum for Science (Education Reform Act, 1988) included statutory attainment tests for children in Key Stage 1 (5- to 7-year-olds). The tests pressurised teachers to produce children who would be measured and consequently labelled by test results. This is contrary to contemporary pedagogy that views the culture of 'teaching to the test' as detrimental to children and to the wider community. The benefits of assessing children's emerging skills for diagnosis and planning are desirable in order to meet individual needs, but certainly not for the production of publicised league tables. Young children largely learn through the medium of play, and it is therefore inappropriate to start formal approaches to higher skills and knowledge when children's experiences are restricted to individual stages of development.

In the early 1980s, primary science focused mainly on the development of 'process' or scientific skills. The Education Reform Act (1988) identified science as a core subject within the primary school curriculum, alongside mathematics and English. Science in the primary curriculum recognised the balance and interrelationship between conceptual understanding, process skills and attitudes, although assessment emphasised knowledge and understanding. Unfortunately, subsequent documentation gave less and less importance to scientific attitudes and the nature and history of science. The curriculum appears to reflect changing societal views and political discourse regarding what constitutes science, good education and the nature of Early Years science.

Science has now grown to become a cultural way of knowing and our lives are inextricably entwined and controlled by scientific rationality. Early childhood education has expanded considerably since the 1980s and is now included in the debate on appropriate preschool science education. The value of learning about science at such an early age is to help children interact with natural phenomena and promote development of creative enquiry. Pre-science provides skills for children to investigate their environment, promote creativity and curiosity, develop language used for describing and communicating ideas or observations, and understand the world around them. In Early Years and primary education the role of the science educator is to encourage freedom to explore without imposing traditional scientific enquiry. This allows children to build on and retain values of their own natural curiosity, experience and understanding, with guidance, of creating an enquiry that draws upon accepted scientific knowledge. Creative thought and new ideas generated by the child are seen as the embryonic stage of developing skills and thought processes that will later be the guide to specific subjects and disciplines that incorporate a scientific approach within their traditional boundaries. Not all scientists agree with this pedagogical approach, as it is seen as having limited usefulness in creating future scientists (Chaille and Britain, 2003).

The current National Curriculum specifies the essential ingredients in the school science curriculum. However, there are still mixed and incomplete messages about the teaching and learning of science within Early Years education due to the need to test knowledge and understanding. This creates difficulties because the criteria and the assessment process actually focus on knowledge rather than on understanding. Clearer interpretation of what is appropriate for young children is required through clarification of documentation and the inclusion of affective (emotional, personal, attitudinal) development. In the statutory framework for the Early Years Foundation Stage (DfE, 2014) and Development Matters in the Early Years Foundation Stage (Early Education, 2012), very little emphasis is attached to promoting science and technology. This needs to change if young children are to fully appreciate their environment and develop the conceptual understanding, skills and attitudes essential for lifelong learning in a world now dominated by science and technology.

For young children, explorations will often lead to more systematic investigations but skills such as questioning, finding out, observing and 'talking about' are the first steps in an age-appropriate model for children's exploration of their world. Science is a complex interrelationship between conceptual understanding, processing skills and attitudes, and this process, added to the complex nature of young children's learning, makes it very difficult to assess using 'tests'. The aim of pre-scientific understanding should therefore incorporate a learning purpose for acquiring knowledge and skills in scientific literacy and developing appropriate attitudes to enhance scientific thought.

Promoting science: a pause for reflection

Do you think that enough is done to promote the learning of science and technology at all levels in schools today?

What balance should there be between 'scientific skills' and 'scientific knowledge' in teaching and learning science?

What should the role of 'testing' be in the acquisition of scientific skill and knowledge?

Visionary pedagogy for Early Years science

The visionary pedagogy for Early Years science requires Early Years and primary teachers to understand how science works rather than understanding theories of science. The concepts of inquiry skills used in everyday activities and across all subject areas will promote 'spontaneous sciencing' (Chaille and Britain, 2003). By incorporating science as the root of everyday things and events, scientific knowledge will become a natural component of a child's way of knowing. This in turn will promote learning and development through attitudes of open-mindedness and the quest for evidence, alongside children's natural propensity of curiosity and exploration of their environment. Adult intervention in this process therefore allows opportunity for enrichment of the child's experiences and their desire for understanding (Davies *et al.*, 2014). The child's perception of this process will be influenced by the cultural value placed on scientific thinking. Curiosity towards natural phenomenon may be praised or punished through the use of language or tone of voice. Complimenting a child on their new-found knowledge by stating that they may, for example, become a fantastic footballer, doctor, vet or dancer is commonplace but I rarely hear a child extolled as a budding future scientist. Impressions of the value which society places on roles are created early in childhood and if the word *science* or *scientist* is not mentioned in the home or other learning environments it will relegate the subject to a position of low importance. Once again it is cultural attitudes towards science that have an impact upon how society in general views science, and this in turn may influence Early Years practice. For science to be valued it needs to fit in with the cultural environment. In this way a natural acceptance of science is constructed that will help develop the foundations of familiarity and lifelong interest towards scientific knowledge. You do not need to be a trained scientist to teach a scientific approach to young children, but it is necessary to develop an understanding of ways of working to facilitate children's thinking and scientific language. It should be noted that to survive in our world everyone is a scientist in their own right, as we use scientific methodology throughout the day when engaged in, for example, domestic (food and nutrition), behavioural (social and cultural), education (learning), technology (gadgets!) and environmental (from recycling to green footprint) activities.

For the Early Years teacher it is important to develop confidence in the delivery of science. Rogers (2012) investigated Early Years teachers' views on how science was being taught within the Early Years Foundation Stage and concluded that great value appeared to have been placed on science as instrumental in helping children understand their environment. However, the article also identified teachers' low confidence or lack of enjoyment in the subject of science. Negative views of science in an environment where social attitudes are formulated restrict a child's foundations of learning. This creates a continuum of historical cultural perceptions of the value of science. To achieve effective spontaneous sciencing, the Early Years teacher will need to have secure subject knowledge and awareness of how science is embedded in all that we do. The introduction of GCSE English, maths and science as a statutory requirement for Early Years educators and teachers may in some ways help alleviate lack of confidence in the teaching of science, although ongoing professional development is to be supported for those who demonstrate lower levels of understanding. To effectively promote scientific literacy may require teachers and Early Years educators to reflect on their own understanding and attitudes towards science. Learning activities to develop young enquiring minds will be given greater emphasis if both teacher and child have 'fun' discovering pre-scientific thoughts and ideas.

Zeece (1999) supports the suggestion that fostering scientific learning to encourage children to observe, explore and experiment in the early childhood setting does not need specialised equipment. By applying constructivist pedagogy it allows the teacher to recognise opportunities within their natural environment to encourage children to pause and observe, reflect and explore. By doing so it emphasises the philosophy that 'science' is all around us. Learning in a social situation allows a child to change the way in which they experience the phenomenon within their world (Bowden and Marton, 1998), and the integration of knowledge through different genres may allow a child to respond in various ways to encourage a starting point of interest, development of self-reliance and a sense of participation. Table 9.1 lists the concepts of science typically taught alongside issues of the wider world and creative ways of knowing, using an oak tree as the subject matter. Social discourse is extended to a wider social framework, and sense making through narrative becomes a personal journey for the child.

Table 9.1 Traditional and contemporary teaching of science concepts

Scientific methodology: traditional approach	Pre-scientific literacy: wider world and creative ways of knowing through play (e.g. oak tree)	Pre-scientific thinking: ecosystems	Scientific concepts: chemistry, physics and biology
Systems (groups or collections having some influence on one another)	Oak tree as part of ancient forest (ancestors, cultural history)	Oak tree as part of the ecosystem	Oak tree as a living organism
Models (representation of real objects or phenomena)	Non-fiction literature plus stories, songs and poems relating to oak trees (English and European folklore)	Shape of leaves Flowers and pollination	Drawings Words Physical modules Categorisation
Constancy and change (how things change over time)	Fallen oak branches make powerful wands Planting an acorn in the forest or garden	Summer and autumn leaves Influence of the environment	Growth and decay Seasons
Scale (focusing on characteristics and comparisons)	Games or dance around the tree (largest tree species in England) Lightning damage makes oak trees ideal for climbing and hiding	Height and span of tree – compare to self	Size, quantity, distance and weight of oak trees
Patterns and relationships (structure and organisation of matter)	Creating artwork and jewellery from leaves, fallen branches and acorns (oak design found in many old churches)	Pattern of leaves Roots	Properties in nature, comparisons, patterns in nature Age and environmental conditions according to trunk rings
Cause and effect (explanations for phenomena)	Legends of gods associated with the oak tree (e.g. Thor)	Ecosystem and global warming	Shadows, freezing/melting, gravity, draught, flooding, conductor of electricity
Structure and function (relationship between characteristic and action)	Mythical creatures such as the Oak Fairy or Green Man who resided within the oak tree	What other creatures or plants live in, around or under the tree.	Plant structure Photosynthesis
Variations (discontinuous and continuous properties)	Listening to how the oak tree 'whispers' when the wind blows Sit under the oak tree and imagine what it would be like to be part of the tree	Sound of rustling leaves Colours on leaves and bark	Colours of different species of oak tree Disease Fungi
Diversity (variety of types)	Touch, smell, feel and see – what makes the oak tree unique	Other tree species nearby	Seeds, leaves, flowers, living organisms Different species of oak

Science literacy and lifelong learning

To ensure that children develop prerequisites for lifelong learning, understanding scientific concepts is essential. Predictions for the future imply that the workforce will be divided into those who have science-based knowledge and those who do not. For those without such knowledge, career opportunities may be extremely limited, as advanced computerised systems continue to replace the human workforce. Preparing children to survive in a culture where scientific and technological advancement is rapid requires a framework or curriculum that supports early experiences of setting and achieving learning goals rather than performance. Incorporating play-based activities to explore the world allows for a contemporary and diverse approach to the initial concept of scientific thinking through child-centred exploration, experimentation and explanation (Table 9.2). As active learners, children will have opportunities to exercise their curiosity and construct meaning and understanding of their environment. While a contemporary approach may not appear to be directly focused on scientific thought, it allows for scaffolding to take place through spontaneous sciencing with the use of open questions to prompt reflective thinking and the process of theory building. In addition, it allows science to become integrated within technology, mathematics, literacy, social studies and the arts, thereby fostering interaction among all disciplines.

Discovering the world of natural science through playful interactions allows a child to formulate their own hypothesis based on logical and categorical means (Bruner, 1997). The child also needs to experience social interaction to begin a discourse when seeking and experiencing natural phenomena. Pedagogical practice must therefore promote co-learning to allow the child to change or challenge their

Table 9.2 A comparison of traditional and contemporary approaches to science-based learning

Traditional approach	Contemporary approach
Science laws and principles	Science is active exploration of the environment
Teacher is the authority	Teacher is a facilitator
Curriculum set by teacher	Child-centred learning
Large group instructions	Individual or small group investigations
Evaluation based on set answers	Evaluation based on multiple criteria
Content based on science theory	Content connected to children's experiences
Predetermined parameters	Open-ended study
Protocols set when collecting data	Multiple ways to collect and record data
Science viewed as separate subject from others	Science integrated with other subject areas

Adapted from Zeece (1999).

Table 9.3 Questions to foster scientific thinking

	Scientific thinking	Type of question	Examples
	Attention to significant details	Attention focusing	What is it doing? How does it feel? What colour is it? How does it move?
	Precise information	Measuring and counting	How many? How much? How heavy?
	Analysis and classification	Comparison	How are they alike? How are they different?
	Exploration of properties and events; also encourages predictions	Action	What if …?
	Planning and trying solutions to problems	Problem-posing	How could we …?
	Reflection on experiences and construction of new ideas	Reasoning	Why do you think …? Can you explain that?

Figure 9.1 Fostering exploration: 'What can you see?'

Figure 9.2 'A snail moving!'

Adapted from Martens, (1999).

own predictions through the act of borrowing competence from the experienced other. Co-learning also allows the Early Years teacher to develop an understanding of how a child thinks and what strategies they are using (Säljö, 2000). Listening and responding appropriately to the child, to promote confidence and value, will assist in building their self-confidence and self-esteem crucial for future co-learning. Variations in ways of explaining a situation or phenomenon lead to becoming aware of critical features that may be identified, and this prepares a child for understanding and using a scientific thought process in future situations. The child therefore becomes aware of concepts of science and this will lead them towards knowledge of scientific language. It is at this stage where the seeds for lifelong learning are planted and nurtured by shared enthusiasm for exploration and knowledge.

Meaningful science activities are those which are relevant to children's daily lives. This will facilitate children to make connections between what they already know and what they are learning. Sense-making discussions instigate children's awareness of their own learning and concept development, and this promotes the restructuring of alternative ideas into scientific models of thought. Contemporary environmental issues are frequently highlighted in the mass media, influencing social and cultural lifestyles and daily experiences. Exploring the natural world through the discipline of environmental science is therefore an ideal starting place for children and teachers to investigate the world of science from a human-centred point of view, using issues that dominate our current and future way of life.

Questions to foster scientific thinking: a pause for reflection

Look again at the categories of questions that promote scientific thinking. Think of one scientific activity that you could use with children (choose any age group) and plan a series of questions based on all the categories.

Would you use all of the questions to promote learning within one activity? Are some types of questions more likely to promote a change in thinking than others?

Why does asking questions foster scientific thinking? Why not just give children the answers?

The future learning environment

The aim of Early Years and primary science is to formulate a pedagogy that will support the development of skills that will promote children to become active and informed members of society. In a culture where scientific and technological advances seem set to change ways of living, it is vital that all citizens acquire scientific literacy so that they may be active participants in future global communities. The notion of scientific literacy is not new (Murphy *et al.*, 2005) and it allows the practitioner or teacher to concentrate on developing skills and conceptual knowledge. Most importantly, children need to learn to value and respect themselves and the environment in which they live – rather than suffer the consequences and guilt of living in a world where global warming and pollution dictate how they must survive. Discovering the world through the discipline of environmental science allows for recognition of what is happening to the planet as well as helping provide answers to how to live in harmony with the environment. Environmental science incorporates the study of the physical, chemical and biological processes that take place in our world, as well as the social, political and cultural factors (Table 9.4).

It is important to provide children with the essential early experiences they need if they are to develop sound scientific literacy. These early experiences will include using skills such as observing and sorting while playing with a range of different materials found within the manufactured world of the home or the natural outdoor environment (Platz, 2004; Eshach and Fried, 2005). To effectively build science understanding, young children need opportunities for sustained engagement with materials and conversations that focus on the same set of ideas over weeks, months and years (NRC, 2007). Using contemporary environmental issues as a topic focus will allow a child to engage with scientific literacy within both formal and informal settings. Observing and recording topics such as life cycles of plants or animals engages biology, zoology, chemistry, habitats, ecology, global climate change and

Table 9.4 Environmental science is an interdisciplinary field of study. Each discipline may then be subgrouped into areas of specific specialism. More than one science will be applied to any given situation

Environmental science		
Physical and chemical	**Biological**	**Information sciences**
Chemistry	Biology	Natural resource management
Physics	Zoology	Conservation
Nuclear science	Oceanology	Water pollution
Atmospheric science	Soil science	Air pollution
Geodesy (applied mathematics)	Ecology	Ecosystems and habitats
Limnology (study of inland waters)	Health science	Environmental health
Geology	Social science	Sustainable development
Mineralogy	Palaeontology	Global climate change

conservation to be explored through multiple activities, including everyday life situations, play-centred learning and time to talk (NAEYC, 2013). The learning experience may be adapted to engage young children for an extended period of time to assist in opportunities to discover, examine, explore, investigate, make predictions and test their knowledge of the natural environment. The introduction of environmental science as the basis for scientific literacy and thinking also allows children, families and practitioners to develop behaviours that support sustainable development. The UN Decade of Education for Sustainable Development (UNESCO, 2007) integrated principles, values and practices into all aspects of education in an attempt to raise social awareness of limited natural resources and the effects of global warming on the world.

Within early childhood education the emphasis must be on developing education for sustainable development (ESD) through the principle of setting standards and 'practising what you teach'. This includes developing strategic plans for sustainability, examining the setting's ecological footprint, minimising waste, practising sustainable consumption, and engagement with the local and wider environment. Demonstrating a culture of positive behaviours and promoting social participation will influence the attitudes of young children towards caring for the environment that will hopefully support a culture of sustainable development now and in the years to come. The topics link well to outdoor play, and the natural environment is ideal for observing natural history and supporting scientific literacy. Role play at being an ecologist, environmental scientist, conservationist, geologist or zoologist would certainly enhance children's understanding and perceptions of 'a scientist'. All that is needed is an enquiring mind, a magnifying glass and an enthusiastic adult to lead the way to a fun-filled adventure in the world of science.

Recommended reading

Aitken, J., Hunt, J., Roy, E., Sajfar, B. and Featherstone, S. (2015) *A Sense of Wonder: Science in Early Years Education.* London: Bloomsbury Publishing.

Dunne, M. and Peacock, A. (eds) (2015) *Primary Science: A Guide to Teaching Practice* (2nd edn). Croydon: Sage.

Johnston, J. (2014) *Emergent Science: Teaching Science from Birth to 8.* Abingdon, Oxon: Routledge.

Louis, S. (2008) *Knowledge and Understanding of the World in Early Years Foundation Stage.* Oxford: Taylor and Francis.

Stead, D. and Kelly, L. (2015) *Inspiring Science In The Early Years: Exploring Good Practice.* Milton Keynes: Open University Press.

Useful websites for resources and support materials

The Association for Science Education; www.ase.org.uk

Primary Science Teaching Trust; www.pstt.org.uk/funding-and-projects.aspx

The Woodland Trust. Educational activities for children; www.woodlandtrust.org.uk/

Trees for Life: Restoring the wildness; www.treesforlife.org.uk/forest/mythology-folklore/

Wellcome Trust: Educational resources for all age groups; www.wellcome.ac.uk/

References

Barrow, L.H. (2006) A brief history of inquiry: From Dewey to standards. *Journal of Science Teacher Education*, 17(3), pp. 265–78.

Bowden, J. and Marton, F. (1998) *The University of Learning.* London: Kogan Page.

Bruner, J. (1997) Celebrating divergence: Piaget and Vygotsky. *Human Development*, 40(2), pp. 63–73.

Chaille, C. and Britain, L. (2003) *The Young Child as Scientist* (3rd edn). Boston, MA: Allyn and Bacon.

Davies, D., Collier, C., Earle, S., Howe, A. and McMahon, K. (2014) *Approaches to Science Assessment in English Primary Schools* (full report, teachers' summary and executive summary). Bristol: Primary Science Teaching Trust.

Department for Education (DfE) (2014) *Statutory Framework for the Early Years Foundation Stage.* Runcorn: Department for Education.

Department of Education and Science (DES) (1978) *Primary Education in England: A Survey by HM Inspectors of Schools.* London: HMSO.

Dewey, J. (1910) Science as subject matter and as method. *Science*, 31, p. 27.

Early Education (2012) *Development Matters in the Early Years Foundation Stage (EYFS).* London: Early Education.

Education Reform Act (1988) London: HMSO.

Eshach, H. and Fried, M.N. (2005) Should science be taught in early childhood? *Journal of Science Education and Technology*, 14(3), pp. 315–36.

Isaacs, N. (1962) The case for bringing science into the primary school. In W. Perkins (ed.), *The Place of Science in Primary Education.* London: British Association for the Advancement of Science, pp. 4–22.

Kilmer, S.J. and Hofman, H. (1995) Transforming science curriculum. In S. Bredekamp and T. Rosegrant (eds), *Reaching Potentials: Transforming Early Childhood Curriculum and Assessment, Vol. 2.* Washington, DC: NAEYC, pp. 43–63.

Kirkup, G., Zalevski, A., Maruyama, T. and Batool, I. (2010*) Women and Men in Science, Engineering and Technology: The UK Statistics Guide 2010.* Bradford: UKRC.

Martens, M.L. (1999) Productive questions: Tools for supporting constructivist learning. *Science and Children*, May, pp. 24–7, 53.

Murphy, C., Beggs, J., Russell, H. and Melton, L. (2005) *Primary Horizons: Starting Out in Science.* London: Wellcome Trust. Available at www.wellcome.ac.uk/primaryhorizons (accessed 29 January 2016).

National Association for the Education of Young Children (NAEYC) (2013) *All Criteria Document, 17–18.* Available at www.naeyc.org/files/academy/file/AllCriteriaDocument. pdf (accessed 22 April 2016).

National Research Council (NRC) (2007) *Taking Science to School: Learning and Teaching Science in Grades K–8.* Washington, DC: National Academies Press.

Organization for Economic Cooperation and Development (OECD) (2014) *PISA 2012 Results in Focus: What 15-year-olds Know and What They Can Do with What They Know.* OECD. Available at https://en.unesco.org/unesco_science_report (accessed 5 April 2016).

Piaget, J. (1952) *The Origins of Intelligence in Children.* New York: International University Press.

Platz, D.L. (2004) Challenging young children through simple sorting and classifying: A developmental approach. *Education,* 125(1), pp. 88–96.

Plowden, B. (1967) *Children and their Primary Schools.* London: HMSO.

Pramling, N. and Samuelsson, I. (2001) 'It is floating 'cause there is a hole'; A young child's experience of natural science. *Early Years*, 21(2), pp. 139–49.

Rogers, V. (2012) Early Years: Where does science fit in? *Primary Science*, 123 (May/June), pp. 28–30.

Säljö, R. (2000) *Learning in Practice: A Socio-cultural Perspective.* Stockholm: Prisma.

Solomon, J. (1993) *Teaching Science, Technology and Society: Developing Science and Technology Series.* Bristol: Taylor and Francis.

UNESCO (2007) *The UN Decade of Education for Sustainable Development: 2005–2014: The First Two Years.* Paris: UNESCO.

UNESCO (2015) *Science Report: Towards 2030.* Paris: UNESCO. Available at http://en. unesco.org/unesco_science_report (accessed 27 March 2016).

Vygotsky, L. (1986) *Thought and Language.* Cambridge, MA: MIT Press.

Zeece, P.D. (1999) Things of nature and the nature of things: Natural science-based literature for young children. *Early Childhood Education Journal*, 26(3), pp. 161–6.

Supporting physical development

Health and well-being through the use of outdoor environments

Kristy Howells

Chapter overview

This chapter will examine what physical activity is and the importance of children being active linked to the recommended WHO (2010) and NHS (2013) levels for Early Years and primary-aged children. It will:

■ Explore the difficulties in understanding the different levels of physical activity both for the child and for the observer.

■ Identify where within the curriculum guidance for both Early Years Foundation Stage and the Primary Curriculum physical activity exists and question the potential lack of guidance from a practitioner's or teacher's viewpoint.

■ Consider how physical activity benefits physical development. It will examine how physical activity can help learning within physical education, as well as how physical activity and crossing the midline can help learning.

■ Propose how the outdoor environment and in particular playtime can help physical activity and physical development.

■ Highlight the importance of role models within physical activity and consider the use of a whole school or setting approach to physical activity and physical development.

This will enable the reader to begin and evaluate the physical learning opportunities provided by the educational environment and thus amend and improve practice.

> ## Questioning theory in practice: a pause for reflection
>
> What really is physical activity?
>
> If you were watching your children, how would you describe their physical activity?
>
> How would you explain physical activity to the children?

Physical activity defined

Physical activity has been defined in numerous ways, it is however a 'complex behaviour variable' which can vary 'from day to day, in intensity, frequency and duration and consists of both unavoidable activity and variable activity' (Winsley and Armstrong, 2005, p. 65). These suggestions follow Armstrong's (1998) previous work, where he stated that 'physical activity is a complex behaviour and the accurate assessment of young people's physical activity is extremely difficult' (p. s9). For the purpose of this chapter, physical activity is generally regarded as 'any bodily movement resulting in energy expenditure' (Sirad and Pate, 2001, p. 440). However, this definition is extended to include, as Oliver *et al.* (2007b) suggest, 'fine (e.g. painting and sculpting) and gross (e.g. running and skipping)' motor skills (Oliver *et al.*, 2007b, p. 47).

Recommended physical activity levels

Physical activity of at least a moderate intensity level for 60 minutes a day has been recommended for its health benefits (such as improving cardiorespiratory and muscular fitness) for children by the Department of Health (DoH, 2005, 2011) and by the World Health Organisation (WHO, 2010). In England, the DoH (2005) set out delivery recommendations by the Minister of Sport and the Minister for Public Health for increasing levels of physical activity within the whole of the population. The Chief Medical Officer's recommendations were devised from a review of scientific evidence on the contribution of physical activity for health and well-being (DoH, 2004). The DoH (2011) extended the recommendations and suggested that additional moderate to vigorous activity beyond 60 minutes and up to several hours would impart greater health benefits for children. The WHO (2010) highlighted that 'physical inactivity levels are rising in many countries' (p. 7) and identified the 'prevalence of noncommunicable diseases and the general health of the population' (p. 7). The WHO Secretariat reviewed scientific evidence and used it to develop the recommendations. Moderate physical activity has been described as when the body begins to sweat and breathing increases (Topendsports, 2011). Examples of types of activities that would be regarded by the NHS (2011b) and the DoH (2011) as being at a moderate intensity are brisk walking which increases to jogging, running, playing football, bike riding and other games.

The guidelines from the NHS (2011a) give more detail; they recommend that children have at least an hour a day of moderate to vigorous physical activity, but also that on three days a week, children should do muscle- and bone-strengthening activities. Previously, activities for bone health and muscle strength had only been advised for completion twice a week (DoH, 2005). The recommendations also included suggested activities that could be completed within the primary school setting and Early Years setting within physical education lessons or within playtime. These suggestions included push-ups, gymnastics, sit-ups, swinging on playground equipment, rock climbing and games such as tug of war (NHS, 2011a). For the purposes of bone strengthening, the NHS (2011a) suggested activities that were again accessible for young children particularly during playground break time and these included hopscotch, hopping, skipping and jumping, skipping with a rope, running, gymnastics, football, volleyball and tennis. Recommendations have also been made with regard to the types of activities that require moderate physical activity for most children. These included walking to school, playing in the playground, skateboarding, rollerblading, walking the dog, riding a bike on the flat or over a few hills and pushing a lawn mower (NHS, 2011a). The vigorous intensity activities that were suggested as suitable for most children included playing chase (if allowed within the primary school setting: *Daily Mail*, 2007), energetic dancing, aerobics, running, gymnastics, football, martial arts such as karate and riding a bike fast or over hills (NHS, 2011a). It could be proposed that these recommendations (NHS, 2011a) were an improvement on the previous ones (DoH, 2005) in terms of them offering specific examples of activities. These examples make the recommendations more understandable, meaningful, more applicable and therefore potentially more achievable, especially within a primary school setting, although more difficult within an Early Years setting. The suggested activities included those that could easily occur within playground time or before and after school, meaning that the focus would no longer be solely on specific physical education lessons and therefore broadening the time in which children can successfully reach the recommended levels of daily activity.

Questioning theory in practice: a pause for reflection

How should you or could you record physical activity of your children?

Can you use observation tick boxes? Will you tick off the same as a colleague?

Can you video analyse and decide on the different levels of physical activity expressed by the children?

Difficulty in profiling physical activity levels

Children's physical activity is rarely lengthy and is more often than not made up of intermittent and spontaneous patterns, making activity profiling difficult (Waring *et al.*, 2007; Kolle *et al.*, 2009). Transitions between light and moderate physical activity levels may be sporadic as children move between these frequently and the different physical activity levels are not sustained for a long period of time, thus making it really difficult to understand and share with the children. Children spend half of their waking hours – up to seven out of 14 hours – within the primary school setting (Owens *et al.*, 2000) and more within early childhood settings. Therefore, school life and time within early childhood settings has the potential to have a significant impact upon primary-aged children's lives due to the amount of time spent at school and in the early childhood settings (Howells, 2011).

Precise physical activity quantification in preschools in particular is vital according to Oliver *et al.* (2007a) to establish physical activity prevalence and the associations between activity and health outcomes. Oliver and colleagues (2007a) proposed that research into physical activity in preschools is much understudied and they have found that preschool children report low levels of vigorous activity and high levels of physical inactivity. This links to Okely's (2011) findings who reported that children are living more of a sedentary lifestyle and are not participating in the recommended physical activity requirements. Yet as a teacher or an Early Years practitioner it is your responsibility to promote physical activity and physical development within your setting to help support the children to reach as many of the daily recommended physical activity goals as possible.

Physical activity guidance within the curriculum (or lack of it)

Within the new Primary Education Curriculum for England (DfE, 2013) there is a focus on sustained physical activity in physical education and healthy lifestyles in personal, health, social and emotional lessons, but there is no curriculum guidance about what sustained physical activity is and how it is defined. The NHS (2013) guidance on birth to age 5 suggests that children should not be inactive for long periods, and specifies light and energetic activities; however, there is a suggested period of time of 180 minutes but the guidance again does not specify how this should or could be measured, so how can practitioners know if this is occurring? Yet, Cramer, the Chief Executive of the Royal Society of Public Health, has recently stated that 'School education from a young age should focus on the importance of active lifestyles and healthy diets to ensure our society is one that understands the relationship between diet and good health' (Cramer, 2015).

How physical activity benefits children's development

Oliver and colleagues (2007b) propose that physical activity has been visibly recognised as being fundamental to health and well-being in school-aged children. Janz and colleagues (2001) found that physical activity improves children's bone health, and Fisher and colleagues (2005) suggest that physical activity is important in the development of fundamental motor skills. Reilly (2011) considers that the benefits of physical activity are beyond just the physical but also include psychological well-being, social competence and emotional maturity. Lindsey and Colwell (previously, in 2003) also indicated the importance of physical activity in improving social competence. Steiner Waldorf Education (2011) highlighted that physical activity is a young child's approach to thinking. Johnson and Dinger (2012) encourage 3-year-olds to have motion, novelty, adventure, and to engage the world with their whole bodies, while at age 5 we need to encourage children to play, move and to explore to learn about being a risk taker. Emily (a preschool manager) has illustrated these milestones with her children Jack and Henry (see Figures 10.1 to 10.8).

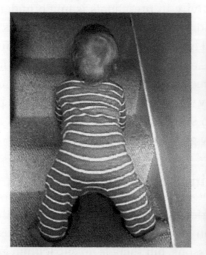 

Figures 10.1 and 10.2 Learning through climbing: pulling the body upward

Figures 10.3 and 10.4 Learning through touch: feeling, sensing, embracing

Figures 10.5 and 10.6 Learning through play: sliding and holding

Figure 10.7 Learning through adventure: exploring

Figure 10.8 Learning through new experiences: touch and wonder

Physical activity and learning within physical education

Jess and Dewer (2004) propose that the place for children to learn how to move is within primary physical education lessons, while Wellard (2012) highlights it as a place for children to become comfortable with their own bodies, and Laker (2001) suggests it as a place to learn how to cope with losing. Children are able to learn from physical education lessons in a variety of ways: physically, socially, affectively and cognitively (Price, 2008). Cools and colleagues (2011) suggest that the 'development of fundamental movement skill' is a 'key factor in promoting long term physical activity' (p. 1). Lubans and colleagues (2010) also proposed that there was a positive association between fundamental skill 'competency and physical activity' levels (p. 1019). Fairclough (2003) suggested that there are multiple aims of physical education lessons, including those that are similar to Lubans et al. (2010) such as development of motor skills, but also suggested that creative and artistic expression, self-realisation, moral development and social development are able to be completed through physical education lessons. The number of skills and areas to be developed during a physical education lesson seem to be numerous and ever increasing. Fairclough (2003) suggested that it is important to ensure that children are able to complete skills. They highlighted that this was particularly important for preschool children aged 3 to 5.

Different activities can help develop movement in a variety of different ways; for example, gymnastics is concerned with control, coordination and challenges, which in turn helps children to understand strength, suppleness and stamina, and also helps to promote children's spatial awareness (Pica, 2004) and decision making, which may then be applied to other activities (Broomfield, 2011). Swindlehurst and Chapman (2008) suggest that gymnastics and dance are also important for developing non-locomotor movement skills such as 'twisting, stretching, turning and bending' (Swindlehurst and Chapman, 2008, p. 30). These skills help develop basic skills of balance and coordination (Jess and Dewar, 2004). These in turn are then used within other activity areas such as athletics and games to improve the overall performance of the child. Yet, in opposition to Swindlehurst and Chapman, (2008), O'Neill and colleagues (2012) highlighted the importance of, in particular, dance classes in terms of activity levels. They suggested that dance provided valuable opportunities to be physically active, especially for girls; although this research was completed with adolescent girls, further research would be needed to examine this in more depth with younger children, such as infants. Robison (2012) suggested that swimming is one of the best physical activities for children, as children can build confidence in the water and can also be active while having fun. Swimming is often reported as being memorable by children, as it can often involve walking to the local swimming baths or catching a bus, and taking up a large chunk of the day. Leeder (2003, p. 1) discussed this phenomenon of trips outside the school as being 'memorable'.

Active rest is needed when developing and learning new skills, as it allows for the skill being learned (particularly in young children) to move from the cognitive stage of skill acquisition into the autonomous stage, where the children are able to complete the skill with more proficiency (Fitts and Posner, 1979). Within the Early Years Foundation Stage Curriculum (DfE, 2008) and the National Curriculum (DfEE/QCA, 1999), it is acknowledged that children are developing physical skills, but it is also recognised that they need to develop communication, language and literacy. They need to be able to articulate what they and others are performing, rather than just being able to perform the action. They are sentient, interactive

Table 10.1 Examples of key vocabulary

Words to describe motion	Stop	Start	Forwards	Backwards	Sideways	Space
Words to describe actions and ways of moving	Rolling	Crawling	Shuffling	Jumping	Skipping	Control
Words to describe feelings	Happy	Sad	Jolly	Stormy	Lonely	Excited
Words to describe what happens to body when exercising	Hot	Red cheeks	Breathing more	Tummy moves	Sweating	Tired

beings, not automatons. One of the strands of the National Curriculum for Physical Education (DfEE/QCA, 1999) is to be able to evaluate and describe performance; therefore, the children need opportunities within the lessons to be able not only to evaluate their actions and those of others, but also to develop the key vocabulary (see Table 10.1) needed to allow them to describe and analyse these performances.

Physical activity, crossing the midline and learning

Roeber and colleagues (2012) highlighted the importance of physical activity and movement for children's development and proposed that children who have difficulties in physical activities, such as crossing the midline, may be excluded from social activities, impacting upon play, social competence and decreased self-esteem. The Early Years has been identified by Timmons *et al.* (2012) as a critical period for promoting physical activity, but they also highlighted that the amount of physical activity needed for healthy growth and development is unclear. Field (2010, p. 7) proposed that:

> by the age of three, a baby's brain is 80% formed and his or her experiences before then shape the way the brain has grown and developed. That is not to say, of course, it is all over by then, but ability profiles at that age are highly predictive of profiles at school entry. By school age, there are very wide variations in children's abilities and the evidence is clear that children from poorer backgrounds do worse cognitively and behaviourally than those from more affluent homes.

Fedewa and Ahn (2011) completed a systematic review and identified that when children undertook physical activity interventions three times a week they found a strong influence on children's cognitive and achievement outcomes. They also found that those children with learning disabilities who struggle in particular with mathematics and reading improved vastly when physical activity interventions were introduced. This could be due to a lack of midline crossing activities as the children developed.

> ### Questioning theory into practice: a pause for reflection
>
> How can I use my outdoor environment to help support children's learning?
>
> Is the outdoors more beneficial than the indoors?
>
> What area do your children use or want to use more? Can you promote this area to encourage physical activity and development?

Use of outdoor equipment to encourage physical activity and development

Infants have been shown to spend up to a quarter of their school day in the playground (Ridgers *et al.*, 2006); therefore it is vitally important to consider what is occurring within the playground to encourage physical activity and physical development. The Kent NHS Overview and Scrutiny Report (2006) suggested that playground play should be encouraged by providing hopscotch grids and basketball hoops in playgrounds. However, the concept and idea of encouraging children may not allow all children to achieve the necessary moderate and above moderate physical activity levels needed within the day to stay healthy. More structured sessions may be needed for some children. A way to increase children's levels of physical activity within the school day is by developing playground play through improving the playtime environment, in order to help tackle inactivity, boredom and bad behaviour (Brady *et al.*, 2008). The Kent County Council (KCC) (2006), as an example of initiatives within the past 10 years, suggested that physical activity could be improved through their playground improvement scheme. The KCC (2006, p. 1) gave schools a grant at that time of £5,000 to purchase facilities for school playgrounds that would 'increase sporting opportunities, develop skills based activity and raise levels of physical activity'. The KCC's (2006) evaluation found that 83 per cent of schools within the scheme stated that, through the grant, they had increased sporting opportunities during playtime and that this had led to greater physical activity. However, it should be noted that lunchtime playground supervisors who were supervising the children during these playtimes may not have been qualified or have been contracted to organise physical activities for the children, unless some of the grant money was spent on developing the staff's knowledge and understanding of age-appropriate learning. Participation to include all children was not planned or structured; the children were just encouraged to complete such activities during playtimes, so there may be children who chose to sit on the side and observe rather than participate.

Movement and physical activity around the playground could be encouraged through the use of the simple addition of brightly coloured markings on the playground and interesting and exciting new additions such as playground and adventure equipment. These additions encouraged children to participate in 'running, jumping and balance', ultimately helping to 'develop stamina, suppleness and flexibility' (KCC, 2006, p. 1). Although an increase in activity levels was reported by schools and observed through the case study visits, the scheme evaluation also reported that this increase varied from school to school. The greatest increase in activity was found when children understood the purpose of the new equipment or line markings and how to use them. Yet, the biggest limiting factor was the lack of equipment, to be used in conjunction with the new line markings; for example, markings for tennis were placed in playgrounds, but the schools struggled to fund tennis rackets for more than one class within the school (KCC, 2006). Stratton (2000) suggested that opportunities did occur for physical activity in the playground setting. He compared physical activity before and after the painting of fluorescent markings on the school playground. He found through heart rate monitor recordings that the new markings had a positive impact on increasing physical activity levels, and suggested that playgrounds are important for physical activity and that markings and other factors that encourage opportunities for physical activity should be extended within school time.

Indoor versus outdoor

Ridgers and colleagues (2011) suggested that time spent outdoors is associated with increased physical activity. Within preschool and infant learning, young children are permitted more often to a free flow in their movement from one learning experience to another (Werner *et al.*, 2012) and move between the outdoor and indoor learning environments freely in their choice of learning. In both environments infants can enquire into and explore their learning both physically and socially (Vygotsky, 1962). Ward and Roden (2008) recommended that enquiring is completed on a daily basis, as this equips infants with the capabilities to discover information throughout life. This also allows them to be active agents in their own learning (Baynes, 1996; Piaget, 1951).

The charity, Fields in Trust (2011), reported that outdoor recreational spaces such as playing fields on school sites were under threat, particularly during difficult economic times, and planning applications to build on such playing fields had more than doubled since 1999 when there were 625 applications, to 1,322 applications in 2009. At the aforementioned rate there would soon be neither playing fields nor playgrounds in schools, as they would only have to provide suitable outdoor space, rather than, as the previous strict rules stated, space that was dependent on the number of children at the school and of an area of at least 5,000 square metres (Harrison, 2012). In Manchester, the council has banned ball games in the street and ASBOs have been given to children for playing football (Lashley, 2008). It comes as no surprise, therefore, that children may find it difficult to reach their recommended physical activity target (DoH, 2005; WHO, 2010) if they are not encouraged or are even prevented from utilising and seizing every opportunity to be physically active in activities of their choice (such as football) during break times or outside of schools/settings. It is really important that we continue to encourage the use of outdoor spaces and ensure new settings, and that schools are built with space for outdoor learning and physical activity to occur.

Questioning theory into practice: a pause for reflection

What can you do yourself as an educator/teacher/practitioner?

How can you walk the talk?

Are you practising and showing the children how to be physically active yourself?

What can everyone within the setting/school do to support this type of learning?

The importance of positive role models

Price (2008) believed that these benefits of physical activity, physical education and physical development to the whole child were not to be underestimated. He suggested that physical education played a strong role in children's 'physical, social, affective and cognitive development'. Alder (2000) identified enjoyment as the key to children's learning, with Hirt and Ramos (2008) suggesting fun as being potentially the central focus of physical education lessons. Yet, the National Association for Sport and Physical Education (2005) identified that fun is a subjective principle. They highlighted that fun is 'not a widely accepted goal or objective' (p. 26) and nowhere within the National Curriculum for Physical Education (DfEE/QCA, 1999) was 'fun' defined as an expected outcome. Dismore and Bailey (2011) suggested that 'fun has not always been considered an appropriate outcome of Physical Education' (p. 499). Just because a child is having fun does not in itself guarantee that progression is being made in the learning or in the child's physical development. At best, physical education lessons can play a role in shaping the character of a child, forming a supportive, honourable, considerate individual (Flemming and Bunting, 2007). Children may be able to create and consolidate friendships through using communication skills to construct and develop positive relationships (Flemming and Bunting, 2007). Raymond (1998) highlighted that requiring 'silence' and an inherent lack of communication in physical education lessons is a misconception. He suggested that there was rarely a need for silence, though it was often used as a tool, or demanded within the lessons, by teachers who were lacking in confidence and wished to feel in control of the learning environment within physical education. It is important that children have a positive experience of physical education and physical development during school from preschool to primary and onward to increase confidence and, in particular, self-esteem. Pupils will then understand the benefits of regularly participating in physical activity and will feel comfortable about wanting to continue with such activities throughout life. Therefore, there is a need for positive, motivated and enthusiastic role models, in particular the class teachers within a primary school setting (Howells, 2007).

The development of sportsmanship is key within physical development and physical activity, such as discouraging children from shouting 'losers' at each other for the rest of the day if they have won a game. The use of positive encouragement and feedback and by getting children to recognise and praise each other are important skills to be developed within sessions with the children. Laker (2001) supported this and suggested that physical education lessons were ideal settings for allowing children to explore how to cope with winning and losing to develop sporting behaviour. The results from a survey performed by Richardson (2011) suggested that two-thirds of school children aged between 8 and 16 reacted badly when they lost and their parents also behaved badly when watching their children lose. Sulking, getting angry and crying (Richardson, 2011) were the most common behaviours displayed by parents and children alike. The area of emotional development clearly still needs to be worked on within both the primary and secondary school setting, and is therefore an important element of physical development and physical education lessons. This is currently being addressed in part via the Spirit of Cricket initiative aimed at teaching young people 'how to win and lose politely' (Richardson, 2011, n.p.), but it does not tackle the behaviour of the parents. Yet, Fairclough and Stratton (2006) proposed a view that was against developing sportsmanship within the role of physical education, as they felt that cognitive and social development were 'hindrances' to the physical gain and 'less relevant'. Gilliver (2003) seemed to suggest a middle ground between Fairclough and Stratton (2006) and Doherty and Brennan (2007) by proposing that children could learn the cognitive and social elements associated with the National Curriculum for Physical Education (DfEE/QCA, 1999) through being physically active.

Whole school/setting approach to physical activity and physical development

Gidlow and colleagues (2008) considered the physical activity levels of children in both primary and secondary school and found that, in particular, younger children were more physically active outside of the school day. They suggested that physical activity within school needed to be promoted but did not suggest the types of physical activity that could be encouraged or where within the school or setting day this could occur. Hills and colleagues (2007) also discussed the important role that schools and settings have in helping to increase physical activity levels and in combating obesity in general. According to the Healthy Schools Initiative (2009, n.p.), the aim of their physical activity guidance is to 'support the whole school approach to promoting healthy active lifestyles' and this should be an 'integral part of daily life in a health-promoting school'. It is important to identify the whole school approach to physical activity. Rees and colleagues (2001) recommended that for those 'wishing to implement effective physical activity interventions, a whole school approach can promote greater involvement in physical activity' (p. 6). They suggested that it is important to involve all members of the school community, including peer-led initiatives, in particular with regard to choosing the activities on offer. Focusing on the fun of the activity helps improve self-confidence, rather than focusing on mastering all skills within the activity (Rees *et al.*, 2001). Gorely and colleagues (2009) completed an intervention programme involving a whole school approach and found that those children in the intervention schools had significantly increased the total time children spent at moderate to vigorous physical activity levels compared to those in the control schools where the whole school intervention approach did not occur. The interventions included physical activity events such as one-mile school runs/walks, using pedometers and accelerometers and recording fruit and vegetable consumption; however, they concluded that more work is needed to promote fruit and vegetables, as consumption levels were relatively low. Gorley and colleagues (2009) also suggested moving towards a whole school approach to involve parents and carers to help increase physical activity of children.

Conclusion

This chapter has outlined the importance of planned physical activity for children of all ages as appropriate to their stage of development. Authorities, such as the WHO, the Department of Health, and education departments, have been increasingly voicing their concerns about the lack of physical activity in children's lives, with the result of possible health disorders in the future. It is therefore essential that teachers and practitioners understand that physical development in all its forms should be encouraged and planned for within educational environments. This includes fine and gross motor skills, both of which may be observed in everyday classroom activities, planned physical lessons and in the playground and outdoor play areas for children. The chapter highlights the need for teachers and practitioners to support children's learning through the use of a key vocabulary describing physical activity that allows children to communicate their activities, to be active role models and to strategically plan activities to ensure that all children are engaged in appropriate physical exercise whenever possible. The starting place for such awareness is through the evaluation of existing practice, and this chapter suggests starting places for observation and not being afraid to use the outdoor environment within the educational setting to help support children's physical development and physical activity.

Recommended reading

The following three texts are provided as follow-on reading:

Howells, K. (2012) Chapter 13: Placing an importance on health and physical activity. In G. Griggs (ed.), *An Introduction to Primary Physical Education*. Abingdon, Oxon: Routledge (pp. 207–20).

Driscoll, P., Lambirth, A. and Roden, J. (eds) (2015) *The Primary Curriculum: A Creative Approach* (2nd edn). London: Sage (pp. 137–55).

Doherty, J. and Brennan, P. (2007) *Physical Education and Development 3–11: A Guide for Teachers*. Abingdon, Oxon: Routledge.

References

Alder, H. (2000) *The Ultimate 'How to' Book: Strategies for Personal Achievement*. Aldershot: Gower Publishing.

Armstrong, N. (1998) Young people's physical activity patterns as assessed by heart rate monitoring. *Journal of Sports Sciences,* 16, s. 9–16.

Baynes, K. (1996) *HOW CHILDREN CHOOSE: Children's Encounters with Design*. Loughborough: Loughborough University.

Brady, L-M., Gibb, J., Henshall, A. and Lewis, J. (2008) *Play and Exercise in Early Years: Physically Active Play in Early Childhood Provision*. London: Department for Culture, Media and Sport.

Broomfield, L. (2011) *Complete Guide to Primary Gymnastics*. Champaign, IL: Human Kinetics.

Cools, W., De Martelaer, K., Samaey, C. and Andries, C. (2011) Fundamental movement skill performance of preschool children in relation to family context. *Journal of Sports Science,* 29(7), pp. 649–60.

Cramer, S. (2015) Comment. In J. Gallagher, *Parents 'Rarely Spot Child Obesity'*. Available at www.bbc.co.uk/news/health-32069699 (accessed 2 April 2015).

Daily Mail (2007) Children banned from playing tag in school playground. Available at www.dailymail.co.uk/news/article-435233/Children-banned-playing-tag-school-playground.html (accessed 21 December 2007).

Department for Education (DfE) (2008) *Early Years Foundation Stage*. Available at http://nationalstrategies.standards.dcsf.gov.uk/node/132718 (accessed 25 March 2010).

Department for Education (DfE) (2013) *The National Curriculum in England. Framework Document for Consultation. February 2013*. Available at http://media.education.gov.uk/assets/files/pdf/n/national%20curriculum%20consultation%20-%20framework%20document.pdf (accessed 1 March 2013).

Department for Education and Employment (DfEE)/Qualifications and Curriculum Authority (QCA) (1999) *The National Curriculum. Handbook for Primary Teachers in England. Key Stages 1 and 2*. London: HMSO.

Department of Health (DoH) (2004) *Physical Activity, Health Improvement and Prevention At Least 5 a Week. Evidence on the Impact of Physical Activity and its Relationship to Health. A Report from the Chief Medical Officer*. London: Department of Health, Crown.

Department of Health (DoH) (2005) Choosing activity: A physical activity action plan. Available at www.dh.gov.uk/prod_consum_dh/groups/dh_digitalassets/@dh/@en/documents/digitalasset/dh_4105710.pdf (accessed 26 October 2009).

Department of Health (DoH) (2011) *Physical Activity Guidelines for CHILDREN AND YOUNG PEOPLE (5–18 YEARS)*. Available at www.dh.gov.uk/prod_consum_dh/groups/dh_digitalassets/documents/digitalasset/dh_128144.pdf (accessed 31 August 2011).

Dismore, H. and Bailey, R. (2011) Fun and enjoyment in physical education: Young people's attitudes. *Research Papers in Education,* 26(4), pp. 449–516.

Doherty, J. and Brennan, P. (2007) *Physical Education and Development 3–11: A Guide for Teachers.* Abingdon, Oxon: Routledge.

Fairclough, S. (2003) Physical activity levels during Key Stage 3 physical education. *British Journal of Teaching Physical Education,* 34(1), pp. 40–5.

Fairclough, S.J. and Stratton, G. (2006) A review of physical activity levels during elementary school physical education. *Journal of Teaching in Physical Education,* 25(2), pp. 239–57.

Fedewa, A.L. and Ahn, S. (2011) The effects of physical activity and physical fitness on children's achievement and cognitive outcomes: A meta-analysis. *Research Quarterly for Exercise and Sport,* 82(3), pp. 521–35.

Field, F. (2010) The Foundation Years: Preventing poor children becoming poor adults. *The Report of the Independent Review on Poverty and Life Chances.* London: HM Government.

Fields in Trust (2011) *Loss of Sites.* Available at www.fieldsintrust.org/Loss_of_Sites.aspx (accessed 24 January 2012).

Fisher, A., Reilly, J.J., Kelly, L., Montgomery, C., Williamson, A., Paton, J. and Grant, S. (2005) Fundamental movement skills and habitual physical activity in young children. *PubMed,* 37(4), pp. 684–8. doi: 0.1249/01.MSS.0000159138.48107.7D.

Fitts, P.M. and Posner, I. (1979) *Human Performance.* Westport, CT: Greenwood Publishing Group.

Flemming, T.M. and Bunting, L. (2007) *PE Connections: Helping Kids Succeed through Physical Activity.* Leeds: Human Kinetics.

Gidlow, C.J., Cochrane, T., Davey, R. and Smith, H. (2008) In-school and out-of-school physical activity in primary and secondary school children. *Journal of Sports Science,* 26(13), pp. 1411–19.

Gilliver, K. (2003) Quality physical education. *British Journal of Teaching Education,* 34(1), pp. 129–31.

Gorely, T., Nevill, M.E., Morris, J.G., Stensel, D.J. and Nevill, A. (2009) Effect of a school based intervention to promote healthy lifestyles in 7–11 year old children. *International Journal of Behavioural Nutrition and Physical Activity,* 6(5). doi: 10.1186/1479-5868-6-5.

Harrison, A. (2012) *School Playing Fields: 31 Sales Approved.* Available at www.bbc.co.uk/news/uk-19291911 (accessed 21 December 2012).

Healthy Schools Initiative (2009) *Physical Activity Guidance Documents.* Available at http://resources.healthyschools.gov.uk/v/32f5e04c-9d22-4d55-9f8d-9cbc00f37ae8 (accessed 14 December 2009).

Hills, A., King, N. and Armstrong, T. (2007) The contribution of physical activity and sedentary behaviours to the growth and development of children and adolescents: Implications for overweight and obesity. *Sports Medicine,* 37(6), pp. 533–45.

Hirt, M. and Ramos, I. (2008) *Maximum Middle School Physical Education.* Leeds: Human Kinetics.

Howells, K. (2007) A critical reflection of the opportunities and challenges of integrating the Every Child Matters (ECM) agenda into teaching physical education (PE). *Primary Physical Education Matters,* 2(1), pp. ii–iii.

Howells, K. (2011) An introduction to physical education. In P. Driscoll, A. Lambirth and J. Roden (eds), *The Primary Curriculum: A Creative Approach.* London: Sage, pp. 118–36.

Janz, K.F., Burns, T., Torner, J., Levy, S., Paulos, R., Willing, M. and Warren, J. (2001) Physical activity and bone measures in young children: The Iowa Bone Development Study. *Pediatrics,* 107, pp. 1387–93. doi: 10.1542/peds.107.6.1387.

Jess, M. and Dewar, K. (2004) Basic moves, developing a foundation for lifelong physical activity. *The British Journal of Teaching Physical Education,* 35(2), pp. 24–7.

Johnson, J. and Dinger, D. (2012) *Let Them Play: An Early Learning (Un)Curriculum.* St Paul, MN: Redleaf Press.

Kent County Council (KCC) (2006) Kent County Council, Sports Development Unit, *PE and School Sport, Playground Improvement Scheme, Impact and Monitoring Report.* Available at http://209.85.229.132/search?q=cache:XZZ70sYYdygJ: www.kentsport.org/schools/ documents/PlaygroundMonitoringReportex-photos.doc+kent+children%27s+physical+ activity+levels&cd=3&hl=en&ct=clnk&gl=uk (accessed 25 October 2009).

Kent NHS Overview and Scrutiny Report (KNOSR) (2006) *Tackling Obesity: NHS Overview and Scrutiny Joint Select Committee Report Parts 1 and 2.* Available at www.kent.gov.uk/ NR/rdonlyres/D42DE05E-2825-4290-ACFC-F5DF1D284F8C/8520/tacklingobesityjan08. pdf (accessed 11 September 2008).

Kolle, E., Steene-Johannessen, J., Klasson-Heggebø, L., Andersen, L.B. and Anderssen, S.A. (2009) A 5-yr change in Norwegian 9-yr olds' objectively assessed physical activity level. *Medicine and Science in Sports and Exercise,* 41(7), pp. 1368–73.

Laker, A. (2001) *Developing Personal, Social and Moral Education through Physical Education: A Practical Guide for Teachers.* London: Routledge.

Lashley, B. (2008) *Council Bans Ball Games in Street.* Available online at http://menmedia. co.uk/manchestereveningnews/news/s/1032821_council_bans_ball_games_in_street_ (accessed 1 February 2008).

Leeder, A. (2003) *Tips for Trips.* London: Continuum.

Lindsey, E.W. and Colwell, M.J. (2003) Preschoolers' emotional competence: Links to pretend and physical play. *Child Study Journal,* 33, pp. 39–52.

Lubans, D.R., Morgan, P.J., Cliff, D.P., Barnett, L.M. and Okely, A.D. (2010) Fundamental movement skills in children and adolescents: Review of associated health benefits. *Sports Medicine,* 40(12), pp. 1019–35.

National Association for Sport and Physical Education (2005) *Physical Education for Lifelong Fitness: The Physical Best Teacher's Guide* (2nd edn). Leeds: Human Kinetics.

National Health Service (NHS) (2011a) *Physical Activity Guidelines for Children and Young People.* Available at www.nhs.uk/Livewell/fitness/Pages/physical-activity-guidelines-for-young-people.aspx (accessed 17 August 2011).

National Health Service (NHS) (2011b) *What is Light, Moderate and Vigorous Exercise?* Available at www.nhs.uk/chq/Pages/2419.aspx?CategoryID=52&SubCategoryID=145 (accessed 2 February 2011).

National Health Service (NHS) (2013) *Physical Activity Guidelines for Children and Young People.* Available at www.nhs.uk/Livewell/fitness/Pages/physical-activity-guidelines-for-young-people.aspx (accessed 15 July 2015).

O'Neill, J.R., Pate, R.R. and Beets, M.W. (2012) Physical activity levels of adolescent girls during dance classes. *Journal of Physical Activity and Health,* 9(3), pp. 382–8.

Okely, A. (2011) Sedentary behaviour recommendations for early childhood. In *Encyclopedia on Early Childhood Development.* Available at www.child-encyclopedia.com/sites/default/files/textes-experts/en/483/sedentary-behaviour-recommendations-for-early-childhood.pdf (accessed 27 May 2015).

Oliver, M., Schofield, G.M. and Kolt, G.S. (2007a) Physical activity in preschoolers. Understanding prevalence and measurement issues. *Sports Medicine,* 37(12), pp. 1045–70.

Oliver, M.O., Schofield, G.M., Kolt, G.S. and McLachlan, C. (2007b) Physical activity in early childhood: Current state of knowledge. *New Zealand Research in Early Childhood Education Journal,* 10, pp. 47–68.

Owens, J.A., Spirito, A., McGuinn, M. and Nobile, C. (2000) Sleep habits and sleep disturbances in elementary school aged children. *Journal of Developmental and Behavioural Paediatrics*, 21(1), pp. 27–36.

Piaget, J. (1951) *Play, Dreams and Imitations in Childhood.* New York: Norton.

Pica, R. (2004) *Experiences in Movement: Birth to Age 8* (3rd edn). Canada: Thomson, Delmar Learning.

Price, L. (2008) The importance of physical education in primary schools. In I. Pickup, L. Price, J. Shaughnessy, J. Spence and M. Trace (eds), *Learning to Teach Primary PE.* Exeter: Learning Matters, Chapter 1.

Raymond, C. (1998) *Coordinating Physical Education across the Primary School: The Subject Leader's Handbook.* London: Routledge, Falmer.

Rees, R., Harden, A., Shepherd, J., Brunton, G., Oliver, S. and Oakley, A. (2001) *Young People and Physical Activity: A Systematic Review of Research on Barriers and Facilitators.* London: EPPI – Centre, Social Science Research Unit, Institute of Education, University of London.

Reilly, J. (2011) Physical activity in early childhood. In *Encyclopedia on Early Childhood Development.* Available at www.child-encyclopedia.com/sites/default/files/textes-experts/en/483/physical-activity-in-early-childhood-topic-commentary.pdf (accessed 27 May 2015).

Richardson, H. (2011) *Britain's Pupils are Bad Losers, Survey Suggests.* Available at www.bbc.co.uk/news/education-12938578 (accessed 30 April 2011).

Ridgers, N., Stratton, G. and Fairclough, S.J. (2006) Physical activity levels of children during school playtime. *Sports Medicine,* 36(4), pp. 359–71.

Ridgers, N.D., Carter, L.M., Stratton, G. and McKenzie, T.L. (2011) Examining children's physical activity and play behaviours during playtime over time. *Health Education Research,* 26(4), pp. 586–95.

Robison, S. (2012) *Free Primary School Swimming Lessons Scheme Extended.* Available at www.bbc.co.uk/news/uk-scotland-16998634 (accessed 13 March 2012).

Roden, J. (2008) Raising and analysing questions and use of secondary sources. In H. Ward, J. Roden, C. Hewlett and J. Foreman (eds), *Teaching Science in the Primary Classroom: A Practical Guide* (2nd edn). London: Sage, Chapter 4.

Roeber, B.J., Tober, C.L., Bolt, D.M. and Pollak, S.D. (2012) Gross motor development in children adopted from orphanage settings. *Developmental Medicine & Child Neurology,* 54(6), pp. 527–31.

Sirad, J.R. and Pate, R.R. (2001) Physical activity assessment in children and adolescents. *Sports Medicine*, 31(6), pp. 439–54.

Steiner Waldorf Education (2011) *Guide to the Early Years Foundation Stage in Steiner Waldorf Early Childhood Settings.* Available at www.foundationyears.org.uk/files/2011/10/Guide_to_the_EYFS_in_Steiner_Waldorf_settings1.pdf (accessed 28 May 2015).

Stratton, G. (2000) Promoting children's physical activity in primary school: An intervention study using playground markings. *Ergonomics*, 43(10), pp. 1538–46.

Swindlehurst, G. and Chapman, A. (2008) Teaching dance: A framework for creativity. In J. Lavin (ed.), *Creative Approaches to Physical Education: Helping Children to Achieve Their True Potential.* London: Routledge, pp. 29–54.

Timmons, B.W., Leblanc, A.G., Carson, V., Connor Gorber, S., Dillman, C., Janssen, I., Kho, M.E., Spence, J.C., Stearns, J.A. and Tremblay, M.S. (2012) Systematic review of physical activity and health in the early years (aged 0–4 years). *Applied Physiology, Nutrition and Metabolism*, 37(4), pp. 773–92.

Topendsports (2011) The Sport and Science Resource. *METs.* Available at www.topendsports.com/weight-loss/energy-met.htm (accessed 25 January 2012).

Vygotsky, L.S, (1962) *Thought and Language.* Cambridge, MA: MIT Press.

Ward, H. and Roden, J. (2008) *Teaching Science in the Primary Classroom.* London: Sage.

Waring, M., Warburton, P. and Coy, M. (2007) Observation of children's physical activity levels in primary schools: Is the school an ideal setting for meeting government activity targets. *European Physical Education Review,* 13(1), pp. 25–40.

Wellard, I. (2012) Body-reflexive pleasures: Exploring bodily experiences within the context of sport and physical activity. *Sport, Education and Society*, 17(1), pp. 21–33.

Werner, P.H., Williams, L.H. & Hall, T.J. (2012) *Teaching Children Gymnastics* (3rd edn). Champaign, IL: Human Kinetics.

Winsley, R. and Armstrong, N. (2005) Physical activity, physical fitness, health and young people. In K. Green and K. Hardman (eds), *Physical Education Essential Issues.* London: Sage, pp. 65–77.

World Health Organisation (WHO) (2010) *Global Recommendations on Physical Activity For Health.* Available at http://whqlibdoc.who.int/publications/2010/9789241599979_eng.pdf (accessed 3 October 2010).

History, geography and learning about the world

Janice Gill

Chapter overview

This chapter will introduce the ideas, theories and policies concerned with the teaching and learning of history and geography, including requirements from the current EYFS and National Curriculum documents. The main aim of the chapter is an attempt to explain why and how these subjects should be taught in schools. The key issues of learning facts versus developing skills will be considered. There will be suggestions taken from case studies that illustrate ways to support children's learning in a creative manner, demonstrating that learning from first-hand experiences is significant in developing children's understanding and the building of a sound knowledge base in these subject areas. The chapter concludes by asserting that there is a place for learning about history and geography in the primary classroom.

Introduction

Currently, we seem to be continually reflecting on our past and our heritage. In recent years we have celebrated numerous anniversaries of significant events: major battles of the First World War (1914–18) and the Second World War (1939–45), the Battle of Trafalgar (1805), Waterloo (1815) or Magna Carta (1215). In 2016, celebrations for the anniversary of Shakespeare's birthday and the 950th anniversary of the Battle of Hastings took centre stage; we may have watched major televised events marking, for example, the Queen's Golden Jubilee (2002), Andy Murray winning Wimbledon (2013) or Britain winning the Davies Cup in Tennis (2015) for the first time in over 70 years. If we look at recent film releases, we can identify those which are based on historical events; for example, *Monuments Men* (based on the German Third Reich's hoarding of art treasures) and *Suffragettes* (telling of the early twentieth-century fight for women's rights by the Pankhursts) and those which are fictitious; for example, *Robin Hood*. Television also provides numerous programmes to spark our interest in recent and past history as well as more personal histories; for example, *Antiques Roadshow*, *Cash in the Attic*, *Who Do You Think You Are?*, *Time Team*, *Time Crashers*, *Walking through History*; and there are series based on historical fiction set in different periods of the past, including *Poldark* or *Wolf Hall*. There are also programmes aimed specifically at children; cartoons such as *Mike the Knight* and those based on the best-selling books, *Horrible Histories*. From time to time we are also able to follow media coverage of the discovery of a major historical find, for example, the remains of Richard III (2015) ... We are surrounded by evidence of our past.

There is also continual interest in all things geographical. Friends and family may live in different countries; we can use social media to maintain contact with them or we can use different search engines to find out more about the country or even book a holiday there. The world seems to have somehow grown smaller with the advances in technology making things more immediately available. Access to information about different places in its simplest form may consist of 'Travelogues', television programmes which take a journey to and investigate different countries. Of course, it should be remembered that throughout history there have been people keen to explore the world around them: the Romans who founded and lost a great Empire, the Angles, Saxons and Jutes who invaded England from Northern Europe, the Vikings who set forth from Scandinavia, Marco Polo, Christopher Columbus, Magellan, Vasco de Gama, Sir Walter Raleigh, Captain Cook, David Livingstone, Sir Walter Scott, etc. The advent of film, radio and television in the late nineteenth and early twentieth century certainly helped raise greater awareness of faraway places, and in the late 1950s this was developed into the idea of a 'Travelogue' by Alan Whicker and then Michael Palin (*Around the World in 80 Days* and others). More recently, these programmes have been undertaken by celebrities such as Joanna Lumley, Sue Perkins, Stephen Fry, Warwick Davies, Griff Rhys Jones and Michael Portillo. Prunella Scales and Timothy West have explored the canals in the UK and a number of chefs, for example, Antonio Carluccio and Gino d' Campo, have explored Italy's different foods, and even the Hairy Bikers have taken their cookery skills to places near and far! These programmes are very often accompanied by different types of publications which may motivate people to travel and explore different countries. TV schedules also detail a number of programmes exploring, for example, the natural landscape, such as *Coast*, or natural disasters – earthquakes, tsunamis, floods and famines – as well as various appeals to support the victims of these disasters, such as 'Comic Relief'. Today, a variety of information about different areas of 'Geography' is readily available online, and closer to home the rise of websites such as Google Earth means we can literally look into our own backyards and neighbourhoods. Aerial photography is also popular (and often features heavily in news reports of bombing raids in other countries), and publications such as *Britain from the Air* have enjoyed commercial success. Photography or IT simulations may also feature in local news stories that discuss planning applications, new roads or housing/industrial developments. Other geographical areas of interest that may appear in the media include cliff falls revealing fossils, national stories concerning the siting of new airports/extensions to runways, new proposals for high-speed train travel, or currently the migrant crisis (which affects us globally). Geography, as well as history, is a key part of our everyday life.

Issues in teaching history and geography

There are a few issues to be considered however before we even think about how to plan for teaching and supporting children's learning in the classroom, and six key issues are discussed in this section.

History and geography in education: a pause for reflection

Before reading on, consider your own perspectives.

We can now readily access historical and geographical information through a variety of different media; knowledge is at our fingertips, but what is the situation in schools?

■ How did you learn about these subjects?

■ How has your previous learning influenced your views as an adult?

■ What should be taught and how can we best support children's learning in these areas?

Issue 1: Our own knowledge and understanding of history and geography

What do these subjects mean to you and what images, thoughts or feelings do they evoke? Are your feelings based solely on experiences of being taught history or geography in school or have you been influenced by the media or an interest beyond school? No doubt some people, including educationalists, may ask what the point is of learning about these 'old, dry and boring' subjects, and even question how they came to be included in a school curriculum. Answers to philosophical questions such as these go beyond the remit of this chapter, but the subjects have been included in the school curriculum since at least 1902 (the aim of teaching history at this time was to foster patriotism and teach the evolution of British democracy) and are still valued by the policy makers who make decisions as to what children should be taught. In history, the value in learning about the past is that it allows us to make sense of our lives today and develop an understanding of how we have come to be:

How do you know who you are unless you know where you've come from?
How can you tell what's going to happen, unless you know what's happened

before? History isn't just about the past. It's about why we are who we are –
and about what's next.

> (Sir Tony Robinson cited in the *National Curriculum Handbook for*
> *Primary Teachers in England*, 1999, p.103)

Similarly, the value to learning geography is promoted as being a part of our everyday
lives and that it allows us to make sense of the world; understanding the different
environments in which we live and the types of changes which affect our lives:

> What is our knowledge worth if we know nothing about the world that sustains
> us, nothing about natural systems and climate, nothing about other countries
> and cultures?

> (Jonathon Porritt cited in the *National Curriculum Handbook for*
> *Primary Teachers in England*, 1999, p.108)

Issue 2: When to actually teach history and geography in a very busy curriculum

Government policies continue to try to address concerns about the poor standards
of literacy and numeracy skills among school leavers; more recently, free English
and mathematics GCSE classes have been funded for those who do not have these
qualifications. The drive to raise standards in literacy and numeracy also impacts
upon children in the EYFS, KS1 and KS2; children are formally assessed with Early
Learning Goals in the EYFS and then with SATs in English, mathematics and
science at the end of KS2. School test results are published in league tables and
used as a benchmark by OFSTED inspectors in their evaluation of a school's
performance. If children are not making sufficient progress, then the school's report
will not be satisfactory. This presents a dilemma to those making decisions about
how to cover the full breadth of curriculum subjects within school; are teachers
expected to concentrate on raising standards in mathematics and literacy to the
exclusion of other areas of the curriculum, or are there ways in which the school
can follow a broad and balanced curriculum and still raise expected standards? It
all rather depends on the confidence of the school managers and more so on what
they value as to the proportion of time which is allocated to history and geography,
and indeed other arts subjects in the curriculum which the children follow.

Issue 3: Whether to teach history and geography as separate, discrete subjects or within a cross-curricular topic, integrated studies or humanities

In the recent past, 'history' and 'geography' were perceived as discrete subjects
taught at secondary school, but now aspects of history and geography are included
in the EYFS as part of knowledge and understanding of the world and as study

units within KS1 and KS2. Few primary schools actually choose to teach these as discrete subjects, although for purposes of planning and assessment the key learning objectives for each subject area will be used so that the subject's distinct nature is not lost. Cooper (2002, p. 134) suggests that there is much overlap between history and geography; both subjects draw on the use of investigation of different sources:

> To find out how people live, their work, leisure, beliefs, homes, food and clothes. They are based on the same organising concepts which run through societies: agriculture, manufacture, trade communication, social structure and belief systems.

Cooper (ibid.) also indicates that there are distinct differences between the two subjects:

> History focuses on interpreting the causes and effects of changes over time. Geography is more concerned with the interactions between people and their natural and man-made environment, with the influences of land forms and climate on settlement and daily life.

Some schools may choose to blend or incorporate aspects of history and geography into a 'topic' or project such as 'Egypt' (a cross-curricular-based approach). Others may include Citizenship or Personal, Social and Health Education (PSHE) along with Religious Education as part of 'Humanities' or 'Integrated Studies', for example, following projects such as 'Our Locality' or 'Rivers'. It does not matter how the subjects are studied or even that young children may not actually understand that they are studying 'history' and 'geography'; what is important is that children are actually allowed time to develop their historical and geographical knowledge skills and understanding.

Issue 4: Teacher confidence, both in subject and pedagogical knowledge

It is all very well having a depth of knowledge in history or geography, but it is not at all helpful to children if the appropriate methods are not chosen to enthuse and motivate their learning. Teachers' confidence is often very dependent on their own past experiences and resultant attitude towards their own knowledge, skills and understanding of these subject areas. A lack of teacher confidence may either result in more thorough planning and preparation for teaching or learning based perhaps on pre-published plans and materials which are 'safe'. This may result in dry, tedious activities and lessons where calculated risks are not taken, or it may mean that the teacher becomes dependent on the teaching of facts; transmitting knowledge. Thorough planning would include taking time to conduct research about a 'topic', considering the children's personal experiences, prior knowledge and interests; determining age-appropriate activities which are exciting, fun and based on an enquiry-based approach; interpreting and making deductions from a range of different resources; being mini-detectives, etc. It needs to be remembered that a teacher cannot be an expert in all subject areas, but that thorough preparation and planning as well as personal enthusiasm can play a significant role in creating an enjoyable environment for children that promotes active learning. If the thought of children undertaking an enquiry-based approach to a topic is causing a headache, be brave and take a risk, as this approach actually enables children to take much greater ownership of their learning.

Issue 5: Deciding how to teach history and geography

This issue is concerned with whether to focus on the teaching of facts (that is, knowledge, using more 'traditional' teaching methods) or the development of skills and understanding (using more of a problem-solving, enquiry-based approach to learning), or both.

The learning of facts, mainly by rote, was one of the main methods of learning in Victorian times; this is wonderfully epitomised by Dickens' character Mr Gradgrind in *Great Expectations* who states: 'Now what I want is, Facts … Facts alone are wanted in life.'

The issue of facts versus skills and understanding has been debated for many years; one of the most recent significant arguments about this topic was in 1988 when the National Curriculum was first established amid fears that the teaching of history and geography would disappear altogether at this time. The then Minister for Education, Kenneth Baker, suggested that children should learn about the main events in British history: the development of the British Empire and Parliament and democracy, the lives of British monarchs and the important events of their reigns, and the implications of the Industrial Revolution and the British Empire for the world. Opposing this idea was a group of historians supported by Skidelsky (1991), who argued that learning skills and studying the lives of ordinary people and different aspects of world history would be far more interesting and meaningful to children, especially given the multicultural society in which we live. However, both sides had overlooked the fact that there was actually a need to teach and support children's learning through using methods which allowed for the interrelation of knowledge, skills and understanding.

Interestingly, the same issue seems to emerge each time there is a suggestion to review the content of the National Curriculum. Even today, there are still some politicians who are keen that children should learn facts to the exclusion of all else. Political influence on the curriculum is deep-rooted; it stems from a mistrust of so-called 'progressive' teaching methods employed in some schools in the past. The National Curriculum of 1988 eventually adopted a type of compromise position between the teaching of facts and skills and understanding; but a more traditional approach to teaching and learning is evident. It is seen to support the raising of standards (whatever these are) and preparing children for a life of work, and to assist the country in competing against other world economies. This is still the case with the new statutory requirements of 2014. There is however some truth in the need to learn facts; children need to learn some facts to form a basis for enquiry from which they are able to develop understanding. However, when talking about historical facts, additional caution is required; such facts are often based on an interpretation of the past and so in the light of new evidence a fact may change; for example, King Richard III was often portrayed as a hunchback until a recent discovery and excavation of his skeleton. The use of more advanced technology quickly disproved what had been previously accepted as a fact. Many would thus argue that it is not simply a case of teaching facts or developing skills and understanding in history and geography but to use methods which incorporate a blend of both.

Issue 6: Determining how children actually learn about history and geography

This issue also concerns the methods that should be used to teach children history and geography, and has been the subject of much discussion. Should they be taught knowledge (facts) using more traditional pedagogical methods or be facilitated in their learning strategies by being encouraged to develop their skills of enquiry and understanding by using 'less traditional' and more 'creative', exploratory pedagogical approaches? This decision may well need to be based on the practitioner's knowledge of the theory of learning. The term 'more traditional' methods in this instance is based on behaviourist theories, with characteristics based on transmission-style teaching; these methods are very much 'practitioner orientated'; the practitioner 'delivers' information and children 'receive' the practitioner's view of knowledge; children may copy ideas from presentations or texts with little engagement or understanding; they are passive in their learning. In contrast, 'less traditional' (rather than 'progressive' as some methods were termed in the mid-twentieth century) may be understood to be based on constructivist, social constructivist or nativist (or liberal, alternative) theories of learning. These theories are described as 'child-centred': the practitioner facilitates children's learning by organising different activities, encouraging problem solving, developing the skills of enquiry, and presenting opportunities for children to investigate, to ask and answer questions; in other words, children are actively involved in their learning.

It may be helpful here to reflect on what actually constitutes an 'outstanding' learning experience, perhaps something like the following:

- Knowledge of and relationship with the children.

- Enthusiasm for the subject.

- Good subject knowledge.

- Thorough planning, organisation and preparation.

- Interesting use of a range of different resources.

- Encouraging children to find out through a variety of activities.

- Ability to assess the children's knowledge, skills and understanding and plan for the next steps in the children's learning.

So, in order to plan for the effective support of children's learning in history and geography, practitioners need to reflect on how to address the six issues outlined above as well as to consult the statutory curriculum requirements for the age group for which they are responsible, which follows in the next section.

Early Year Foundation Stage expectations

The Statutory Framework for the Early Years Foundation Stage (EYFS) (DfE, 2014, p. 5) supports children's learning from birth to age 5.

> It sets the standards that all early years providers must meet to ensure that children learn and develop well and are kept healthy and safe. It promotes teaching and learning to ensure children's 'school readiness' and gives children the broad range of knowledge and skills that provide the right foundation for good future progress through school and life.

The framework establishes four guiding principles to help practitioners support children's development and learning in Early Years settings. These are to recognise that each child is *unique*, to encourage the child to form *positive relationships*, to provide the child with an *enabling environment* and to acknowledge that '*children develop and learn in different ways and at different rates*' (DfE, 2014, p. 6).

The EYFS 'curriculum' consists of seven areas of learning and development; the first three are known as prime areas and are expected to arouse children's curiosity and excitement. These are:

- Communication and language development.

- Physical development.

- Personal, social and emotional development.

The prime areas are expected to be 'strengthened and applied' within the following four specific areas:

- Literacy development.

- Mathematics.

- Understanding the world.

- Expressive arts and design.

The specific area which concerns the teaching and learning of history and geography is contained within 'Understanding the world'. Practitioners are expected to guide 'children to make sense of their physical world and their community through opportunities to explore, observe and find out about people, places, technology and the environment' (DfE, 2014, p. 8).

The Early Learning Goals (ELG) provide an insight into what children might learn in the EYFS. The following description for 'Understanding the world' might be considered to be developing historical skills, knowledge and understanding:

> People and communities: children talk about past and present events in their own lives and in the lives of family members. They know that other children don't always enjoy the same things, and are sensitive to this. They know about similarities and differences between themselves and others, and among families, communities and traditions.
>
> (DfE, 2014, p. 12)

The following ELG may be considered to be developing geographical skills, knowledge and understanding:

> The world: children know about similarities and differences in relation to places, objects, materials and living things. They talk about the features of their own immediate environment and how environments might vary from one another. They make observations of animals and plants and explain why some things occur, and talk about changes.
>
> (Ibid.)

It can be seen that there is little evidence here of a requirement to teach children facts; instead there is a clear opportunity to plan to develop children's knowledge, skills and understanding in a cross-curricular fashion using an enquiry-based approach to learning 'through playing and exploring', 'active learning', 'and creating and thinking critically' (DfE, 2014, p. 9.). How this might be undertaken will be outlined below. First, let us take a cursory glance at the expectations for children's learning from the National Curriculum for Key Stage 1 and then Key Stage 2.

National Curriculum history Key Stage 1 and 2 expectations

Whereas the EYFS framework seemingly allows practitioners to develop children's historical and geographical knowledge, skills and understanding in a variety of ways, with no set content, themes or topic areas, the National Curriculum requirements for Key Stage 1 (KS1) are a little different; teachers are given greater guidance as to the content they should cover, with the NC stating:

Pupils should be taught about:

■ Changes within living memory. Where appropriate these should be used to reveal aspects of change in national life.

- Events beyond living memory that are significant nationally or globally; for example, the Great Fire of London, the first aeroplane flight, or events commemorated through festivals or anniversaries.

- The lives of significant individuals in the past who have contributed to national and international achievements. Some should be used to compare aspects of life in different periods; for example, Elizabeth I and Queen Victoria, Christopher Columbus and Neil Armstrong, William Caxton and Tim Berners-Lee, Pieter Bruegel the Elder and LS Lowry, Rosa Parks and Emily Davison, Mary Seacole and/or Florence Nightingale and Edith Cavell.

- Significant historical events, people and places in their own locality.

(DfE, 2014, p.182)

In addition, the National Curriculum require pupils to 'develop an awareness of the past, using common words and phrases relating to the passing of time' as well as being able to place people and events into a chronological framework. It suggests that vocabulary is developed to encourage children to ask and answer questions to demonstrate their understanding as well as learning about how historians find out about the past (DfE, 2013, p. 182).

Despite the guidance, the content of the KS1 history curriculum is quite broad; it allows teachers a choice in determining *what* exactly should be taught as well as *how* it should be taught. The use of the phrase '*taught about*' differs from '*taught that*' in that it enables teachers to choose a variety of different methods to support the development of children's historical understanding. To use the phrase '*taught that*' may have encouraged a fact-based, 'transmission' style of teaching. This may inadvertently lead to some earlier lesson plans to be continued in use in a repetitive cycle. Resources may have been collected over time, and mode of delivery well established in a particular topic area. With the emphasis in schools revising and working on core, assessed subjects, some reliance on 'tried and tested' methods that meet the National Curriculum orders may continue.

In terms of ways in which to develop children's historical understanding; there is a focus on historical skills: the use of sources, asking/answering questions, identifying similarities and differences, and interpreting the past. There is also a focus on developing knowledge: use of common words and phrases, knowledge of significant events and people, and a balance of skills, knowledge and understanding. What is particularly interesting about the 2013 requirements is the emphasis on developing a sense of chronology. In the original 1988 National Curriculum this was omitted and was much criticised; children could study any period of time in any order, for example, the Tudors, and not know how this period of history related to others. During the 1950s and 1960s many primary school children were taught a sense of chronology from the historical textbooks written by R.J. Unstead (his texts have since been heavily criticised for bias, stereotyping and gender issues). There was a straightforward progression based on a series of textbooks; first-year juniors learned about 'Cavemen to Vikings', second-year juniors studied 'Medieval Times', third-year juniors learned about the 'Tudors and Stuarts', and fourth-year juniors studied the 'Georgians and Victorians'. Somehow learning about historical periods in chronological order was lost in 1988, but it is now back with a vengeance; chronological understanding is further emphasised in the KS2 requirements:

> Pupils should continue to develop a chronologically secure knowledge and understanding of British, local and world history, establishing clear narratives within and across the periods they study.
>
> (DfE, 2013, p.183)

The chronology is emphasised by the requirements placed on this timeline (see Figure 11.1).

In addition, the period for study is open to more choice for the school, with demands for:

- A local history study.

- A study of an aspect of history or a site dating from a period beyond 1066.

- A non-European society that provides contrasts with British history – one study chosen from: early Islamic civilization, including a study of Baghdad c. AD 900; Mayan civilization c. AD 900; Benin (West Africa) c. AD 900-1300.

(DfE, 2013, pp. 184–5)

This opens up areas of study for more recent history with, for example, the events of the Second World War being a firm favourite.

Although the content of the KS2 history curriculum is quite prescribed, and there appears to be a narrower choice of topics, these can all be studied in some depth, and how to do this, whether as a discrete subject or in a cross-curricular approach, is according to teacher choice. There does appear to be a greater emphasis on developing historical concepts (and thus knowledge), although there is still a focus on the use of historical sources; on the skills of devising and answering questions, and of interpreting and communicating findings. Developing both knowledge and skills is seen to support children's historical understanding.

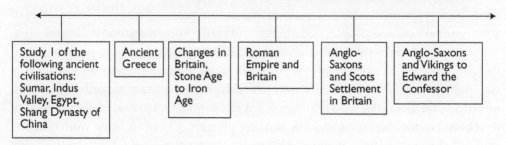

Figure 11.1   Diagram of chronology: a timeline helps build a secure understanding of events across time

National Curriculum Geography Key Stage 1 and 2 expectations (DfE, September 2013)

Key Stage 1

Again, in contrast to the EYFS, the National Curriculum requirements for KS1 (2013) provide clear guidance as to the content which should be taught:

> Pupils should develop knowledge about the world, the United Kingdom and their locality. They should understand basic subject-specific vocabulary relating to human and physical geography and begin to use geographical skills, including first-hand observation, to enhance their locational awareness.
>
> (DfE, 2013, p. 185)

More specifically, the National Curriculum lists four areas of study with very specific terminology and resources to be used as the learning tools. These four areas cover world locational knowledge (e.g. names of continents and oceans), place knowledge based on a comparison study of a small area of the United Kingdom with a non-European area, an understanding and knowledge of human and physical geography (e.g. seasons, names of key physical features) together with a list of geographical skills and fieldwork activities to be developed and experienced (DfE, 2013, pp. 185–7).

The use of the term 'taught to' seems a little more formal, and indeed the first section of the programme of study states 'name' – indicating the need for children to learn some facts. There is some prescription; teachers are expected to develop certain concepts and skills; however, the context in which this is done and the methods that could be employed are according to teacher choice. The study unit encourages the development of knowledge, skills and understanding.

It should be remembered that prior to the National Curriculum in 1988, the content and methods used to teach geography in the primary sector were very varied, and followed the learning and teaching beliefs of the time; teaching may have been based on an area of a topic (for example, Tutor Exploration), studying the weather, or using the immediate locality. Distant places may have been studied through the use of television programmes, picture slideshows or textbooks. The programmes of study for geography from the National Curriculum (1988) actually prescribe the teaching of a number of different areas which in the past would have been more familiar to those in the secondary sector; for example, physical geography (coastal erosion, rivers and volcanoes), and human geography (regions of the British Isles). Today, the curriculum provides many opportunities to learn about different aspects of the locality and distant places, and it reflects the many changes that have taken place in society. The movement of different peoples across the world through immigration, migration and those seeking asylum means that there are an incredible variety of different cultures represented in our schools and a wealth of knowledge and experience to utilise; advances in technology mean that information about global issues such as weather, floods, tsunami, volcanic eruptions, and how to monitor these events, is readily available; satellites now provide instant images of places near and far. There are many more immediate sources available to enthuse teachers in planning, and there are many different ways in which these sources may be used to support children's learning.

At Key Stage 2 (KS2), children are expected to extend their knowledge and understanding of geographical concepts and further develop their skills, but the context in which this is undertaken and the methods which could be employed are according to teacher choice:

> Pupils should extend their knowledge and understanding beyond the local area to include the United Kingdom and Europe, North and South America. This will include the location and characteristics of a range of the world's most significant human and physical features. They should develop their use of geographical knowledge, understanding and skills to enhance their locational and place knowledge.
>
> (DfE, 2013)

In a similar way, KS2 lists the four areas of knowledge that need to be taught, building upon the knowledge contained in KS1 documentation. Again, it is very specific as to content, although it leaves the 'how' of the learning strategy to the teacher.

How to develop knowledge skills and understanding

It may be clearly seen that the National Curriculum requirements for geography advocate that developing both knowledge and skills supports children's geographical understanding. Taking into consideration the EYFS and National Curriculum requirements, as well as the six key issues highlighted in the previous section, the next step is to consider pedagogy: which teaching and learning strategies should be used to develop children's historical and geographical knowledge skills and understanding?

How do children learn about history and geography? Piaget would suggest that children need to work from *concrete* experiences; work with objects; artefacts, and to be active in their learning. Bruner would recommend working in a similar fashion, using an *enactive* form of learning, while Gardner would refer to this as a *kinaesthetic* way of learning, Dewey (1998), among others, would advocate learning from *first-hand experience*. So, in terms of which methods could be used to stimulate children's interest, the choice is relatively clear: there is a need to take a child-centred approach to *facilitate* children's learning; providing different activities whereby children are *doing* something; examining objects; exploring ideas through drama and stories, or working outside of the classroom. However, it is also important not to provide the children with activities that are too difficult or too easy: an appropriate age- and ability-related challenge.

Vygotsky (and Bruner) would also encourage the use of language to support such active learning, either by children talking to or asking questions of each other to help them make sense of an idea or through the involvement of a *more knowledgeable other* who may help to *scaffold* a child's learning. The practitioner or teacher would need to stand back from the activity and observe, but would always be ready to intervene and pose questions; to *work within the zone of proximal development* to elicit responses and from this to support the children to move on to the next step in their learning; this enables teachers to assess children's learning in a *formative* manner.

Building knowledge through experience: a pause for reflection

Consider how you support a child's learning at a particular age/stage using the different theoretical ideas put forward in this section using the following steps:

1 Think of an artefact, resource or story.

2 What activity would this promote? (e.g. free-play, a game, drama, artwork or poster)

3 How would you stimulate 'talk', discussion or a question-and-answer session?

4 What key vocabulary would you use?

5 What would you want the child to learn from this experience?

It is actually not enough for the practitioner or teacher to just provide activities for children. They also need to encourage children to develop the skill of asking questions, finding out answers and communicating these to others. Children need to use their imaginations; they need to pretend to be detectives, find clues, interpret these clues and reach a conclusion (deduction and inference); this makes learning much more fun! So instead of children being presented with information, they should be encouraged to find out for themselves: an *enquiry-based* approach to learning.

As we have seen, there are a number of key concepts in history and geography which children need to learn about. In history, an awareness of time and chronology, cause and effect, change and continuity, interpretation, use of historical sources and communication are important, and in geography, the concepts of space, place, scale, connectedness, cultural awareness and diversity, physical and human processes, environmental impact and sustainability are a fundamental part of understanding the subject. Of course, there is some overlap between historical and geographical concepts, as there is within other subject areas; time, place and scale could equally relate to mathematics or art. Although the concepts may be dealt with separately or within subject barriers, it is also important to consider these concepts within the holistic development of children's learning.

Within these key concepts there are of course a whole range of other concepts (for example, time: decade, era, epoch, century; physical and human processes:

weather and climate, goods transport, travel, settlements); many are difficult to grasp without experience.

So where does the practitioner/teacher begin? The starting point should always be the child's experience; what do they already know or understand? At an early age a child has a view of the world which has been formed by his or her experience. Smith (1976) would call this the *theory of the world in the head*. A child's understanding is very different to an adult's; an adult has had more experience. The practitioner or teacher needs to work from the level of the child's understanding and support them in finding out new things. It is no good, for example, talking to children about the rainforest if their only experience is of being in an urban 'jungle'. Likewise, Palmer (1994, p. 2) suggests that we need to take into consideration that 'each child has a unique relationship with the world in which he or she is growing up; a relationship based on feelings, experiences, and interactions with people places objects and events'. Understanding this relationship is key to building an appropriate learning opportunity for the child.

Developing key concepts: further examples

Time and chronology

Time is a rather difficult concept; it is an abstract concept; think about occasions when time appears to mean nothing to children; the excitement before major celebrations and the use of the phrase 'sleeps'; travelling on a journey and being asked 'Are we there yet?'. Practitioners in the Early Years will be familiar with teaching children the days of the week and using simple charts to record the names. Then they may progress to learning months of the year and perhaps the seasons. On a daily basis young children do note the passing of time; they quickly get used to certain routines they understand – morning, snack time, dinner (or lunch) time and afternoon – and are able to recognise that evening time comes when it is 'nearly dark'. They may even recognise the position of hands on an analogue clock meaning that a certain event will happen. They will learn about today, tomorrow and yesterday. A simple way to reinforce the understanding of the passage of time is to take photographs of a classroom at different times of the day and ask the children to arrange the photographs in the correct order, which should prompt a great deal of discussion! Teachers need to use as many visual sources as they can in order to effectively support children's learning of the concepts of time and chronology: timelines, charts, models and pictures. Stories and nursery rhymes can also support children's sequencing skills and reinforce ideas about 'before' and 'after'. Through undertaking different activities involving the use of visual sources, young children will soon begin to understand differences; in recognising things which are old and new or similar and different, for example, they can always identify their own favourite cuddly toy or teddy bear! An early assessment task provided by the QCA in 1993 asked children to compare two objects, one old, one new, by drawing them, and then children were asked to draw an object in three different time periods: 'at the time when I am growing up', 'at the time when (e.g. my mummy was a little girl)' and 'at the time when (e.g. my granny was a little girl)'. This, as Cooper (2002, p. 58) comments, will help 'to refine their understanding of concepts of very old, old and new'. Activities which encourage children to approach their understanding in this way would certainly help them develop a sense of time and chronology.

Older children also need access to a range of resources to deepen their understanding of chronology. Cooper (2002) advocates that in planning to develop historical understanding, teachers start from what is known, and then consider ideas from within living memory before those which are beyond living memory. If you look at the way in which the primary curriculum is sometimes organised, this is actually not often reflected in practice, with children in Year 3 often studying an aspect of early history (invaders and settlers, for example, the Romans), and Year 6 studying the Second World War. However the curriculum is arranged, children need to be able to refer to a visual timeline to understand how the period of history they are studying fits in with others. A simple assessment for chronological understanding is to cut up perhaps 12 pieces of card with pictures of artefacts on one side and an historical period on the other (Bronze Age, Medieval Times, Tudors, Edwardians, etc.), and to ask the children to place them in order. Be warned that there may be some children who have a ruler with the correct sequence of the Kings and Queens of England to hand. Children will also learn more about a particular period of time through the imaginative use of photographs and pictures; artefacts, including film, objects and old newspapers; stories, drama and role play (to support the development of empathy), as well as making visits to different places of interest, including art galleries and museums.

Many key concepts in history will develop as children's knowledge and understanding increases; for example, the concepts of cause and effect (knowing why an event happened and what the impact was: what changed? For example, why did the Second World War occur and what was its effect?), and continuity and change (understanding similarities and differences; making comparisons, for example, using and comparing old toys, newspapers, even logos from food and drink products). An effective book to develop the concept of change over time is *A Street through Time* by Anne Millard, illustrated by Steve Noon. Other concepts will develop as children begin to use skills of enquiry: asking questions, interpreting information from different sources, formulating answers and communicating their ideas.

Developing enquiry skills: being the detective

A simple activity often used to 'hook' children into developing enquiry skills is to produce a carrier bag, shopping trolley, wastepaper basket, suitcase or dustbin bag and place into it a selection of objects (artefacts). For example, consider using old receipts, bus/train tickets, ornaments, foreign coins, a small book, a photograph, a postcard or a wrapper from a cereal bar. The practitioner could engage in role play to make the activity more exciting; for example, taking on the role of an elderly lady with a suitcase or, as one ITE student explained, he dressed up a bit like a surgeon, donning rubber gloves, mask and an apron, and presented a group of children with a rubbish sack smeared in mud and announced that it had been dug up from a grave; the sack contained 'grave goods'! The aim is to provide the children with some resources about which they need to answer a set of questions:

- What is the object?

- What does it tell us about the person?

- Who might the object belong to?

The children are led easily into developing their skills of enquiry as they consider the resources before them, pull together their thoughts about the connections between the objects, draw upon their experiences and use inference and deduction skills to paint a picture of a person and their life. Children enjoy this type of activity, often conjuring up fascinating characters. When they are asked to present their thoughts to their peers, it is intriguing to note how different some of the children's conclusions are, and this of course leads into discussion of the issue of interpretation. How can we ever be really sure of anything when it is all a question of interpretation? Such an activity is almost guaranteed to captivate children's imagination and they can then be given other resources to work with, applying their new-found skills to any aspect of history.

Using historical sources: artefacts, pictures, photographs, etc.

Historical sources are usually known as *primary* or *secondary* sources. *Primary sources* were written or created during a certain period of time and provide a record of something from the past which enables us to study history. Anything which survives from the past may be understood to be a primary source. *Secondary sources* are resources which are based on the primary sources; anything which reconstructs or interprets the past providing an impression or story of a particular event. We need to be aware that some primary sources, such as newspapers and autobiographies/memoirs, may contain bias (look out for male prominence or articles influenced by politics), or present a distorted view of an event. Something called *tertiary* sources also exists; for example, textbooks which can often be seen to be based on secondary sources. An interpretation of an interpretation may not be the most effective way of learning about the past … it is important to note that however many sources you have, you have to *infer* meaning from them and your conclusions should always be seen to be inconclusive because further evidence may emerge.

Some examples of sources are:

- Visual: pictures, photographs, paintings, film, maps.

- Artefacts: toys, coins.

- Buildings.

- Oral sources: people.

- Written sources: postcards, school reports, diaries, letters.

- Books: legends and folktales, poems, stories.

- Songs, including nursery rhymes.

When children are encouraged to talk to one another about an object, it enables them to look at things with a critical eye and helps them not only develop their questioning skills, but also their general language skills, especially those of deduction and inference. Children should be supported in asking both closed and then more open questions, perhaps devising key questions for others to answer about a source they are using. The practitioner should always ask children to discuss their conclusions and suggest why they have reached those conclusions.

Some key questions to be used with children are:

- What do we know for certain?

- What don't we know?

- What is there still to be found out?

- How reliable is the evidence?

Looking at the reliability of the source and asking further questions helps develop criticality:

- Is the source authentic?

- Is it biased?

- When and how was it made? What for? For whom? Why?

- If you refer to another source does this agree with your source?

When using sources such as an artefact (e.g. an old iron), it is important for children to look very closely at an object and to conduct a thorough examination. Collingwood (cited in Cooper, 2002) suggests that any questions that are posed need to relate to 'the significance and purpose of' an object and then 'to the people who made them' (p. 96). Children can be asked to do the tasks listed in Table 11.1.

If using paintings or portraits, additional questions may be posed: asking children to consider the background of the picture, looking closely at the subject of the work, at what is going on, being held/carried, expressions on faces, etc. With some objects, to aid really close observation, children could be encouraged to draw the object or focus on a small detail which interests them, or to support their understanding they could be encouraged to provide labels for the objects to inform others as part of a display, or use the object in role play or drama activities.

Table 11.1 Questions to prompt a thorough examination of an object

Describe the object	Guess how it was used	Make general assumptions
How does it feel?	What was it for?	Would there have been many/few of these?
What does it look like?	How was it used?	Would it have been valuable?
What is it made of?	Who would have used it?	What can we tell about the people who
How was it made?	When would it have been	made it/used it?
Has it been used (signs of	used?	What can the object tell us about the past?
wear and tear?)		

The use of oral evidence (that is, from a visitor's recollection of a significant event or a memoir/diary entry) should also be considered as an historical source; it is usually meaningful because it concerns someone's personal experience and may help children better understand an aspect of the past; for example, children may be encouraged to use surveys or interviews to ask a parent or guardian about their childhood. Visitors need to be selected carefully and perhaps asked to refer to artefacts to support them in talking about their memories. Any oral evidence needs to be treated with a little caution.

The main difficulty of course is that our memories change over a period of time and unless recollections can be verified by other sources they are not wholly reliable. With memoirs/diary entries it rather depends on how soon after an event it is written as to how reliable the information is. However, it should not be forgotten how exciting using this form of evidence may be for children or the learning that can emerge from undertaking such activities. Using any form of historical source promotes questions and interpretations which are fundamental skills in developing historical understanding.

Accessing memories: a pause for reflection

What happens when you discuss a childhood memory of an event with a colleague? How far is the account changed or embellished? Consider the issues involved in the reliability of oral evidence.

Story/drama

By now it may be seen that the past can be interpreted in many different ways and it is also *represented* in a variety of ways. An example of this is through using stories. In the Early Years, a practitioner may use a story such as a fairy- or folktale, myth or legend to provide a stimulus for children. A story helps feed a child's imagination; children can conjure up images in their minds and this helps in developing simple skills of interpretation; if you asked a child to draw a picture of what they had imagined as you were reading a story there would be a variety of different interpretations.

Using stories: a pause for reflection

Reflect on the story of *The Three Little Pigs*. How can this story help develop historical skills and understanding?

What other traditional stories can be used in this way?

Practitioners need to consider the language of the story: the first little pig, the second little pig … (use of ordinal numbers); how the story provides a sequence of events and how it marks the passage of time. The story also provides an opportunity to think about cause and effect: what happened with the house of sticks when the wolf 'huffed and puffed'? Teachers can ask the children how the characters feel (empathy) and to suggest what the wolf thought and felt about things (exploring different points of view). Later on in KS2 this simple activity could well lead to being able to discuss, for example, the Battle of the Spanish Armada (1588), and the different perspectives of the Commander of the Spanish Armada and the Commander of the English Fleet. Children should also be encouraged to question if the characters are real or imaginary (a recent survey (2015) by English Heritage suggests that children know more about fictitious characters than real ones), to ask why people in the past acted as they did, and to discuss the differences between a fact and a point of view. There are different versions of some folktales; if the practitioner asks children (or even colleagues!) they may talk about different endings for the story of *Little Red Riding Hood* (here similarity and difference could be explored). These activities support children's understanding that there are different interpretations or versions of the same event. Children can be introduced to stories at a young age and gradually progress to stories about historical events, fictional stories set in the past and, by the end of KS2, to considering eye-witness accounts of an historical event (for example, extracts from Pepys' diary of the Great Fire of London from 1666). As can be seen, using stories can develop a significant number of skills as well as understanding in history, and both children's skills and understanding can be easily accessed through writing, drawing, observations and even drama.

Drama and role play

Drama and role play provide enjoyable and imaginative opportunities for children to engage with many aspects of history. From an early age, children enjoy dressing up and taking part in 'pretend play'; some enjoy nothing more that wearing a helmet and wielding a sword, pretending they are a knight, perhaps copying a favourite cartoon character like Mike the Knight or donning a striped T-shirt, hat and eye patch acting out the part of a pirate. Drama does not have to mean a large class making a great deal of noise in a small space; it can include small group activities such as freeze frames and tableaux and role play. It can also be undertaken in the classroom using puppets, or through role play or hot seating. Drama activities support children in developing empathy through 'exploring emotions, attitudes relationships and situations outside their direct experience' (Cooper, 2002, p. 25) where children can 'put themselves in another person's shoes'. Drama activities also help develop children's communication skills (adults can also intervene to support the development of children's language, vocabulary and of course different concepts). Participating in drama activities may in fact contribute to children's growth in self-confidence across many different subject areas.

Field trips

The value of field trips can never be underestimated. If you ask friends what they remember about being taught history in primary school they may well recall a visit to an historical place of interest more than any other memory. There is something about going on a walk, coach or train to a place further afield; organising clothes, bags, food, pocket money and camera; the feelings, the excitement; not being able to sleep well the evening before. However, in recent years, school visits have featured heavily in the national press because unfortunate accidents, health and safety regulations (risk assessments and Disclosure and Barring (DBS) checks) have generated a considerable amount of paperwork, and the costs of taking children away from the school site have increased, with schools being advised to ask for voluntary donations in order that every child is able to participate. However, if you value how such trips can change some children, you *will* find ways to take them out!

Field trips do not have to mean travelling far; begin with the school building and its grounds, and then go outside the school gates to the street, the park, church or local attraction. After this, think about travelling beyond the immediate area to a place further afield.

Field trips: a pause for reflection

Extend the idea of field trips to consider how you might use reconstructions (through drama, theme parks, museums, re-enactments, TV and film) to engage children and give them the 'virtual-reality' experience of a field trip.

What might be the advantages and disadvantages of such activities?

Conclusion

This chapter has raised some of the key issues teachers and practitioners should consider when planning historical and geographical learning experiences for children. These issues go beyond consideration of teaching a set of facts and are fundamental to all learning situations illustrating the need to capture the interest of the child and to allow them to fully engage in active learning for themselves. A range of pedagogical methods has been suggested, with hands-on exploratory and imaginative situations using artefacts and oral histories or stories as a starting place to support children's knowledge and understanding of human behaviours within the world today as well as in the past. The chapter has shown that much of the learning of history and geography overlaps with and supports other curriculum subjects and could be described more in terms of skills and attitudes than of subject knowledge, although this, of course, is important. Developing skills that can compare one feature with another, interpret motives and data, accurately observe and record phenomenon, identify a sequence and pose questions are all skills that are essential not only for history and geography but for other curriculum areas, as well as being valuable life skills. History and geography as curriculum subjects are not only stimulating in their own right, but are essential for understanding the people and places around the world that we all inhabit.

Recommended websites

There are many organisations that provide inspiration for history and geography topics; try some of the suggestions below to see what is available.

Table 11.2 Recommended websites

Geography websites	History websites
Comic Relief	BBC History
Fair Trade	British Library
Geographical Association	English Heritage
Geography Teaching Today	Historic England
Google Earth/Street View	Historic Palaces
Learning through Landscapes	Historical Association
Multi Map	History Today
National Geographic	National Archives
Oxfam	National Trust
Primary Geographer	Primary History
Unicef	
Royal Geographic Society	
WWF	

References and further reading

Andreetti, K. (1993) *Teaching History from Primary Evidence.* London: David Fulton.

Barnes, J. (2007) *Cross-curricular Learning 3–14: Developing Primary School Practice.* London: Paul Chapman Educational.

Bruner, J.S. (1963) *The Process of Education.* Cambridge, MA: Harvard University Press.

Bruner, J.S. (1971) *The Relevance of Education.* New York: Norton.

Carr, E.H. (1961) *What is History.* Basingstoke: Palgrave Macmillan.

Catling, S. and Willy, T. (2009) *Teaching Primary Geography QTS.* Exeter: Learning Matters.

Claire, H. (1996) *Reclaiming Our Pasts.* Stoke-on-Trent: Trentham Books.

Cooper, H. (2002) *History in the Early Years.* London: Routledge/Falmer.

Cooper, H. (2006) *History 5–11: A Guide for Teachers* (2nd edn). Abingdon: Routledge.

Cowdrey, M. (2012) *Children's Learning in Primary Schools – A Guide for Teaching Assistants.* London: Routledge.

Davies, J. (1998) *The Subject Leader's Handbook – Coordinating History across the Primary School.* London: Falmer.

Dewey, J. (1998) *Experience and Education: The 60th Anniversary Edition.* Indiana: Kappa Delta.

DfE (2013) *The National Curriculum in England: Key Stages 1 and 2 Framework Document.* Available at www.gov.uk/government/uploads/system/uploads/attachment_data/file/425601/PRIMARY_national_curriculum.pdf (accessed 21 April 2016).

DfE (2014) *Statutory Framework of the Early Years Foundation Stage: Setting the Standards for Learning, Development and Care for Children from Birth to Five.* Available at www.foundationyears.org.uk/files/2014/07/EYFS_framework_from_1_September_2014__with_clarification_note.pdf (accessed 21 April 2016).

Dickens, C. (2012) *Great Expectations (Penguin English Library).* London: Penguin Classics.

Gardner. H. (1993) *Frames of Mind: The Theory of Multiple Intelligences.* London: Fontana.

Hoodless, P. (2008) *Teaching History QTS.* Exeter: Learning Matters.

Martin, F. (2006) *Teaching Geography in Primary Schools.* Cambridge: Chris Kington.

Millard, A. (2012) *A Street through Time.* London: Dorling Kindersley.

Murphy, P. (1999) *Learners, Learning and Assessment.* London: Sage.

Palmer, J. (1994) *Geography in the Early Years.* London: Routledge.

Phinn, G. (2015) *The Best Days of our Lives: Schooldays.* Skipton: County Publications.

Piaget, J. (1962) *The Language and Thought of the Child.* London: Routledge & Kegan Paul.

Pickford, T., Garner, W. and Jackson, E. (2013) *Primary Humanities Learning through Enquiry.* London: Sage.

Rosen, M. (2014) *Good Ideas: How to Be Your Child's (and Your Own) Best Teacher.* London: John Murray.

School Examinations and Assessment Council (1993) *History from Photographs.* London: NFER- NELSON.

Skidelsky, R. (1991) *History, What is its Future?* E271 Curriculum and Learning. Milton Keynes: Open University Press.

Smith, F. (1976) *Reading.* Cambridge: Cambridge University Press.

Vygotsky, L. (1986 translation newly revised and edited by Alex Kozulin) *Thought and Language.* Cambridge, MA: MIT Press.

Index